Using Pag

Macintosh® Version

C.J. Weigand

CORPORATION
LEADING COMPUTER KNOWLEDGE

Using PageMaker®:

Macintosh® Version

Copyright © 1989 by Que® Corporation

All rights reserved. Printed in the United States of America. No part of this book may be used or reproduced in any form or by any means, or stored in a database or retrieval system, without prior written permission of the publisher except in the case of brief quotations embodied in critical articles and reviews. Making copies of any part of this book for any purpose other than your own personal use is a violation of United States copyright laws. For information, address Que Corporation, 11711 N. College Ave., Carmel, IN 46032.

Library of Congress Catalog No.: 89-60288

ISBN 0-88022-411-8

This book is sold *as is*, without warranty of any kind, either express or implied, respecting the contents of this book, including but not limited to implied warranties for the book's quality, performance, merchantability, or fitness for any particular purpose. Neither Que Corporation nor its dealers or distributors shall be liable to the purchaser or any other person or entity with respect to any liability, loss, or damage caused or alleged to be caused directly or indirectly by this book.

92 91 90 89   8 7 6 5 4 3 2 1

Interpretation of the printing code: the rightmost double-digit number is the year of the book's printing; the rightmost single-digit number, the number of the book's printing. For example, a printing code of 89-1 shows that the first printing of the book occurred in 1989.

Using PageMaker: Macintosh Version is based on Versions 3.01 and earlier.

ABOUT THE AUTHOR

C.J. Weigand

C.J. Weigand is a retired Navy submarine officer and popular author, speaker, and consultant on Macintoshes and desktop publishing. He has written many articles and reviews that have been published in *MacWeek*, *Macintosh Today*, *Computer Graphic*, *MACazine*, *Personal Publishing Magazine*, and other publications. For more than two years, Weigand served as senior editor of two magazines—*MACazine* and *Personal Publishing*. He is currently editor-at-large for *Personal Publishing Magazine*.

Publishing Manager
   Lloyd J. Short

Product Director
   Karen A. Bluestein

Production Editor
   Kelly D. Dobbs

Editors
   Jo Anna Arnott
   Alice Martina Smith

Technical Editor
   L.H. Loeb, D.D.S.

Editorial Assistant
   Stacie Lamborne

Indexed by
   Sherry Massey

Book Design and Production
   Dan Armstrong   Diana Moore
   David Kline   Cindy L. Phipps
   Lori A. Lyons   Dennis Sheehan
   Jennifer Matthews

Composed in Times Roman
by Que Corporation and Cromer Graphics

DEDICATION

To our country's Founding Fathers, whose far-reaching vision guaranteed our fundamental rights to freedom of speech and freedom of the press.

Contents at a Glance

Introduction.. 1

Part I The Basics

Chapter 1	The Publishing Process—An Overview............	9
Chapter 2	PageMaker Basics...............................	35
Chapter 3	Creating a Document...........................	59
Chapter 4	Quick Start: Creating a Newsletter...............	79

Part II Working with Text

| Chapter 5 | Text Basics................................... | 97 |
| Chapter 6 | Formatting Text............................... | 123 |

Part III Graphics and Printing Techniques

Chapter 7	Graphics Basics................................	155
Chapter 8	Formatting and Enhancing Graphics	177
Chapter 9	Printing Techniques............................	197

Part IV Creating Different Types of Publications

Chapter 10	Planning Page Layouts	223
Chapter 11	Designing a Newsletter.........................	251
Chapter 12	Designing Other Publications	263

| Appendix A | Dealing with a Commercial Printer .... | 277 |
| Appendix B | Installing PageMaker and Configuring Your System................................... | 281 |

Additional Tips and Techniques.................. 285
Quick Reference 291

Index   321

TABLE OF CONTENTS

Introduction 1
    Desktop Publishing—What's It All About? 1
    Why PageMaker? 2
    Who Should Use This Book? 3
    How To Use This Book 3
    What Is in This Book? 4

I   The Basics

1   The Publishing Process—An Overview 9

    Desktop Publishing 9
        Planning 10
        Writing 11
        Producing Layouts 11
        Reviewing 12
        Printing 12
    Planning Your Publication 13
        Planning the Layout 14
        Developing a Style 15
        Evaluating the Cost 16
    Preparing Your Publication 17
        Software You Need 17
            Word Processing Software 17
            Graphics Software 18
        Text Considerations 20
            Story Length and Publication Content 20
            Selecting a Typeface 20
        Graphics Considerations 21
            Using Artwork 21
            Clip Art—Pros and Cons 22
            Scanned Images 22
            A Few Words about Copyright 23
            Original Artwork 23
    Bringing It All Together 24
        Arranging Three Key Elements 24
            Headlines 25
            Text 25

	Graphics	26
	Making Your Layout Work	27
	Balance, Symmetry, and Order	27
	Adding Emphasis with a Dominant Element	28
	Proofing Your Publication	28
	Printing Your Publication	30
	Choosing the Right Output Device	30
	Choosing the Right Print Shop or Service Bureau	32
	Chapter Summary	32
2	**PageMaker Basics**	**35**
	Before You Begin	35
	Opening PageMaker	36
	Creating a Document	37
	Determining Page Size and Orientation	38
	Selecting the Starting Page and Number of Pages	38
	Using the Double-Sided and Facing Pages Options	39
	Setting Margins	40
	Changing a Document	40
	Viewing the Publication Window	41
	Using the Pasteboard	41
	Using the Toolbox	42
	Using the Pointer Tool	42
	Using Diagonal-Line and Perpendicular-Line Tools	43
	Using the Text Tool	43
	Using the Square-Corner Rectangle, Rounded-Corner Rectangle, and Circle Tools	44
	Using the Cropping Tool	44
	Using Rulers	46
	Using Page Icons	48
	Viewing Your Publication	49
	On-Line Help: The Guidance Desk Accessory	53
	Saving Your Work	54
	Printing Your Publication	56
	Chapter Summary	57
3	**Creating a Document**	**59**
	Setting Document Defaults	59
	Changing Program Defaults	60
	Changing File Defaults	61
	The Magic of Master Pages	62
	Laying a Solid Foundation	67
	The Layout Grid	67
	Changing Columns	70

		Using Guides...	73
		Rulers and Measurements..........................	74
	Chapter Summary..		77

4 Quick Start: Creating a Newsletter 79

	Opening PageMaker..		79
		Setting Up Master Pages	80
		Positioning the Logo...................................	81
		Creating a Page-Number Block..................	82
	Preparing and Loading Text		84
	Preparing and Placing Graphics		85
	Refining the Document		86
		Working with Short Text............................	86
		Creating a Table of Contents.................	87
		Using Drop Caps	88
		Selecting Fonts	89
		Using Rules and Snap To Guides	91
		Editing Your Work	91
	Saving and Backing Up...................................		92
	Printing Your Work		92
	Chapter Summary...		93

II Working with Text

5 Text Basics 97

Importing and Copying Text into PageMaker	97
Preparing Text	98
Importing Text	101
Using Text Placement Options......................	102
Using Text Flow Options	104
Manual Flow..	105
Automatic Flow	106
Semiautomatic Flow................................	108
Changing Text-Flow Modes	109
Using the Clipboard	109
Creating and Editing Text	110
Fonts and Type styles...................................	112
Font Types	114
Font Sizes..	115
Type Styles..	115
Position and Case....................................	116
Typing Special Characters	117

ix

	Kerning Type	119
	Automatic Kerning	119
	Manual Kerning	120
	Exporting Text	121
	Chapter Summary	122
6	**Formatting Text**	**123**
	Performing Simple Layout Tasks	123
	Creating Columns	123
	Inserting and Removing Pages	124
	Rearranging Text Elements	126
	Adjusting Guides	127
	Resizing Text Blocks	128
	Using the Pasteboard	131
	Formatting Paragraphs	132
	Leading	133
	Spacing	135
	Indents and Tabs	135
	Setting Indents	136
	Setting Tabs	138
	Hyphenation	141
	Automatic Hyphenation	141
	Prompted Hyphenation	141
	Discretionary Hyphenation	142
	Aligning Text	143
	Adjusting Word Spacing	144
	Using Style Sheets	147
	Style Sheet Basics	147
	Defining and Editing Styles	148
	Importing Styles	150
	Assigning Styles	150
	Overriding Styles	151
	Chapter Summary	152

III Graphics and Printing Techniques

7	**Graphics Basics**	**155**
	Graphics Supported by PageMaker	155
	Using Paint Images	155
	Using PICT Images	157
	Using EPS Images	157
	Using Scanned Images	159

	Importing Graphics	161
	Using the Place Command	162
	Using the Clipboard	165
	Using PageMaker's Drawing Tools	166
	Drawing Lines	167
	Drawing Boxes and Circles	169
	Applying Shades and Patterns	169
	Modifying Graphics	170
	Resizing and Reshaping Images	171
	Cropping Images	173
	Moving Images	174
	Exporting Graphics	175
	Chapter Summary	175
8	**Formatting and Enhancing Graphics**	**177**
	Flowing Text around Graphics	177
	Using Text Flow and Wrap Options	178
	Specifying a Text-Wrap Standoff	180
	Creating a Custom Boundary	182
	Manually Wrapping Text	184
	Working with Scanned Images	185
	Image Control	186
	Modifying TIFF Files	187
	Modifying Paint Files	191
	Working With Color	191
	Defining Colors	193
	Applying Colors	195
	Chapter Summary	196
9	**Printing Techniques**	**197**
	Getting Ready To Print	197
	Using the Print Options	199
	Creating Multiple Copies	200
	Making Reductions, Enlargements, and Thumbnails	201
	Creating Proof Prints	202
	Changing Printer Specifications	203
	Tiling Large Documents	204
	Understanding Downloadable Fonts	205
	Using Printer Drivers and APD Files	206
	Smoothing Graphics	208
	Printing in Color	208
	Preparing Color Overlays	208
	Using Cutouts	209
	Using Commercial Printers	211

	Using the Linotronic	212
	Proofing before Printing	212
	Outputting Directly to Film	213
	Using the Linotronic	214
	Creating PostScript Files	215
	Using Offset Printing	217
	Selecting the Proper Paper	218
	Chapter Summary	218

IV   Creating Different Types of Publications

10   Planning Page Layouts — 223

Communicating Ideas Effectively	223
Achieving the Right Look	224
Understanding Structure	226
Making the Story Fit	228
Using White Space	230
Using Contrast, Balance, and Symmetry	231
Creating Headlines	234
Using Type Effectively	236
Using Attention-Getting Graphics	238
Using Boxes, Rules, and Other Design Elements	240
Creating Drop Caps	242
Creating Drop Shadows	244
Using Electronic Whiteout	244
Using Templates	245
Using Prepackaged Templates	245
Creating Your Own Templates	246
Working With Templates	247
Avoiding Layout Mistakes	248
Chapter Summary	249

11   Designing a Newsletter — 251

Designing the Banner and Masthead	251
Choosing the Right Format	252
Using a Single-Column Format	253
Using Multiple-Column Formats	253
Using Boilerplate	256
Achieving a Consistent Look	256
Using Type and Editorial Text	257
Using Borders and Rules	258
Using Special Visual Effects	259

	Using Screens	259
	Using Reverse Type	260
	Using Photographs	260
	Using Halftones	261
	Using Captions and Credits	261
	Chapter Summary	261
12	**Designing Other Publications**	**263**
	Working with Short Documents	263
	Creating Overhead Transparencies	264
	Creating Brochures and Price Lists	265
	Creating Handbills, Fliers, and Mailers	266
	Creating Greeting Cards	269
	Creating Certificates	269
	Creating Stationery and Business Cards	270
	Managing Large Publications	272
	Designing Successful Ads	274
	Chapter Summary	276
A	**Dealing with a Commercial Printer**	**277**
B	**Installing PageMaker and Configuring Your System**	**281**
	Installing Guidance	283
	Changing MultiFinder's Memory Allocation	284

Additional Tips and Techniques 285

Recovering from a Crash 285
Converting PageMaker Pages into EPS Files 286
Using Your Word Processor To Update Stories 286
Improving Laser-Printed Output 287
Placing Stubborn TIFF Files 287
Drawing Quick White Lines 287
Adding Signatures to Documents 287
Reflowing Text Blocks from the Top 288
Adding Color with Kroy 288
Easy Binding with Unibind 288
Keeping Updated with *ThePage* 289
Going Online for Information and Support 289

Quick Reference 291

Working with Files 291
Working with Graphics 293

Working with Pages	296
Facing Pages	296
Numbering Pages	297
Page Elements	298
Working with Rulers and Guides	299
Working with Text	301
Changing Type Specifications	303
Formatting	305
Hyphenating	307
Importing and Exporting	308
Spacing	310
Wrapping Text	312
Leading	313
Using Styles	314
Working with Color	315
Printing	318
Index	**321**

ACKNOWLEDGMENTS

This book wouldn't have been possible without the loving and generous support of my wife Carol. A special, heartfelt thanks to her.

Special thanks also go to Douglas "Sandy" MacKay of Packer Printing in Mystic, Connecticut, for always being on call and willing to share so many valuable insights.

Finally, many thanks to Karen Bluestein of Que Corporation who fought so vigorously for this project and then helped see it through to fruition.

Trademark Acknowledgments

Que Corporation has made every effort to supply trademark information about company names, products, and services mentioned in this book. Trademarks indicated below were derived from various sources. Que Corporation cannot attest to the accuracy of this information.

Ashton-Tate is a trademark of Ashton-Tate Corporation.

CompuServe Information Service is a registered trademark of CompuServe Incorporated and H&R Block, Inc.

Cricket Draw is a trademark of Cricket Software, Inc.

Encapsulated PostScript (EPS) is a registered trademark of Adobe Systems, Inc.

FullPaint is a trademark of Ann Arbor Softworks, Inc.

ImageWriter, LaserWriter, MacDraw, Macintosh, MacPaint, and MacWrite are registered trademarks and Finger, MultiFinder, and System are trademarks of Apple Computer Inc.

Linotronic is a trademark and Times is a registered trademark of Allied Corporation.

Microsoft Word and Microsoft Works are registered trademarks of Microsoft Corporation.

PageMaker is a registered trademark of Aldus Corporation.

PostScript is a registered trademark and Adobe Illustrator is a trademark of Adobe Systems Incorporated.

SuperPaint is a trademark of Silicon Beach Software, Inc.

X-ACTO is a registered trademark of Hunt Manufacturing Co.

CONVENTIONS USED IN THIS BOOK

The conventions used in this book have been established to help you learn to use the program quickly and easily. As much as possible, the conventions correspond with those used in the PageMaker documentation.

Commands, menu names, and dialog boxes are written with initial capital letters. Words and letters that the user types are written in *italic* or set off on a separate line. Options in dialog boxes and on-screen messages are written in a `special typeface` and capitalized as they appear on-screen.

Introduction

Desktop Publishing—What's It All About?

Some people consider desktop publishing to be a passing fad; others view desktop programs as harbingers of things to come. Whatever your thoughts on the subject, Desktop Publishing has dramatically changed the way written communications are prepared. Today, almost anyone can become an instant publisher with a personal computer like the Macintosh, appropriate software to create text and graphics, a page-makeup program like PageMaker to bring the various page elements together, and a laser printer to print the final results.

Desktop publishing is doing it yourself—whether you are putting together a mail-order catalog for potential customers or an informal newsletter for company employees. Being able to manage the entire publishing cycle from beginning to end means that you are the one who is in control. No longer must you suffer typesetters who introduce errors into your work or printers who habitually miss deadlines. No longer do you have to pay extra for incorporating last minute changes into your publications or turn away a client who needs an important document produced the same day.

Besides the control offered by desktop programs, desktop publishing's phenomenal growth has been fueled by a second consideration—doing it yourself costs less. Running stencils on a mimeograph machine also is an economical way to publish your ideas, but the inferior print quality visibly detracts from your attempt to get your message across. Desktop publishing with a laser printer, however, yields near-typeset quality documents. If you use a Linotronic ImageSetter, the results are indistinguishable from the results obtained with traditional typesetting methods.

In the Information Age, the proliferation of new publications sometimes seems overwhelming. More material than ever before is being published from the desktop. Each person has an insatiable desire to communicate thoughts and ideas to others, and desktop publishing enables you to do so more quickly and less expensively than ever before.

Why PageMaker?

PageMaker is the standard against which other page-layout software must be compared. The program is the first choice for most desktop publishers, primarily because of the friendly, intuitive user interface. Other page-layout programs make you create separate boxes to hold each element in a publication. Only after you position one of these boxes on-screen can you fill the box with text or graphics. With PageMaker, you can place text and graphics directly on your pages—no boxes are necessary.

If an item on the page doesn't look quite right, you grab the item using the mouse and move or manipulate it—just like working on a real desktop where you can pick up and rearrange items without having to think through the mechanics of what you are doing. Imagine, for example, how much more difficult working at home or in the office would be if you had to keep every item on your desk in a separate container sized exactly to fit. You would soon be up to your eyebrows in all kinds of cardboard boxes. Most page-layout programs, however, take this approach to desktop publishing.

PageMaker is more flexible and easier to use than other page-layout programs. PageMaker possesses an exceptional array of features that make the program attractive to professionals and novices. For example, you can flow text throughout a document with a single click of the mouse, and you can format text automatically—two features that help save time when assembling your publications. You also can wrap text around irregularly shaped graphics, change the contrast and brightness of scanned images by using built-in controls, and apply spot color to text and graphics. Other features enable you to kern type manually or automatically, hyphenate and justify text as you type, control line spacing to within half a point, and much more.

With PageMaker, you get quality without complexity. The new features in the current release of PageMaker (Version 3.01) were added because they were requested by users like you. Each one is included for a reason, and each is important. They can help you perform publishing tasks that previously were considered impossible on a personal computer. By comparison, many of the advanced features found in other programs are features you most likely will not need. For example, one program enables you to adjust leading (the amount of white space between successive lines of type) to within 0.001 point. The best the LaserWriter can do is 1/300 of an inch, or 0.24 point. You would have to print your documents using a high-end typesetting machine and examine incremental changes with a loupe. Most users don't need to go to such extremes when putting together publications like an annual business report or product sales catalog.

PageMaker is an excellent productivity-enhancing tool that you will find yourself relying upon for many tasks. You can use the program to prepare newsletters, fliers, greeting cards, catalogs, sales ads, business and technical reports, books, pamphlets, menus, theater programs, and so on. The program's uses are limited only by your imagination. If you do manual paste-up, PageMaker is a great time-saver. Minor alterations are easy to do, and you can create alternate layouts in just minutes. Major publication changes that previously would have taken days to do can be executed in just hours.

Besides being practical, PageMaker also is fun. You can take chances and experiment with new ideas, layouts, and designs. PageMaker encourages you to be creative, and creative communications is what desktop publishing is all about.

Who Should Use This Book?

Whether you own PageMaker, use the program at work, or plan to buy it soon, you should consider reading this book. If you are new to desktop publishing and feel somewhat intimidated by the complexity of PageMaker's multiple-volume documentation, this book helps you quickly master the basics. Despite PageMaker's apparent friendliness, most first-time users tend to flounder when attempting the simplest publishing tasks and may not understand how to use PageMaker effectively. *Using PageMaker: Macintosh Version* quickly gives you the knowledge and skills you need to produce professional-looking publications every time.

If you are an experienced PageMaker user and want to hone your desktop publishing skills, this book helps you develop the proficiency needed to tackle the toughest assignments. Even the most experienced PageMaker users occasionally have difficulty achieving publishing goals. *Using PageMaker: Macintosh Version* contains step-by-step procedures to help you master new techniques quickly and an abundance of hints and tips to help you develop advanced skills.

How To Use This Book

The best approach is to start at the beginning and read through to the end. You will benefit from the logical progression of ideas and be able to assimilate new concepts as they are introduced. Experienced users may want to skim quickly through the basic material presented in Chapters 2, 3, and 4 and delve right into Part II, "Working with Text." All users, however, should read Chapter 1, "The Publishing Process—An Overview," to gain a more complete understanding of desktop publishing. This chapter gives you a solid foundation upon which to build your publishing skills.

Using PageMaker: Macintosh Version assumes that you are familiar with basic Macintosh terms like "click," "double-click," and "drag." This book also assumes that you have read the user's manual that came with your Macintosh. If you are not comfortable working with menus, windows, dialog boxes, and so on, take time to learn more about them before starting Chapter 1. Inexperienced users can find extra help in Appendix B, "Installing PageMaker and Configuring Your System."

What Is in This Book?

Using PageMaker is divided into four main sections, plus two appendixes, an additional tips and techniques section, and a quick reference section.

Part I, "The Basics," highlights the overall publishing process and explains the fundamentals of document preparation.

Chapter 1, "The Publishing Process—An Overview," provides an overview of the entire publishing process, including planning, preparing, proofing, and printing your publication.

Chapter 2, "PageMaker Basics," introduces you to basic maneuvering techniques, parts of the PageMaker screen display, and the Guidance Desk Accessory.

Chapter 3, "Creating a Document," teaches you how to set document defaults, use master pages, and lay a solid foundation for your documents.

Chapter 4, "Quick Start: Creating a Newsletter," introduces and reinforces some key concepts. After you complete the sample newsletter, you should have enough confidence to get started producing your own publications, even as you continue working through the remaining chapters.

Part II, "Working with Text," teaches you everything you need to know about using text in PageMaker.

Chapter 5, "Text Basics," discusses text sources, preparation, importation, and the proper selection of fonts.

Chapter 6, "Formatting Text," demonstrates the correct application of style sheets. You also learn how to format your publications, including how to use columns, arrange individual elements on the page, and manage white space.

Part III, "Graphics and Printing Techniques," examines PageMaker's graphic handling capabilities and shows you how to harness the power of visual imagery in ways that add impact to your documents.

Chapter 7, "Graphics Basics," introduces you to the different types of graphics and PageMaker's drawing tools. Importing and exporting graphics is discussed, and you learn how to modify your pictures.

Chapter 8, "Formatting and Enhancing Graphics," demonstrates working with scanned images, wrapping text around graphics for special effects, and adding color to your pages.

Chapter 9, "Printing Techniques," discusses all aspects of printing. Printing is the one area that causes the most problems for desktop publishers. You discover what the most common errors are and what steps you can take to avoid them.

Part IV, "Creating Different Types of Publications," ties everything together. You explore various ways to get your message across effectively by using PageMaker. You also gain a deeper understanding of what is important in a good design. This section introduces several proven methods that help your publications attract and hold reader interest. You also see how to create layouts for several types of publications, and you discover techniques for working with book-length documents.

Chapter 10, "Planning Page Layouts," explains how to communicate ideas effectively and lists 10 common mistakes that you should avoid in your designs. This chapter also discusses contrast and symmetry and how to achieve the right look for your documents. You learn how to use prepackaged templates and how to create your own templates.

Chapter 11, "Designing a Newsletter," shows you how to choose the right format, design a masthead, and add visual effects to your newsletters. You also gain some insight into the use of photographs.

Chapter 12, "Designing Other Publications," presents information on creating overhead transparencies, brochures, mailers, certificates, and personal stationary. Design concepts for ads, greeting cards, and other short documents are presented. You also learn document management techniques for longer publications, such as books, business reports, catalogs, and directories.

Appendix A, "Dealing with a Commercial Printer," provides a checklist that will help ensure that your printing jobs get done successfully—the first time.

Appendix B, "Installing PageMaker and Configuring Your System," is provided especially for the benefit of new Macintosh users who need extra help setting up PageMaker.

"Additional Tips and Techniques" contains many useful insights about PageMaker and desktop publishing.

The "Quick Reference" section presents step-by-step instructions for basic PageMaker procedures. Use this section to refresh your memory and to access information quickly.

Each chapter is structured to teach you as much as possible as quickly as possible. You should find *Using PageMaker: Macintosh Version* a straightforward guide that introduces you to the satisfying and rewarding world of desktop publishing and helps you develop the skills needed to create successful publications.

I
The Basics

Includes

The Publishing Process—An Overview

PageMaker Basics

Creating a Document

Quick Start: Creating a Newsletter

The Publishing Process— An Overview

Desktop publishing has been hailed as the perfect solution to every publishing problem. Because of such exaggerations, new PageMaker users often become discouraged when their first attempts at desktop publishing yield less-than-desirable results. "Something magical" doesn't always happen on the first, or even the tenth, try.

Homework is required if you want to produce professional-looking documents. You can become proficient, even with little or no prior experience, but first you must learn the basics. The purpose of this chapter is to give you the fundamentals you need, both practical and philosophical. These fundamentals help you better understand the mechanics of working with your PageMaker software.

Desktop Publishing

Desktop publishing can be divided into five steps:

1. Planning
2. Writing
3. Producing Layouts
4. Reviewing
5. Printing

Examining each step briefly will help you understand how to take a typical publication from initial conception to final distribution.

Planning

Planning is the idea stage in which you set the scope and tone of your publication. The first question you should always ask yourself is, "Who will be reading my publication?" Every subsequent decision you make in some degree follows from the answer to that first question. Other questions to ask yourself include: What is the purpose of the publication? How long should the articles be? Should the writing be formal or informal? Are illustrations called for? If so, how many, and how detailed should the illustrations be? Are photographs needed? Is color an option? How should the material be presented? All these questions and more can be answered readily if you know your audience.

Determining your target audience is not always easy. You have to know something about your readers—their likes, dislikes, interests, prejudices, and ambitions—before you can identify who your readers are. Are they small-business people or Fortune 500 executives? Are they goal-driven individuals, always seeking new challenges or acquisitions, or content with what they have? What is their education level? What are their hobbies? And why should they want to read your publication?

The planning stage is the place to get these answers. By doing your research beforehand, you become better equipped to serve the needs of your readers, and your publication is more likely to succeed. Whether you are preparing a simple flier for a church bazaar or a detailed book about investing in the commodities market, knowing your audience is vital to reaching them with your ideas.

The planning stage also includes delegating tasks. You have to determine who will write, edit, proofread, do the artwork, deal with the printer, track the budget, and be in charge of coffee and donuts. Assigning responsibilities before you start avoids confusion later and makes the entire publishing cycle go more smoothly.

You learn more about planning later in this chapter under "Planning Your Publication." The concept of planning is so important to your success as a desktop publisher that you find references to the planning stage threaded throughout this book.

Writing

Writing quality often determines whether a publication succeeds or fails. Graphics are important, but graphics usually need accompanying text. You may capture a reader's interest with clever illustrations, but if the words don't hold that interest, you lose any chance you may have of getting your message across. The writing stage is the place to organize your ideas into words.

The writing stage also includes the preparation of graphics. Do not let the word "graphics" scare you. A graphic is simply a picture. A graphic can be a hand-drawn illustration, a piece of clip art, a scanned photograph, a design, a fill pattern, or any number of other visual enhancements.

Because graphics heighten interest in the written word, they should complement your text. Remember that you want to capture and hold reader interest. To make that happen, your text and graphics should work together. If purely decorative touches are called for, use them sparingly. The mark of an amateur desktop publisher is the overabundant use of graphic embellishments that fail to add to a publication's content.

For an introduction to some practical aspects of writing and graphics preparation, see "Preparing Your Publication" later in this chapter.

Producing Layouts

Planning and writing are essential, but these steps are only preliminary. The most important step in producing your publication is doing the layout. During the layout phase, you assemble all the disparate pieces into a complete whole by importing text and graphics into your page-makeup program and arranging the elements effectively.

Much of your publication's design is set early in the planning stage. Not until you enter the layout phase, however, do you discover the best way to execute that design. Your choices may depend as much on content as on style. For example, although you may have anticipated using an informal single-column layout for a political newsletter, you may find that the conservative typeface and small pen-and-ink illustrations you selected go better with a formal two-column approach. Although the layout phase requires a certain amount of planning and discipline to achieve good results, this phase also presents an opportunity for creative spontaneity. You can experiment with new ideas, but remember that your ultimate goal is to match your publication's design to your audience's requirements.

Later in this chapter in "Bringing It All Together," you are introduced to several key concepts indispensable to creating effective layouts.

Reviewing

The critical editing is done during the review stage. Although the review cycle begins during the writing stage and continues until your publication is printed, the definitive review is done during this stage. Any publication changes you make afterward can lead to unacceptable delays and result in increased production costs.

The final review should be undertaken by someone not directly responsible for the writing or layout. The closer you are to the preparation and assembly of a publication, the more likely you are to skip over typing, spelling, and punctuation errors. If you have to proof your work, read the text out loud to force yourself to go more slowly and focus on each word. Also explain your layout in detail to someone to help check your work. You may be surprised at how many errors you catch this way that you may have missed during earlier reviews.

The review cycle also is a time to ask whether you have met the goals set during the planning stage. You want to know whether your material works, whether you will reach your intended audience, and whether readers will respond appropriately. Ask a few people who match your audience profile to evaluate your rough layout. They may suggest changes that improve your publication's chances for success.

Under "Proofing Your Publication," in this chapter, you are introduced to a step-by-step approach for making sure that you don't overlook anything during your final review.

Printing

When you reach the printing stage, you are nearly finished. Even if you have done well so far, things still can go wrong. The printing stage is fraught with potential disasters. Many perfectly prepared publications have turned out badly because desktop publishers thought their work was done when their job was ready to be printed.

The quality of a print job directly affects how readers perceive a publication. Surprisingly, many desktop publishers are willing to settle for poor or marginal printing quality. This approach is like getting dressed up in fine evening clothes only to leave the house wearing soiled tennis shoes. You may not create the impression you had hoped for.

You find more about printing later in this chapter under "Printing Your Publication." You also find a detailed discussion about printing in Chapter 9, "Printing Techniques."

Planning Your Publication

Planning your publication can be a team or individual effort. Whether you work within a group or alone, for a client or for yourself, the essential planning steps are the same:

1. *Determine the size of your publication.*

    In addition to page count, determining the size includes selecting page dimensions and defining the image area. The image area is the portion of your page that lies within the margin boundaries. Your text and graphics appear in this area. The wider your margins, the less image area you have to work with and the more pages your publication has to have to hold the same amount of text and graphics. Because the size of your publication is directly related to the final production costs, determining page count and size beforehand and then creating your text and illustrations to fit is a good idea.

2. *Prepare a preliminary layout.*

    Your preliminary layout doesn't have to be elaborate. Its purpose is to give you a rough idea of how your publication goes together. A preliminary layout is more important for lengthy or complex publications than for short ones where most of your work can be done directly on-screen. When doing preliminary layouts, use a pencil to sketch each page on a separate sheet of paper. Simple boxes can be used to show the general arrangement of text and graphics. Think of your preliminary layout as a storyboard. Use the layout as a working guide, and feel free to make changes as you work.

3. *Decide what you need to produce your publication.*

    Determine what software and hardware you will use to prepare text and graphics, how you will print finished pages, if you need outside help, and when your deadlines are.

    Now also is a good time to decide whether to scan in photographs, use spot color for artwork, or opt for typeset-quality Linotronic output. If you are using a commercial printer, obtain a rough cost estimate to include the type of paper, the method of binding, and total number of copies. Knowing your printing costs ahead of time helps you plan and manage your budget.

4. *Make a schedule, and stick to it.*

Of all the advice contained in this book, this piece is probably the most important. Without a schedule, you continually come up against deadlines without accomplishing what you set out to do. A schedule keeps you on track and within budget. If you have a team of people working with you, each person should be given a separate schedule based on a master copy. This process helps to formalize individual responsibilities and ensures that nothing gets overlooked.

Planning the Layout

Your layout is a page-by-page arrangement of all the elements of your publication. Executing an effective layout, like producing a memorable piece of music, can be challenging. Adhering to a few established principles, however, can make doing your layouts easier and still allow you the freedom of individual creativity.

Be consistent. For example, don't switch arbitrarily from three columns on one page to two columns on the next to four columns on the next. With PageMaker, you can modify, change, and experiment with your layouts, but too much inconsistency turns readers away.

Don't confuse consistency with staidness. The elements of your publication can be strewn across your pages with wild abandonment, but even then, you should seek a uniform style.

Err on the conservative side. Too many design elements, a jumble of different fonts and type sizes, and overworking any one technique, like wrapping text around pictures, can detract from the professional look of your publication.

If you are not sure how to get started, try using commercially supplied templates like the ones from Aldus. Templates are preformatted documents that make excellent starting models for creating your own publications. The layouts are already done for you. You supply only the text and graphics.

Use white space as a design element to make your pages seem more inviting. Clean, uncluttered pages are easy on the eyes and help to focus a reader's attention.

Developing a Style

Style is equivalent to personality. You can do several things to give your publications a winning style.

1. *Pick a typeface appropriate to the task.*

   If you are preparing an ad for fine china, for example, you should not choose a display face that looks like stenciled lettering. A stenciled typeface suggests the roughness of boxed cargo. You also should not select a block headline type to announce a church wedding. Instead, use an elegant script face that complements the formality of the occasion. Every typeface has a unique personality. Even subtle differences between selected typefaces can influence the look of a publication. Get to know what typefaces are available, and make sure that the typefaces you use do not clash with your intended messages.

2. *Strive for uniformity in your use of illustrations.*

   Avoid mixing different kinds of images on the same page. A low-resolution bit-map file, for example, doesn't normally sit well next to a high-resolution encapsulated PostScript file. Because artwork and photographs generally reflect the personalities of the creators, use extra care in choosing your illustrations to be sure that they complement the perceived style of your publication.

3. *When you find a layout that works, don't change the layout just for variety.*

   This rule is especially true if you publish a periodical like a newsletter or catalog. Readers find the familiar reassuring. They tend to react negatively to sudden and abrupt changes. If you must make alterations, try to make them gradually. Slight variations in the arrangement of text and graphics from issue to issue help to create interest, but radical departures from the norm can greatly reduce your publication's "recognition" factor.

4. *Select an appropriate paper for your publication.*

   The color, texture, shape, and size of the paper you choose can influence reader perception. For example, you don't want to use ordinary tabloid newsprint to prepare a mail-order catalog of expensive designer clothing. Tabloid newsprint is more appropriate for advertising a bargain sale on work garments.

5. *Keep in mind that style is based as much on substance as on appearance.*

Your ideas and how well you communicate them are most important. Avoid copying the works of others. Study successful publications to learn and adapt new design techniques, but don't just copy layouts you like, or your publications will never develop a unique style.

If you have difficulty finding a style that works, experiment with different layouts. Use different fonts and graphics or try different approaches in your writing. Show your work to others and ask for honest opinions. Direct feedback can help you shape your publications to meet the needs of your readers.

Evaluating the Cost

The cost of producing a publication varies depending on how long you take to create each page. Only you can decide how much your time is worth. Assign an hourly rate to yourself and multiply the rate by the number of hours you plan to spend on a project to get some idea of your labor costs. Don't forget to include training time if required.

Up-front expenses for equipment, amortized over a reasonable period of time, also should be included in your total. Even if you already own the hardware and software, tack on an appropriate rental fee. Otherwise, your cost estimate will be artificially low. If your budget is limited, rent equipment at your local print service bureau. Call ahead to get an accurate cost breakdown of services.

Your biggest expense is likely to be the printing. Paper is expensive, and printing can often equal or exceed all other costs combined. Using a Linotronic ImageSetter also can add from $10 to $15 per original page. Still, that price is less than the roughly $30 to $150 per page you might pay to have typeset work done by a traditional printer.

When you first start doing desktop publishing, you may not save much money. New equipment, software, and training can be expensive and may greatly increase the cost of producing your first few publications. You eventually will recover your original investment, however, and your publishing costs will decrease significantly.

Preparing Your Publication

Most of the preliminary work needed to get your publication ready for layout is done outside of PageMaker. Although you may choose to do some of the work in PageMaker, the bulk of your writing, editing, and drawing should be done using other software. PageMaker is primarily a layout and assembly tool. The program is not a dedicated word processor that can do spell-checks, text searches, and other advanced word-processing tasks or a full-featured drawing program that can prepare detailed artwork. You can use PageMaker to do some of these activities, like editing and formatting text and drawing simple graphic elements. Doing most editing and graphics work in programs specifically designed for such tasks, however, is easier.

Software You Need

As a minimum, you need a word processor for the text and a graphics program (Paint, Draw, EPS) to create and edit illustrations. If you plan to include photographs in your documents, you also want software that enables you to edit scanned TIFF (Tag Image File Format) files. If you want to do any work with display (decorative) type, such as advertisements, you may want to consider buying some third-party laser fonts.

Word Processing Software

Any capable word processor that enables you to save your files as text-only or ASCII (American Standard Code for Information Interchange) is ideal for your writing. Text-only files are stripped of all formatting information, including font types, sizes, and styles. In addition to text-only files, PageMaker directly imports formatted files from a few popular word processors. The current version of PageMaker can read Microsoft Word, Microsoft Works, WriteNow, and MacWrite files and retain most of the original formatting, including paragraph indents and type styles. Future versions of PageMaker may support other word processors.

Text-only files placed within PageMaker are formatted automatically according to the publication default settings you select. In Part II, "Working with Text," you learn how to reformat text within PageMaker. You also learn how to use PageMaker's style sheets to assign formatting to paragraphs.

18   Part I: The Basics

Graphics Software

A graphic is anything except text. A graphic can be a picture, photograph, or design element like a box or rule. PageMaker can import several different graphic formats, including Paint, PICT, EPS (Encapsulated PostScript), and TIFF (Tag Image File Format). Each of these formats has advantages and disadvantages. Figure 1.1 shows examples of these formats.

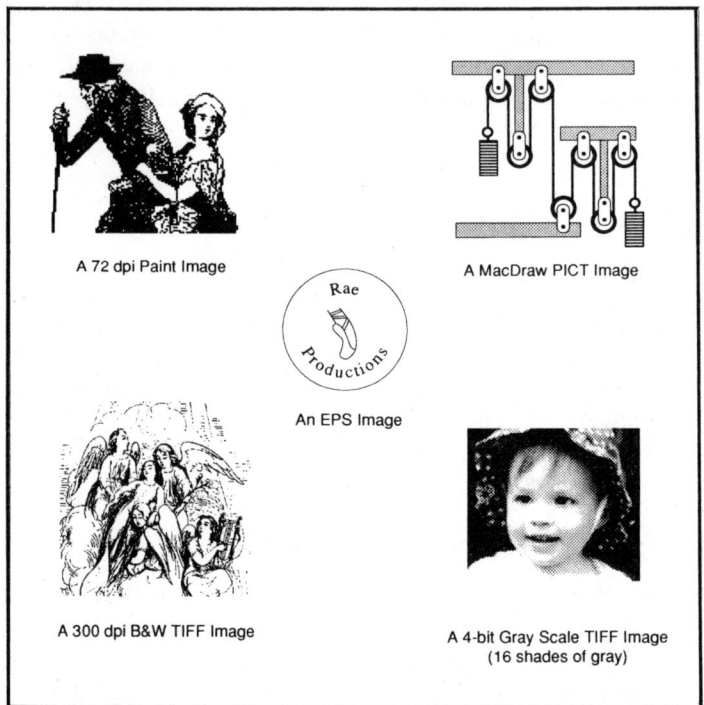

Fig. 1.1.

A sampling of different graphic formats printed on a 300 dpi laser printer.

Paint format, for example, yields a 72 dpi (dots per inch) black-and-white image that matches the bit-mapped (pixel) display of your Macintosh screen. Paint images are easy to create and edit, but their resolution is fixed so that the images do not reproduce well when resized. When scaled to larger sizes, paint images acquire a chunky appearance because each dot making up the image is enlarged separately. When scaled to smaller sizes, the dots run together and the images become muddy looking. Paint images, however, can be rich in detail, and much of today's clip art comes in paint format. Examples of popular paint programs include MacPaint from Claris Corporation, SuperPaint from Silicon Beach Software, Cricket Paint from Cricket Software, FullPaint from Ashton-Tate, DeskPaint from Zedcor, and Canvas from Deneba Software.

The PICT format transfers draw-type files between different kinds of application programs. Draw-type images are described geometrically using mathematical vector notation. Instead of individual dots, these images consist of lines and shapes called objects. Draw-type images reproduce well when scaled, but can sometimes overload your printer's memory if too detailed. These images are easier to create and edit than paint images. Popular drawing programs that enable you to save draw-type files in PICT format include MacDraw from Claris Corporation, SuperPaint, MacDraft from Innovative Data Design, DeskDraw from Zedcor, and Cricket Draw from Cricket Software. Most other Macintosh drawing programs, including programs intended for CAD (Computer Aided Design) work, also enable you to save files in PICT format.

The EPS format permits transfer of high-resolution, device-independent PostScript files between applications. PostScript graphics are the most sophisticated images you can output to a laser printer. These graphics can contain subtle graduations in object shading, curved and pattern-filled text, and other special effects. Macintosh EPS files come in two forms. The first piggybacks a PICT or TIFF screen-display image onto the EPS information to enable you to see and manipulate your graphic on-screen. The second type is a generic EPS file that, when placed in PageMaker, shows only a shaded bounding box containing the file title, creator, and creation date. Whether you want to create or edit EPS graphics, two excellent programs for the Macintosh are Adobe Illustrator from Adobe Systems and Aldus FreeHand from Aldus Corporation. These programs are difficult to master, but the results you can get far exceed the capabilities of most paint and draw programs.

TIFF files are designed primarily to handle scanned images. Like paint files, these files are composed of dots, but they are not limited to 72 dpi. Current TIFF files contain up to 300 dpi and can simulate gray shading by arranging dots in patterns within groupings, or cells. Unfortunately, a single TIFF standard has yet to gain universal acceptance. Several dozen formats are in existence. Every scanner manufacturer seems to have introduced a variation to prevent cross-usage of the company's software. PageMaker, however, imports and displays most black-and-white and gray-scale TIFF files without difficulty. To edit gray-scale TIFF files, you need to use a program like ImageStudio from Letraset or Digital Darkroom from Silicon Beach Software. Black-and-white TIFF files can be worked on using any of several popular paint programs that edit 300 dpi images, including DeskPaint from Zedcor, Cricket Paint from Cricket Software, and Canvas from Deneba Software.

Creating or editing graphics requires separate software. With PageMaker, you cannot edit imported images, and the program's drawing tools are limited to simple design elements. PageMaker, however, does enable you to modify the contrast and brightness of paint and TIFF files. You also can change TIFF gray-scale levels globally and apply custom line screens for special effects. You learn more about these image control features in Chapter 8, "Formatting and Enhancing Graphics."

Text Considerations

A story is a continuous body of text in a publication. A story may be a short piece or feature-length article that runs throughout your publication. The story is the focus of your writing—where your ideas meet the reader. When preparing stories for layout, you should consider several important factors.

Story Length and Publication Content

The number of allotted pages dictates how long your stories can be. You have to decide what to say and how to say it, and you have to make the story fit. In traditional publishing environments, a copyfitter juggles story lengths, resizes graphics, and somehow crams everything together with enough room left over for ads. A copyfitter's layouts generally end up a compromise between what he wants to see included and what he can afford to include.

You probably do your own copyfitting. If your documents are straightforward, balancing story length with content is easy. If you are publishing a multipage newsletter containing dozens of stories and graphics, balancing length and content gets tougher. If stories run a little long or short, you can use some tricks to make them fit without altering the content or your overall layout. You learn some of these tricks in Chapter 10, "Planning Page Layouts."

Selecting a Typeface

The Apple LaserWriter and most laser printers come with a set of built-in PostScript fonts for high-quality document printing. A font is a combination of typeface, type style, and type size. For example, Helvetica Bold 12-point is a font. Most fonts consist of the basic alphabet character set in upper- and lowercase, a selection of diacritics and punctuation marks, numbers from zero to nine, and a few typesetting symbols.

Most built-in LaserWriter fonts are suitable for preparing conservative business documents, but the fonts fall short when used to create publications like leaflets, theater programs, greeting cards, and announcements. For these kinds of publications, you want to use one or more commercial display faces available from companies like Adobe Systems, Casady & Greene, The Electric Typographer, and Dubl-Click Software. You also can design and produce your own fonts using Fontographer, a font generation program from Altsys. Figure 1.2 shows three sample fonts you might choose for your publications.

> Garamond—A serif bookface that makes excellent body copy. It boasts exceptional legibility.
>
> **Helvetica Bold—A popular non-serif font used mainly for headlines and subheads.**
>
> *Flourish—A display face that's ideal for extra-special occasions calling for a touch of elegance.*

Fig. 1.2.

Different typefaces are required for different publishing tasks.

The most important criterion for using any font is that the type not be too noticeable. You want your message to be read. If the font you choose becomes the focus of interest, your message may be ignored. Selecting the right fonts for presenting material is important to get your ideas across. Fonts should complement text by directing reader interest to what you have to say. Fonts and type styles are covered in Chapter 5, "Text Basics."

Graphics Considerations

Graphics in desktop publishing includes illustrations (artwork and photographs) and design elements (rules, boxes, and printer's ornaments). Graphics encompasses everything in a publication not thought of as text.

The graphics you use and their placement are critical to the success of your publication. Too often, graphics are used indiscriminatingly, without much thought being given to how they interplay with other graphics or stories. Professional publishers know that each graphic must count, just as each word in a story or headline must count.

Using Artwork

Without graphics, publications may appear flat and uninteresting. For example, a typical hand-typed business letter is not much of an attention-getter. If you browse through a popular magazine, however, you see graphics used everywhere to illustrate stories, sell products, and highlight information. The text carries the message; the graphics are used to arouse your interest.

You soon will discover that PageMaker is the quintessential medium for assembling documents that include graphics. In later chapters, you learn dozens of ways to enliven your publications with graphics so that they stand out from publications produced by your competition.

Clip Art—Pros and Cons

The term "clip art" comes from the practice of clipping illustrations from books of commercially supplied artwork. These clippings are pasted onto mechanicals (hand-assembled proofs of the final page layouts) to create camera-ready copy. Most of the clip art available to desktop publishers comes prepackaged as on-disk electronic images. These images come in various formats, and you can edit them within any graphics program supporting those formats. You also can use the images as they are by importing them into PageMaker.

Clip art is mainly for people who cannot afford the talents of an artist or illustrator or who don't want to take the time and trouble to create artwork. Even if you have a whole team of artists working for you, however, clip art can come in handy. Tight publication schedules sometimes mean that you don't have time to wait for artwork to be created, and prepackaged clip art offers a convenient shortcut. On-disk clip art, however, is expensive, and the art sometimes is limited in applicability. You may be better off creating your own artwork or scanning existing hard copy, especially if your graphic needs are many and varied. If you don't have a scanner, your print service bureau usually will scan drawings and illustrations for a nominal fee.

Scanned Images

The advent of high-resolution, low-cost scanners for personal computers has made scanning artwork more feasible than relying on disk-based clip art. The advantages of using scanned images are many. You can scan everything from hand-drawn sketches to photographs, and you need scan only what you intend to use. You also have complete control over scan quality. If minor tweaking of a scanned image's contrast or brightness is needed, you can do that within PageMaker. If you need to clean up or modify an image, however, you must use a paint or TIFF graphics program.

Most scanned images consist of line art or photographs. Line art consists of simple lines and curves with shapes devoid of fill patterns (like cross-hatchings or gray shadings). Line art generally is used in a publication to emphasize or expand upon themes or ideas. Technical drawings in equipment maintenance manuals, for example, are a form of line art.

With PageMaker, you can import scanned photos directly into your publications. After importing a photo, you can adjust the contrast, brightness, and gray shading, and create special line-screens for dramatic effect.

A Few Words about Copyright

Artwork and photos can be scanned from many sources, but copyright restrictions may exist on their use. Owning a scanner does not give you license to copy the works of others, unless those works are known to be copyright free and in the public domain.

Commercially supplied clip art that you own in hard copy generally can be used in any way you like. You are not permitted to republish or resell clip art separately as artwork, however, without prior contractual arrangement. Because the laws are sometimes subtle and complex on this issue, erring on the conservative side is best.

For example, a legitimate way to use clip art is to publish a greeting card for friends, relatives, clients, and business associates. You are likely to encounter strong legal opposition, however, if you use that same art to design a greeting card to be sold nationwide in stores or by mail order. Check with the original publisher whenever in doubt.

Original Artwork

The most satisfying artwork is the work you create yourself. Even if you cannot draw a straight line, you may discover hidden talents when you try using one of the many graphic software packages available for the Macintosh. These programs make straight lines and curves easy. Some of these packages even have spray can tools (if you are into graffiti, you can be instantly creative). Creating your artwork means that you can produce just the right art for the job. No more searching endlessly through files of images that don't quite fit your requirements. An example of how to create artwork is shown in figure 1.3.

The same considerations apply to photographs. Buy a camera and take your pictures. Home photographs scan as well as the ones you buy and don't cost you as much. Shooting a couple of rolls of film to get one useful photo should cost less than $25. Buying the same photograph from a stock photo agency can cost as much as $150.

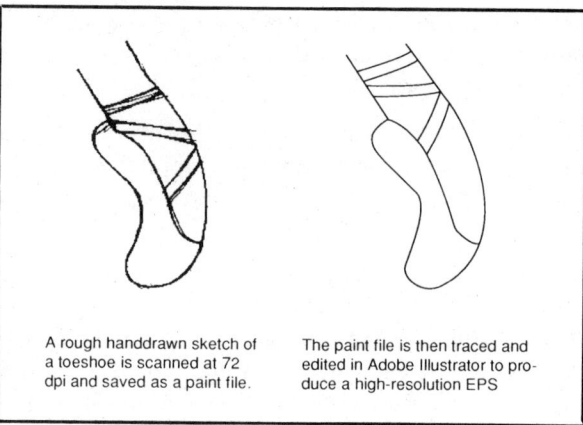

Fig. 1.3.

With a scanner and graphics software, you can produce finished artwork from rough sketches.

A rough handdrawn sketch of a toeshoe is scanned at 72 dpi and saved as a paint file.

The paint file is then traced and edited in Adobe Illustrator to produce a high-resolution EPS

Bringing It All Together

You probably are anxious to begin assembling your pages, but you may be a bit nervous. Don't worry; successful layouts can be done by anyone. Understanding that desktop publishing is primarily a vehicle for communicating ideas is the key to understanding page layout. Everything in the design of your pages should be aimed at reaching your readers. You may want to persuade, entertain, enlighten, or chastise. Your goal is to get your message across.

Arranging Three Key Elements

Every page in a publication represents an arrangement of three key elements:

1. Headlines
2. Text
3. Graphics

Not all three elements always have to be present. For example, a novel may not have any pictures, and a travel guide may contain many pages of photographs without text.

Which elements you use and how you arrange them determine how effectively you communicate your ideas. A stockholders' annual report, for example, may lead off the fiscal section with a bold headline stating "Profits Are Up This Year." This headline followed by a large chart showing steadily increasing revenues quickly conveys the following message: "The company is doing well, and your investments are safe." Elaboration about how profits were obtained may be deemed of secondary importance and printed in small type at the bottom of the page. In this case, the headline and graphic do all the work.

Many combinations of the three key elements are possible. Knowing how to arrange the elements successfully on a page, however, depends on understanding their differing roles.

Headlines

Think of your main headline as your show opener. A headline deserves prominent display because it is read first. If your readers find your headlines interesting, they read on. If not, they may not even glance at the remainder of your text.

Every day, readers are bombarded with messages from every direction—certainly more than they can assimilate at one time. Headlines help them decide what to read. Your headlines, therefore, should be designed to attract attention. Informative, eye-catching headlines can give you a competitive edge.

In Chapter 10, "Planning Page Layouts," you learn how to design headlines to help you communicate ideas more effectively.

Text

Your text is where you express ideas, make arguments, state opinions, and draw conclusions. Your pages frequently may consist of nothing but text, balanced by headers, footers, and a few ruled elements (especially in books, pamphlets, and journals). As a design element, text often shares equal billing with graphics (especially in publications such as catalogs and brochures). Text, however, always defers to headlines and graphics in sales ads, leaflets, product announcements, and other promotional materials.

You can wrap text around an irregularly shaped graphic for stunning effect. You also can mask text within a graphic shape, even within outlined lettering. Small blocks of strategically placed text, set in bold or italic type, can serve as "pull quotes" to heighten story awareness. Curved or rotated text can be used to draw the eye toward an item of interest. You also can use text as a link between elements on a page or to provide continuity in a publication where the main focus is on pictures, as in illustrated how-to manuals and bound collections of artwork or photographs.

Regardless of how good your headlines or graphics are, after you capture reader interest, body copy should take over. Your text should read well and look good. Pay careful attention to text formatting—proper kerning, word and line spacing, hyphenation, justification, and so on are essential to making body copy look presentable. You learn more about text formatting in Part II, "Working with Text."

Graphics

In many ways, the graphic is the most important of the three key elements. Graphics usually are noticed first, even before the headline. Weak graphics can give the impression of a weak publication.

Illustrations should suggest themes expanded on in your text and should help stimulate interest in what you have to say. Graphics that don't add meaning to your publications generally wind up detracting from them. The exceptions are design pieces like rules and boxes that help balance or highlight other elements on the page. Be careful not to overuse rules and boxes, however, or your publications may take on a cluttered look that also detracts.

High-contrast graphics and simple line art usually work best. As the level of detail in an illustration goes up, so does the amount of effort required to understand the illustration. For example, compare the universal skull-and-crossbones symbol on containers of poisonous substances with a complicated electronic schematic. The meaning of the skull-and-crossbones is instantly obvious, even to small children. The meaning of the schematic may take hours or days to decipher.

Of all graphic types, photographs generate the most reader interest. Which, for example, do you prefer to page through, a catalog of designer quilt patterns or a copy of *Life Magazine?* The photographs in *Life Magazine* satisfy our curiosity about ourselves and the world around us. Quilt patterns are just quilt patterns—they tell us little about ourselves.

One often overlooked, but highly effective graphic you can use is the comic strip or cartoon (see fig. 1.4). Humor can be a powerful tool for eliciting reader response. For example, think of the number of people who reach first for the comic section before reading the front page of the Sunday newspaper. Be careful when using humor. What may seem funny to some people fails completely with others. Humor can be a two-edged sword that can deliver your message—or kill the messenger.

Picking the right graphic is rarely easy. Your choices must reflect the nature of your publication and the message you are trying to convey. Your illustrations also must be eye-catching and snappy to entice potential readers. A well-placed graphic often can mean the difference between success and failure for a publication. Desktop publishing is, after all, a form of visual communication.

Fig. 1.4.

A cartoon can be an effective way to convey a message to your readers.

Making Your Layout Work

Headlines, text, and graphics are the three essential ingredients making up any layout. The way you assemble the elements determines how well your composition works. When composing pages, you must think like an artist and apply the fundamental concepts of good design: balance, symmetry, order, and emphasis.

Balance, Symmetry, and Order

Balance represents the equal and harmonious distribution of weight within an environment. Because the weights on pages are composed of visual elements, balance includes the attributes of shape, shade, and size. You can, for example, achieve balance by offsetting darker images with lighter images or a large shape with several smaller ones.

Symmetry affects mood. An asymmetrical arrangement, for example, can sometimes seem jarring and may put off a potential reader. A symmetrical arrangement of the same elements may seem familiar and reassuring.

Order is an outgrowth of balance and symmetry. Order represents the natural progression of the reader's eye across the page as dictated by the placement of elements. You can force the reader's eye to travel left, right, up, or down a page. Because most readers find normal left-to-right and down-the-page flow comfortable, however, try to structure your documents accordingly.

Adding Emphasis with a Dominant Element

If your layout has balance, symmetry, and order, it should work, but you also need emphasis. One dominant element should stand out from the rest.

The dominant element is the one you want the reader to notice first. An element can be dominant by virtue of size, shape, color, intensity, unusualness, placement, or any combination of the preceding attributes. Emphasizing or exaggerating one characteristic is the key. For example, a large, bold headline is usually the dominant element on a newspaper's front page. Sometimes dominance is created unintentionally, as when an excess of fine print becomes the dominant element of a legal contract.

You should have only one dominant element. To have two or more equally strong elements on the same page causes confusion. Your readers won't know where to focus their attention, and they may give up and look elsewhere.

Proofing Your Publication

To be successful as a desktop publisher, you have to proof your work thoroughly. A single typo can be disastrous. Errors, no matter how few or infrequent, can jar the reader's concentration. Typos, spelling mistakes, syntax errors, missing words, wrong homonyms, and missing or incorrect punctuation can be avoided by checking your work or having others review your documents before they are printed.

Watch out for layout errors. Missing or poorly aligned text, meaningless captions, misplaced graphics, and other omissions or inconsistencies can be as devastating as spelling, grammar, and punctuation mistakes. Extra care ensures that your publications always make a favorable impression.

A good way to ensure that you don't overlook anything is to use a checklist like the following:

1. *Read through your publication to check content.*

    See whether each paragraph stands alone in presenting a complete thought and whether successive paragraphs follow logically to a meaningful conclusion. Make sure that you place your most important ideas up front where they are read first. Also make sure that you summarize your ideas to reinforce your message.

2. *Reread each story, checking for misspellings and typos.*

    Look specifically for punctuation errors. List any errors you find and check other stories for the same mistakes. Misspellings, typos, and punctuation errors are often habitual. Increase your awareness of habitual mistakes to prevent repeating them. Whenever in doubt about spelling, don't guess—use your dictionary.

3. *Verify proper capitalization and the spelling of all names.*

    Almost everyone loves to see his name in print. Spell a name wrong, though, and you are not forgiven quickly. If you are preparing an ad, be sure that you include the company name, address, and phone number. Also check product descriptions and prices.

4. *Double-check all symbols, abbreviations, and acronyms.*

    Avoid using them unless you are sure that your readers are familiar with them. If you must use an abbreviation or acronym, make sure that you do so properly. Be sure to explain less commonly known abbreviations and acronyms the first time you use them.

5. *Verify the accuracy of all numbers.*

    Look for transpositions, misplaced decimals, and incorrect totals. One wrong digit can ruin an otherwise perfect job.

6. *Check for consistency.*

    For example, don't use "percent" and "%" interchangeably within the same story. If more than one person contributes to your publication, distribute a style sheet showing preferred usages to help eliminate confusion and make proofing easier.

7. *Verify that headings and subheads are correct and match the text immediately following.*

    Also check that stories continued on later pages pick up where they left off. Look for proper paragraph indentation and spacing and watch for unsightly word gaps in justified columns caused by improper or inadequate hyphenation. Check to make sure that you are using the correct typefaces for headings, subheads, captions, and body text.

8. *Examine your layout for symmetry.*

    Boxes and rules shouldn't crowd text and illustrations, and enough space should be inserted between elements to avoid overcrowding. Make sure that centered items are centered. Do a test print and check the page margins to ensure that none of your material lies outside the printable image area.

9. *Check illustrations.*

    Captions should match illustrations, and each illustration should be in the right place. If you use photographs, check to make sure that you include the proper credits.

10. *After making corrections, proof your publication again to make sure that all changes are recorded properly.*

Use the preceding guide as a starting point for creating a detailed checklist. Let the checklist reflect your special needs and concerns. Whether you use a checklist or not, your ultimate goal should be perfection every time you publish. Using a checklist makes attaining your goal that much easier.

Printing Your Publication

The last step of the publishing process is printing your publication. After a publication is printed, it is ready for distribution. Choose the right output device for the job and the right print shop or service bureau.

Choosing the Right Output Device

For all but the most demanding printing tasks, the output of an ordinary laser printer is fine. Most laser printers yield a minimum 300 dpi resolution, and some offer 400 and 600 dpi.

You can do your printing on a dot matrix printer, but the results you get are far below the quality of laser printing, as you can see in figure 1.5. With a dot matrix printer, you cannot take advantage of the benefits of the PostScript page-description language. Most of the examples and explanations in this book assume that you are using a laser printer or one of the higher resolution Linotronic ImageSetters.

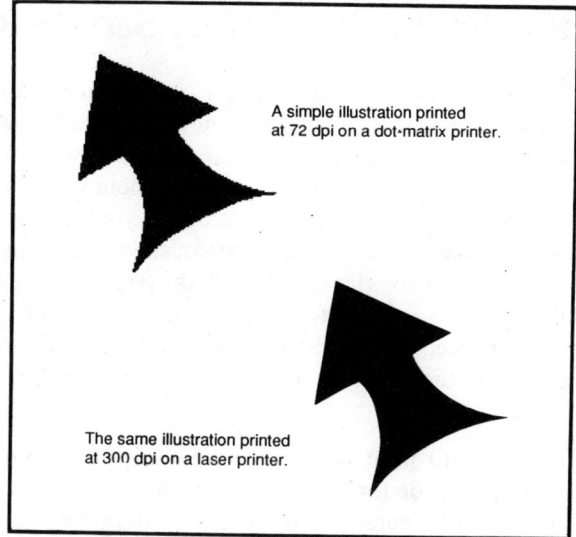

Fig. 1.5.

Laser-printed output is generally superior to output from a 72 dpi dot-matrix printer.

At times, you may prefer to use a dot matrix printer. You can use a dot matrix printer for catalogs, informal correspondence, price lists, fliers, leaflets, and so on. Dot matrix printers can function as proofing devices, although they do not reflect accurately the results you get from a laser printer.

For some jobs, you may want to print color separations and take them to your printer for color reproduction. Color PostScript laser printers can be used but are scarce and expensive. Using a thermal-transfer or ink-jet printer, however, sometimes can produce acceptable results. You also can do limited color printing on some dot matrix printers using a multicolor ribbon and on others using separately colored ribbons for successive passes over the same page. These methods, however, are unwieldy and generally produce poor results. Color pen-plotters sometimes can be used to create quality output, especially when printing simple line art. The newest film recorders also offer you the ability to print high-quality color slides for presentations directly from your computer.

PageMaker supports a variety of laser and other printers through A Printer Description (APD) files. These APD files are text-only documents stored in your System or PageMaker file folder. An APD file tells PageMaker the information needed to work with your printer. Unfortunately, many kinds of printers are not supported by APDs, and to use them you have to buy special connecting cables or printer driver software.

The easiest approach is to print your PageMaker documents using one of the many Aldus-supported PostScript laser printers. If you must use some other device, obtaining good quality output may be difficult or impossible, and may cost you more in time, effort, and money than the results are worth.

Choosing the Right Print Shop or Service Bureau

If you don't have ready access to a laser printer, or if your print job demands high-resolution Linotronic output, you may want to become acquainted with a print service bureau. Print service bureaus usually offer laser-printer and Linotronic printing at a nominal cost per sheet or by the hour. Many bureaus also offer traditional offset printing, including color. If your job requires more sophisticated handling, such as stripping in photos, visit a commercial print shop. Try to find a shop familiar with the Macintosh system and the anomalies of desktop publishing. If you cannot find a commercial printer meeting that description, have your mechanicals or film prepared by a print service bureau operator. Then, deliver them to the print shop with instructions for final processing.

In most cases, you have to print only one master copy of your publication. Remaining copies can be made for a small cost from a high-speed copier using the paper of your choice. Be careful about making alterations late in the print cycle. Author's alterations are subject to extra premiums and often start a new and costly billing cycle. Discuss the entire printing cycle in detail with your printer and agree beforehand on what each item and each step of the process costs. Get a signed estimate before committing. When your copies are printed, they still may need to be cut, folded, and bound before they are ready for distribution. Most commercial print shops and service bureaus can handle these tasks without difficulty.

When looking for a print shop or service bureau, be sure to shop around carefully. You are likely to find a wide variation in printing costs and work quality. Pick a place with a reputation for meeting deadlines and satisfying customers.

Chapter Summary

In Chapter 1, you acquired an overview of the entire desktop publishing cycle, starting with the conceptual stage and ending with a printed document ready for final distribution. You should understand the philosophy behind each step. You learned that publishing is more than putting words and pictures on a page—you need to follow a fundamental set of design principles if you want to achieve consistently good results.

You now know that every layout has three key elements—headlines, text, and graphics. You should have a clear idea of how to make these elements work for you. You also know how to evaluate your work and do those all-important reviews that make the difference between error-free and error-filled publications. You learned how stories and artwork combine to attract reader interest, and you know what it takes to be successful, even when the competition gets tough.

Most importantly, you acquired a deeper appreciation of what desktop publishing is all about. You now are ready to begin learning the mechanics of how to create professional publications using PageMaker.

PageMaker Basics

In this chapter, you learn the basics of working with PageMaker. If you are new to the Macintosh, you may want to review Appendix B, "Installing PageMaker and Configuring Your System." This appendix helps you configure your operating environment so that PageMaker can operate at its best.

If you feel comfortable working with your Macintosh and have installed Page-Maker, you can get started. This chapter introduces you to the main components in the PageMaker environment—the pasteboard, toolbox, rulers, page icons, and page. You learn what these components do and how to use them. You also learn how to move around within your publications and view pages in different magnifications. You discover how to create, open, and edit documents and how to save and print your work. If you get stuck at any point, PageMaker's on-line help can get you moving again.

Before You Begin

PageMaker combines several traditional publishing tools within the framework of one easy-to-use software program. You no longer need T-squares, compasses, triangles, X-ACTO knives, ruling pens, and other traditional implements to prepare your publications. You still have to assemble and review your articles, illustrations, and preliminary layout sketches before getting started, however.

Never skip the prepublication review process. Only when you have all the pieces laid out in front of you should you begin work at PageMaker's electronic drawing table. If you open PageMaker and start importing items and rearranging them on your pages, you may find that finished publications look disorganized. Your publications also take longer to produce if you don't plan. Planning your publications before laying them out is essential to producing quality work.

The recommended way to use this book is to parallel each chapter's lessons with a project you currently are working on. Experiment on a backup copy of your file and apply the different concepts and techniques you learn. Begin each session by gathering all your materials and try to develop a clear idea beforehand of where the publication is going. That way, you have a much better chance of getting there.

Opening PageMaker

You open PageMaker like any other Macintosh program—by double-clicking the PageMaker icon or highlighting the icon and selecting Open from the File menu. The first display you see is the PageMaker startup screen showing the Aldus logo, PageMaker title, program version number, and copyright credits. This startup screen is similar to the one you see when you select About PageMaker from the Apple menu, except that the About PageMaker display also tells you which operating system version you are using and how much memory you have left for other programs to use after PageMaker has loaded (see fig. 2.1). PageMaker requires a minimum of 700K of RAM; you cannot run PageMaker under MultiFinder with other programs if your Macintosh has only 1M of RAM.

> *Note*
> Hold down the Shift key when you choose About PageMaker from the Apple menu to be treated to a slide show listing of key people who played a role in the creation of PageMaker.

Fig. 2.1.

The About PageMaker display.

After PageMaker is loaded, the startup screen remains displayed until you click the mouse or press a key.

Creating a Document

To create a document, choose New from the File menu. PageMaker's Page Setup dialog box appears (see fig. 2.2). In this dialog box, you define your publication's page size and orientation and set page margins. You also use this box to indicate if your document is to have double-sided pages and whether you want to work with facing pages (two pages displayed side by side on-screen at the same time). After you make your selections and click the OK button, PageMaker displays your blank publication in the chosen format.

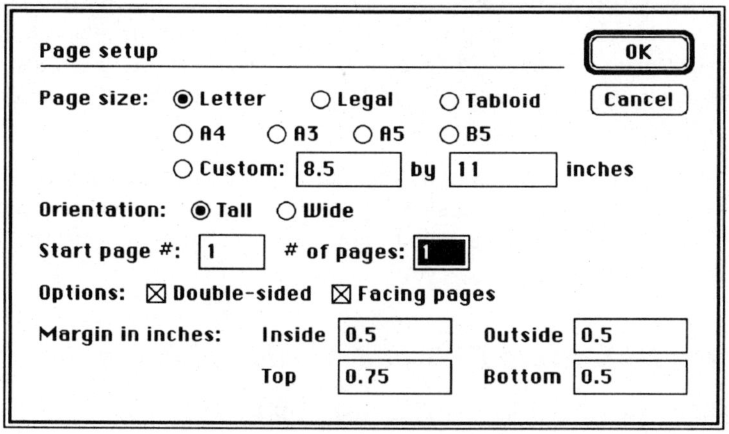

Fig. 2.2.

PageMaker's Page Setup dialog box with options that determine the physical appearance of your pages.

When the Page Setup dialog box first appears, default settings exist for every option. You learn how to create default settings in Chapter 3 under "Setting Document Defaults." You can change any default page specification in the Page Setup dialog box when you open a new document. You also can change these settings at any time by selecting Page Setup from the File menu.

Tip

A quick way to move through any dialog box in PageMaker, instead of clicking your cursor in each field, is to use the Tab key. Every time you press Tab, a new field in the dialog box is highlighted. In a highlighted field, you can type a new value and Tab to the next field. When you reach the last field, pressing Tab moves the highlight to the first field.

Determining Page Size and Orientation

The original default settings in the Page Setup dialog box are for a standard 8.5-by-11-inch vertical page. To select legal (8.5-by-14-inch page), tabloid (11-by-17-inch page), or one of the listed European paper sizes, click the appropriate button in the Page size field. Note that the correct page dimensions appear in the page-width and page-height boxes when you click these buttons. These boxes are not labeled, but they follow the accepted convention of listing the width of the page first. Page dimensions are shown in inches unless you choose a different measurement system such as picas or millimeters with the Preferences command from the Edit menu.

You also can define custom page sizes by typing the desired dimensions in the unlabeled boxes. When you type a number in these boxes, the Custom button is selected. PageMaker can create pages up to 17 by 22 inches in size, but you generally should select a page size no larger than what your printer can handle (consult your printer manual for page-size specifications). If you must print oversized pages, *tile* your output. You learn about tiling large documents in Chapter 9, "Printing Techniques."

For the page Orientation option, you can pick Tall for a vertical page or Wide for a horizontal page. Whatever your choice, the page orientation remains constant. You cannot mix tall and wide page orientations in the same publication.

Selecting the Starting Page and Number of Pages

The Start page # and # of pages settings tell PageMaker on which page to begin numbering your publication and how many pages you initially plan to include. These numbers don't have to be exact. PageMaker creates as many pages as you indicate, and you can change that number later to accommodate changing requirements. You also can change the Start page # setting at any time by choosing Page Setup from the File menu and typing a new value. Once chosen, the # of pages setting, however, is fixed unless you manually add or delete pages with the appropriate menu commands. You learn how to add and delete pages in Chapter 6 "Formatting Text."

You can number pages sequentially from 1 to 9,999, but PageMaker limits you to 128 pages for any one publication. If you plan a publication longer than 128 pages, break the document into separate files. The Start page # setting in the Page Setup dialog box enables you to renumber the separate files to provide a continuous page count when printed.

For example, a 200-page publication must be divided into at least two files. If you make the first file 128 pages long and the second one 72 pages long, you can set `Start page #` for the second file to 129. PageMaker numbers the pages in the second file 129 through 200. When you print both files, the pages of your publication are properly numbered from 1 to 200.

You learn how to set your publication for automatic page numbering in Chapter 3 under "The Magic of Master Pages."

> *Tip*
> The original default setting for `# of pages` is `1` for new documents. By changing that number to a larger value whenever you open a new publication, you may find switching among pages and experimenting with different layouts easier because you don't have to add pages manually. Later, you can add or remove pages as needed to make your total page count come out right.

> *Tip*
> Breaking lengthy publications into multiple parts with fewer than the maximum of 128 pages is a good idea. If you break a 300-page book into three 100-page sections instead of two 128-page sections and one 44-page section, for example, you have room to expand if you have to make editing changes that call for adding text or graphics.

Using the Double-Sided and Facing Pages Options

When you click `Double-sided` in the Page Setup dialog box, PageMaker adjusts the inside margins of facing pages so that they lie next to the inner edge of your publication. In effect, they mirror one another, with odd-numbered pages on the right, and even-numbered pages on the left. If you click the `Facing pages` box, PageMaker displays facing pages on-screen. This option is available only if the `Double-sided` box is checked. With facing pages, you can see your layouts symmetrically while working on both pages.

> *Tip*
> If you are working against a deadline and want to speed up screen redraws when changing page views, don't check the `Facing pages` box. PageMaker takes longer to redraw two pages at a time than to redraw one page.

When using double-sided pages, you usually want to make the inside margin larger than the outside margin to compensate for the page area lost when the publication is bound. Determine beforehand how much of the page is lost in binding, then set the inside margin to center the layout on whatever remains of the width of the page.

Setting Margins

The `Inside` (or left margin for single-sided pages) defines the *gutter* between the binding edge of the page and your layout. Similarly, the `Outside` (or right margin for single-sided pages) defines the space between the outer edge of your page and your layout. `Top` and `Bottom` margins work the same way, except that many desktop publishers let top and bottom margins serve as upper and lower boundaries for flowing columns of text. Headlines, page numbers, and other header and footer material are then placed above or below these margins.

Setting margins is the first step to laying out your pages. You learn more about working with margins in Chapter 6, "Formatting Text."

Before continuing, take a moment to open and close several PageMaker documents. Open publications by using the Open command on the File menu; close documents with the Close command on the File menu or by clicking the close box in the upper left corner of the publication window. Each time a new Page Setup dialog box appears, pick a different page size and orientation. Vary the starting page number and the number of pages. Choose the `Double-sided` and `Facing pages` options, and experiment with a variety of individual margin settings. See what effects your changes have on the page display. This experimentation helps familiarize you with the variations you can achieve using Page Setup.

Changing a Document

To edit an existing publication, choose Open from the File menu. Remember that you have to close any publication you already may have open—PageMaker enables you to work on only one file at a time.

When you choose Open, you see the Open Publication dialog box, which differs from other Macintosh Open dialog boxes in that you can open your original document or a copy of your original (see fig. 2.3). PageMaker normally opens the original file for editing. You can open a copy by clicking `Copy` before you click OK. In either case, the document always opens to the last page and page view you were working with when you closed the document.

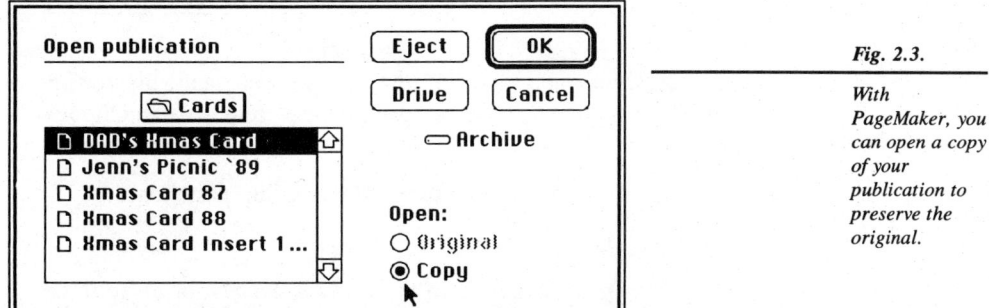

Fig. 2.3.

With PageMaker, you can open a copy of your publication to preserve the original.

With PageMaker, you also can create and save templates. You learn more about working with templates in Chapter 10, "Planning Page Layouts." Whenever you open a template, PageMaker opens a copy and not the original. You can open the original, however—to make formatting changes, for example—by first clicking the `Original` button before clicking OK.

Viewing the Publication Window

When you open a new or existing file, depending on the Page Setup dialog box options selected, one or more pages are displayed in PageMaker's publication window. The publication window is the area of your screen bounded by the rulers (if displayed) and includes the pasteboard and the current page or pages on which you are working. Notice that several other elements also appear on-screen: the pasteboard (PageMaker's equivalent of the drawing table), a toolbox, horizontal and vertical rulers, and a row of numbered page icons that line up along the base of the publication window. These elements, along with the usual menus, scroll bars, and other Macintosh fixtures, are the components of the PageMaker user interface.

Using the Pasteboard

PageMaker's pasteboard is like the surface of a large work table. The pasteboard is the empty space that surrounds the pages of your publication and extends beyond the immediate window boundaries. (You can scale your window to see more of the pasteboard area.) You can leave text and graphics you plan to use in different parts of your publication resting on the pasteboard. You can drag items off your pages onto the pasteboard for safekeeping, and you can later drag them back onto other pages. You also can copy items stored on the pasteboard and paste them onto different pages.

> ***Tip***
> To quickly move a block of text, a design element, illustration, or photograph without cutting and pasting the item to the Clipboard, do the following:
>
> 1. Drag the item onto the surrounding pasteboard.
>
> 2. Turn to the desired page.
>
> 3. Drag the item into position on the new page from the pasteboard.
>
> You can use this shortcut because PageMaker's pasteboard remains constant as you move from page to page. Items stored on the pasteboard remain available no matter what page you turn to in your publication and are saved when you save and close your document. Therefore, you can use the same items the next time you open your publication.

Items stored on the pasteboard do not show up when you print, but they are accessible as long as they lie completely on the pasteboard. If an item barely touches the edge of a page, however, the item stays with that page; it doesn't reappear on the pasteboard when you turn to another part of the publication.

You can create text and graphics directly on the pasteboard by using PageMaker's various tools. Afterward, you can drag the items you created onto your pages. This capability enables you to work with a clear view, unhampered by pages full of columns, grid lines, text, or graphics. As you learn to use the pasteboard, it becomes a great place for creating and editing headlines, cropping and scaling images, customizing graphic boundaries for text wraparound, and experimenting with reversals (white elements against a dark background).

Using the Toolbox

PageMaker's toolbox contains eight tools that can select and modify elements; create and edit text; draw lines, rectangles, and ovals, and crop illustrations. Figure 2.4 labels the various elements in the toolbox.

Using the Pointer Tool

The pointer tool is shaped like an arrow. This tool primarily is used to move and resize graphics and columns of text. But the pointer tool also is a universal tool that changes to take on the characteristics of the other tools, depending on the

Chapter 2: PageMaker Basics **43**

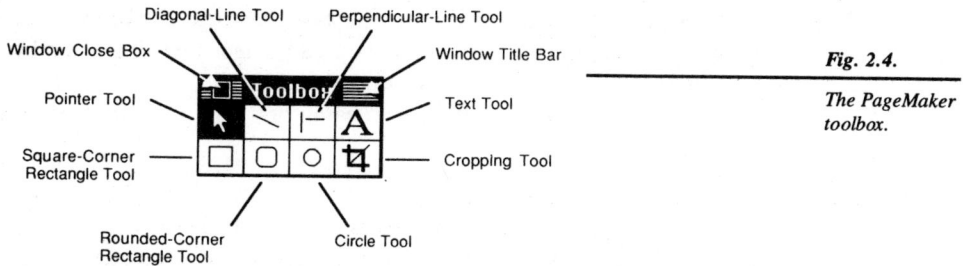

Fig. 2.4.

The PageMaker toolbox.

tool you select and where the tool is positioned in the publication window. Even if another tool is highlighted in the toolbox, the cursor reverts to the pointer tool when you move the cursor off the page-and-pasteboard area to pull down menus, click page icons, and operate scroll bars.

Using Diagonal-Line and Perpendicular-Line Tools

The cursor for the diagonal-line tool is shaped like a crosshair and is used to draw lines, or *rules*, at any angle. Click the center of the crosshair where you want the rule to start and drag until you reach the end of your line. Release the mouse button. Pressing the Shift key as you draw with the diagonal-line tool constrains the tool to horizontal and vertical rules and rules angled at multiples of 45 degrees.

The perpendicular-line tool yields the same results as using the diagonal-line tool with the Shift key: you get horizontal and vertical rules and rules angled at multiples of 45 degrees. The perpendicular-line tool is more convenient to use than remembering to press the Shift key as you draw with the diagonal-line tool.

With both tools, the thickness of the rule you draw is determined by your choice of widths from the Lines menu. Seven widths are available, ranging from hairline to 12 points. Attractive multiple-line border styles and an assortment of dashed lines also are available. You also can reverse any line so that the line appears white against a dark background. By making your menu choices before drawing your lines, you make the choices into default settings that apply to all new lines. If you select an existing line, or group of lines, before choosing a menu command, the menu choice affects only the selections, and the default settings remain unchanged.

Using the Text Tool

The text tool has an I-beam cursor similar to cursors in most word processing programs. Use the text tool to select, edit, and create text. If you position the text tool anywhere within an existing block of text and click once, you can backspace to delete existing text or type new text for insertion at that point. If you click and drag the cursor, you can select text character by character for editing. Double-clicking and dragging selects text on a word-by-word basis; triple-clicking selects an entire paragraph (all text up to and including the carriage return).

When you want to create a block of text of specific width, choose the text tool and click-drag anywhere on the page or pasteboard, away from existing text. (To click-drag, click and press the mouse button on the item while dragging the mouse.) This action produces a columnar boundary that you can type within. As you drag the text tool with the mouse button held down, you see a temporary outline of the dragged-out area on-screen. The outline disappears when you release the mouse button, but the cursor is positioned at the upper left corner of the invisible box you drew. You can start typing immediately. Whatever you type word-wraps to fit the width of your box. If you continue typing, the box expands downward to fit additional text.

Using the Square-Corner Rectangle, Rounded-Corner Rectangle, and Circle Tools

The square-corner rectangle, rounded-corner rectangle, and circle tools all work alike. Each has a cursor shaped like a crosshair, and each is used to draw its representative shape by dragging the cursor with the mouse button pressed. To get perfect squares, rounded squares, and circles, hold the Shift key as you move the cursor.

Using the Cropping Tool

The cropping tool enables you to trim illustrations within PageMaker to improve their appearance and to make them fit in allotted spaces. When you crop (trim) an image, the areas you remove can be recovered later by uncropping or by panning the image within its frame to show a previously cropped portion. Only imported graphics can be cropped, and only one at a time. Graphics created in PageMaker are exempt from cropping, but you can resize and reshape them using the tools with which they were created.

To crop an image, select and position the cropping tool above one of the reshaping handles that appear when you select the image. Press the mouse button and drag the handle inward in the direction you want to crop. Outlying areas of your image disappear. Notice, however, that the graphic doesn't change size. Like cutting a photograph with a pair of scissors, as you trim away the edges, the overall dimensions get smaller, but the picture doesn't change.

To pan a cropped image within its frame, hold the cropping tool above the image and press the mouse button. After a brief instant, the cropping tool changes into a hand tool. Press the mouse button and move the hand tool in the direction you want to slide the image. As long as you continue to press the mouse button, you can move the image in its frame. Release the mouse button when you are satisfied with the display (see fig. 2.5).

Cropping tool

Hand tool

Fig. 2.5.

Cropping and centering imported graphics.

When placed in PageMaker, the first scanned image in figure 2.5 turns out to be larger than the predrawn box into which it was expected to fit. The middle image in figure 2.5 shows how you can use PageMaker's cropping tool to neatly trim the graphic to fit within the box. Note that the size of the image itself doesn't change. In the last image, the cropping tool changes into a hand tool so that you can adjust your display. The image is moved slightly up and to the left to conceal the excess border.

You can hide the toolbox when you want to gain an unobstructed view of your work. Deselect the Toolbox command on the Options menu, or click the window close box in the toolbox. Select the Toolbox command on the Option menu to toggle the toolbox back. The appearance of the toolbox or any other palette (small specialized windows including the toolbox, color palette, and style palette) displayed on-screen does not impede your use of any tool. All palettes "float" above the page, so that when creating a line or box, for example, you can draw from one side of a palette to the other without moving the palette out of the way. If you decide that you want to move a palette, click the cursor in the title bar and drag the palette to another location in the publication window.

Take a moment now to experiment with each of the tools. Use the drawing tools to create a variety of lines and shapes; use the pointer tool to resize and reshape them. Don't forget to try drawing with the Shift key pressed. Draw a few boxes, paste some graphics into PageMaker using the Clipboard and practice cropping the graphics to fit in the boxes. (If you need to review techniques for using the Clipboard, consult the user's manual that came with your software.) Try adjusting each graphic with the cropping tool to center the graphic in its box. Also create some captions using the text tool. Drag out a text box for the first few captions. For the next few, click once on the page and start typing. For the remainder, click once on the pasteboard and start typing. See what happens in each case. You quickly will gain proficiency in using PageMaker's toolbox.

Using Rulers

PageMaker has two rulers: one runs vertically down the left side of the publication window; the other runs horizontally across the top of the window. These rulers are dynamic because they change incrementally to match pages as viewed in different magnifications. Dotted markers travel the lengths of each ruler to pinpoint the exact location of your cursor on the page so that you can precisely position text and graphics. You can hide PageMaker's rulers whenever you don't need them by unchecking the Rulers command in the Options menu. PageMaker's rulers are independent of the page margins.

The Preferences command in the Edit menu enables you to preset your rulers to display measurements in fractional inches, decimal inches, millimeters, picas, and ciceros (a European unit of measure for determining type size). Figure 2.6 shows the Preferences dialog box. You can override the preset measurement values in any of PageMaker's dialog boxes by typing a letter designation for the kind of measurement you want substituted. If your rulers are set for inches and you want to use picas in a particular dialog box, for example, you can type the letter *p* after each value. PageMaker substitutes picas for inches. You learn more about this process in Chapter 3.

Fig. 2.6.

PageMaker's Preferences dialog box.

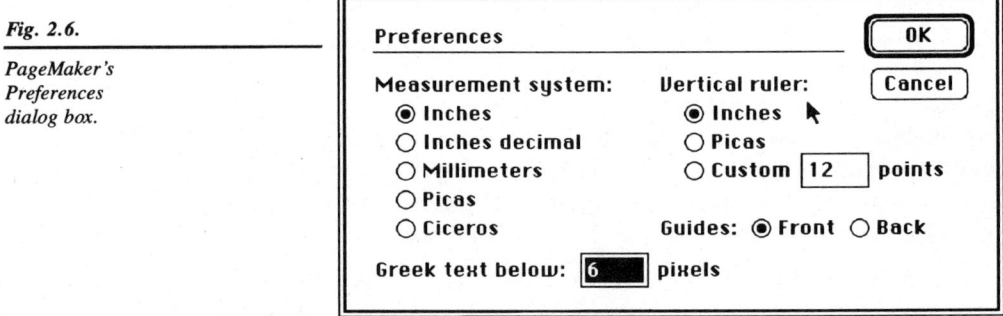

> ***Note***
> Six picas equal 1 inch, and 12 points equal 1 pica. A point is roughly 1/72 inch—equal to one display pixel on your Macintosh screen. (Pixels are the tiny square black dots that make up your screen image.) Twelve pixels of horizontal or vertical spacing represent one pica when laying out your publications.

You can configure the vertical ruler independently from the horizontal ruler by setting the Vertical ruler option in the Preferences dialog box to inches, picas, or a custom point value. Note that the measurement system you select is reflected as the first option for the Vertical ruler settings. The custom point value defines a vertical measurement that corresponds to type leading in points. PageMaker defines *leading* as the distance between the tops of capital letters in successive lines of text.

You also can set publication guides to lie in front of or behind text and graphics by clicking the desired Guides button. You learn how to use guides in Chapter 3.

> ***Tip***
> For whatever value you type in the Custom box, PageMaker spaces the vertical ruler increments to fit an even number of lines of text assigning a leading of the same value. (You learn how to specify leading in Chapter 6, "Formatting Text.") You can use this feature to calculate the depth of a column by doing a simple line count. For this process to work, however, the assigned leading must equal the value you type in the Preferences dialog box. For example, if you type *12* in the Custom box, PageMaker adjusts the vertical ruler to exactly match 12-point leading. Counting the number of ruler increments gives you the vertical line count for type set with 12-point leading.

You can reset the zero markers for both of PageMaker's rulers wherever you like. Resetting the zero markers makes measuring any element on your page easy. Note the crossed lines icon in the upper left corner of the publication window where the rulers intersect (see fig. 2.7). If you position your cursor above the crossed lines icon, press the mouse button, and drag, the cursor changes into a giant crosshair. As you move the cursor on the page, the dotted ruler markers track along for accurate measurement. Wherever you release the mouse button determines the new zero point for your rulers. You can anchor the zero markers in new locations along the rulers by selecting the Zero Lock command on the Options menu.

Fig. 2.7.

Resetting the ruler zero point to make accurate measurements anywhere on your pages.

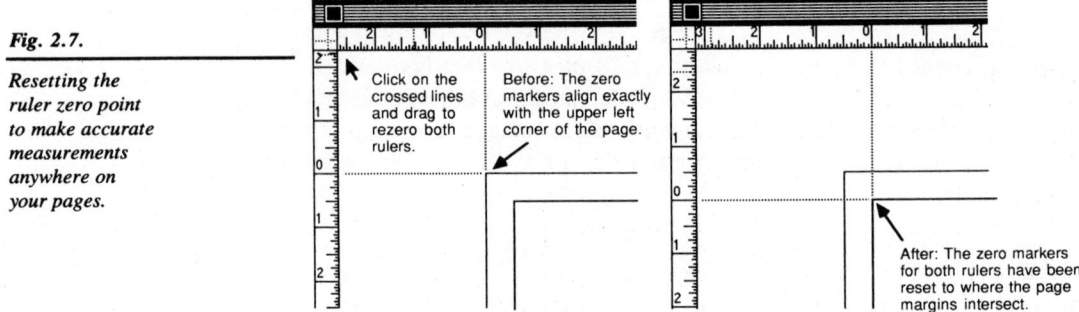

PageMaker's rulers also are the source for nonprinting vertical and horizontal ruler guides. You learn about these rulers in Chapter 3 under "Using Guides."

Using Page Icons

The row of page-shaped icons along the bottom left side of the publication window enables you to browse quickly through a document (see fig. 2.8). When you click a numbered page icon, PageMaker displays that page number. Adjoining pages are shown if you preset your publication for facing pages in the Page Setup dialog box. If your document contains more pages than icons, small arrows appear at each end of the icon row. Click these arrows to scroll through the page numbers one at a time. If you continue to press the mouse button after clicking an arrow, the pages begin to whiz by; release the mouse button to stop them. If you hold down the Command key as you click the right arrow, PageMaker whips you instantly to the end of the row and displays the last page in your publication.

Fig. 2.8.

Changing pages by clicking page icons.

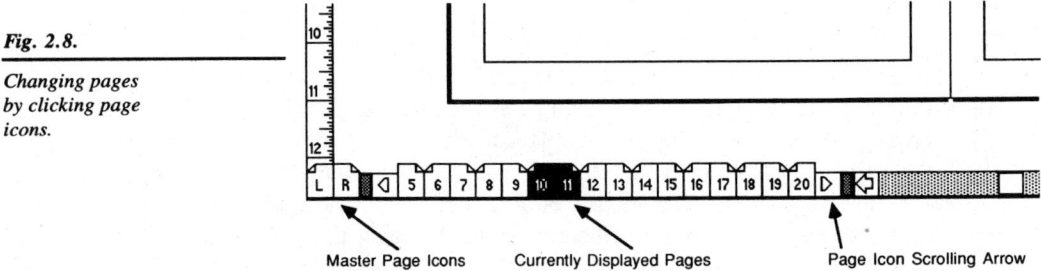

You can jump to any page in your publication by choosing the Go To Page command from the Page menu or pressing Command-G, an equivalent keyboard shortcut. When the Go To Page dialog box appears, type the desired page number and press Return or Enter (see fig. 2.9). (Pressing Return or Enter is the same as clicking the OK button.) To return to the page you just left, choose the Go To Page command and press Return or Enter—PageMaker remembers the last page you were on and displays that number in the dialog box. If you choose Go To Page from the Page menu while pressing the Shift key, Page-Maker steps through each page in sequence starting with page 1. Click the mouse button to stop on any page.

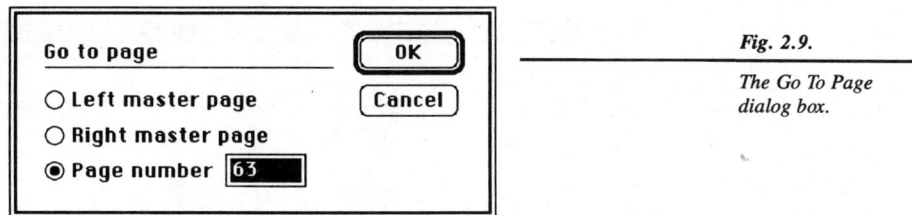

Fig. 2.9.

The Go To Page dialog box.

To move forward in your document one page at a time, press Command-Tab; to skip back a page, press Command-Shift-Tab. If you hold down these keys instead of just pressing and releasing them, you steadily advance forward or backward (but more slowly than if you held down the mouse button after clicking a page-icon arrow).

Take a moment now to open a new document in PageMaker. Accept the default settings, but assign 128 pages to your new publication. Try each of the page-turning techniques discussed in this section. Choose Page Setup from the File menu, check the `Double-sided` and `Facing pages` options, and repeat the exercise. Try clicking the page arrows with the Shift key pressed. Observe carefully what happens. Now try clicking the page icons with the Shift key pressed. Again, observe what happens. These shortcuts enable you to navigate through your publications quickly.

Viewing Your Publication

PageMaker provides seven levels of magnification to zoom in and out on your work. Five are well known; the other two are somewhat obscure, but equally important. If you pull down the Page menu, you see the first five listed as separate entries. In order, they are Actual Size, 75% Size, 50% Size, Fit In

Window, and 200% Size. Each of these viewing commands has a keystroke equivalent, shown in the menu alongside the commands, that you can execute directly from the keyboard.

The Actual Size command means that the page display you see on-screen is the same size as when printed. If you work on a standard 8.5-by-11-inch page, for example, what you see of your page on-screen is shown at actual 8.5-by-11-inch size. With the other viewing commands, you see your pages scaled by some percentage of actual size. Fit In Window reduces your pages, single or facing, so that they fit entirely within the publication window (see fig. 2.10). The size of the publication window can vary from monitor to monitor.

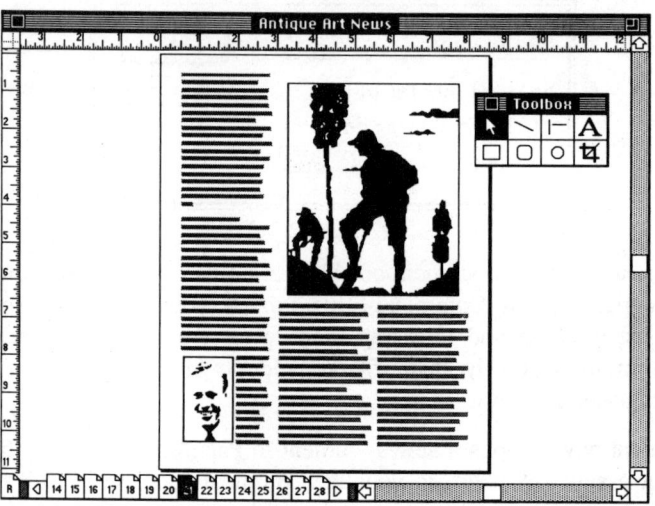

Fig. 2.10.

The PageMaker publication window showing a page in the Fit In Window view.

The remaining two levels of magnification are Fit In World and 400% Size. Fit In World reduces your page and the surrounding pasteboard so that both fit entirely within the confines of the publication window (see fig. 2.11). The 400% Size command zooms in twice as close as the 200% Size command for detailed work. These two viewing commands are accessible only from the Page menu, and only by choosing Fit In Window or 200% Size while pressing the Shift key.

Take a moment to experiment reducing and enlarging page displays with the different viewing commands. Each time you change your view, resize the publication window by dragging the resize box in the lower right corner. Note that the window is redrawn to show everything in the original display. This display is handy when you are working under MultiFinder and want to see all of your page on-screen while viewing another application.

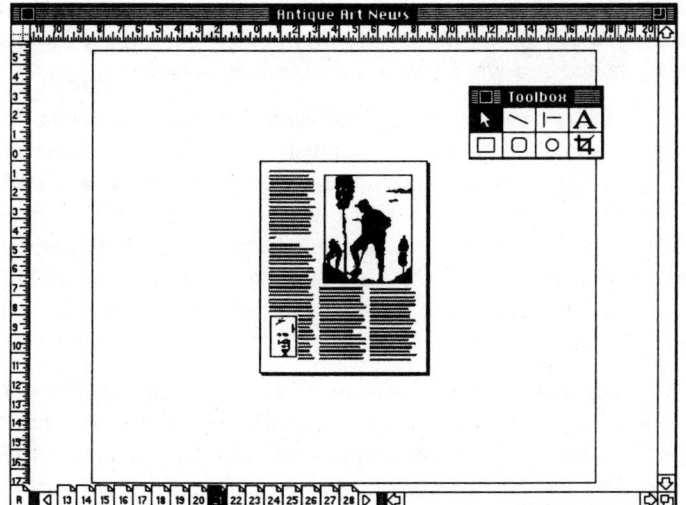

Fig. 2.11.

In the Fit In World view, the pasteboard area surrounding the displayed page is completely revealed.

Enlarged views are indispensable for accurately positioning elements on your pages. They help when you do detailed work, as when trying to align adjoining columns of text. Reduced views, on the other hand, help you do work that requires a more global perspective. Drawing a vertical column line, for example, can be awkward unless you work on a reduced page. Choose the view best for the task at hand so that your work goes more smoothly.

Notice that in reduced views, small text is usually represented by lines of gray shading. This procedure is called *Greeking*. Greeking text at small sizes—when reading is difficult anyway—lets your computer screen refresh more quickly than if each character has to be individually redrawn. Greeking text greatly speeds work in a production environment. PageMaker's default Greek size is six points. You can change the point size below which greeking occurs by typing a new value in the Preferences dialog box's `Greek text below` field (select Preferences from the Edit menu).

Tip

To speed up screen redraws, consider setting the Greek type size to a larger value in the Preferences dialog box. PageMaker takes considerably longer to redraw pages displaying type than to redraw pages with Greeked text.

Another useful way to move about on your pages is to press the Option key and click the mouse anywhere in the publication window. No matter what tool you select, the cursor changes into a grabber hand. If you continue to press the mouse button, you can slide your pages and the pasteboard in any direction. The screen display is updated when you release the mouse button.

Of course, you also can move through your document with the standard horizontal and vertical scroll bars. Most Macintosh programs have these bars, and PageMaker's scroll bars work in the usual fashion. Scroll bars are useful when you have to shift your view only a tiny bit and you don't want to change your page magnification. The actual amount of movement that results when you click a scroll bar varies depending on the view size. You can hide the scroll bars and page icons to see more of your publication by unchecking the Scroll Bars command on the Options menu.

At times, you may want to get to another part of the page that lies outside the immediate viewing window. Using the scroll bars or the grabber hand can be tedious. These movement methods are generally slow, and you cannot see where you're going. You *can* use a shortcut, however. The shortcut works because PageMaker always centers each newly selected view in the area on the page where you last worked. The shortcut also relies on PageMaker's special keyboard shortcuts for jumping between the most commonly used page views. Together, these two features combine to enable you to race around your pages like a jackrabbit. You can click exactly where you want to end up, so that you get there as fast as your screen can refresh instead of fussing with scroll bars, the grabber hand, or assorted menu commands.

If you're working on an actual-size page, for example, pressing Option-Command-Click takes you immediately to the Fit In Window view. Pressing Option-Command-Click again takes you to the Actual Size view, but the page and pasteboard are now centered at the spot where you last clicked in the Fit In Window view. This shortcut gives you an incredibly speedy way to jump instantly from one spot on your page to another.

Similarly, pressing Option-Command-Shift-Click takes you to a 200% Size view with your page centered at the spot where you just clicked. Option-Command-Shift-Click or Option-Command-Click takes you back to Actual Size view.

Tip

Another quick way to get around on your pages is to auto scroll. Select the pointer tool, then click and press the mouse button. Drag the cursor off the screen in the opposite direction you want the window to scroll. Press the mouse button until the desired area of the page comes into view. Your window stops scrolling the moment you release the mouse button.

Chapter 2: PageMaker Basics **53**

Take a moment to experiment with the various keyboard shortcuts that shuttle between different views. Open a new document in PageMaker and draw some boxes and circles on different parts of the page. Use the special keyboard shortcuts to jump quickly from object to object. Try doing the same thing with the scroll bars and grabber hand. Then try pressing the Shift key while using the grabber hand. Note how this action constrains the movement of the display.

On-Line Help:
The Guidance Desk Accessory

Until you gain proficiency with PageMaker, you may forget how to do something. Looking up the solution in PageMaker's manuals or this book is the best way to learn and to refresh your memory. Occasionally, however, you may be in a hurry. For moments like those, PageMaker provides the Guidance desk accessory to supply quick answers to your questions (see fig. 2.12).

Fig. 2.12.

The Guidance desk accessory help screen. Note the special Guidance menu that appears to the right of the PageMaker menu bar.

With Guidance, you can click different parts of the screen display and be transported to another level of information that further explains what you clicked. You have to be careful to click on the right spots; if you don't, you're likely to wind up looking at the wrong display. As an aid to locating the active buttons, each is depicted as a miniature icon. The cursor also changes shape when positioned directly over one of the icons.

To get help with a problem, choose Guidance from the Apple menu. (If Guidance is listed in the PageMaker menu bar, choose Open from the Guidance menu.) Click the topic icons for the items that most closely describe the category of information in which you are interested. Each time you click an additional icon, a new group of subtopics is displayed (see fig. 2.13). Keep clicking icons until you get to the information you need.

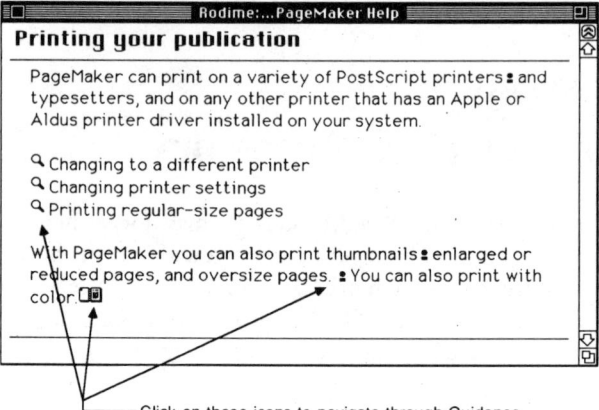

Fig. 2.13.

Miniature icons in the Guidance help display show you where to click for more information.

A supplementary Find command on the Guidance menu (which is added to the right of PageMaker's menu bar whenever Guidance is open) enables you to do text searches for specific topics. You can specify a search based on up to 80 characters of text. Other features include the capability of backtracking through previously viewed screens and the capability to adjust displayed text size for easier reading.

If you have questions about how to install Guidance, review the installation procedure in Appendix B. The appendix explains how to configure your installation so that Guidance is always available as you work in PageMaker but does not take up valuable space under the Apple menu when you work in other programs.

Saving Your Work

With PageMaker, you can save documents in one of two formats: as publications or as templates. You can indicate your preference in the Save As dialog box. If you choose the Save command from the File menu, PageMaker resaves your document under its current name and in the same format as when opened. To save a copy of your document under a different name, or to convert the document into a different format, use the Save As command. If you're working on a new document, the Save and Save As commands produce the Save As dialog box where you can name your file, choose an appropriate format, and tell PageMaker where to store the file on disk.

> ### *Warning*
> With PageMaker, you can replace a publication on disk with a template of the same name; you also can replace a template with a publication of the same name. The only warning you get is the standard dialog box asking if you want to replace the file of the same name. If you want to replace the file, fine. If you click the wrong format button in the Save As dialog box, however, you can wind up writing over your only copy of an important template.
>
> You can prevent this loss by selecting your template in the Finder and choosing Get Info from the File menu. Select the Locked box that appears in the upper right corner of the Get Info dialog box. After you lock the template file in this way, you cannot save changes to the template unless you deliberately unlock it first.

Save your work frequently. You never know when you may suffer a sudden power outage or computer malfunction. Even if you haven't saved your most recent changes, however, you may be able to recover most of your work intact. PageMaker has a built-in automatic feature that can help save the day.

Every time you add or delete pages, change Page Setup specifications, or turn to a new page in your publication, PageMaker does a mini-save. This mini-save produces a complete copy of your publication as the publication exists then. You can revert to the last mini-save version of your file at any time by choosing Revert from the File menu while pressing the Shift key. If you choose Revert without pressing the Shift key, you restore the last version you saved using the Save or Save As command.

> ### *Tip*
> You can force a quick mini-save at any time with a single click of the mouse. Click the highlighted page icon in the row at the bottom of the publication window. Because the highlighted icon represents the current page, no page turning occurs, and you can continue working uninterrupted. You benefit by having protected your most recent changes without having to update and alter your last-saved version.

> ***Tip***
> When you save complete PageMaker documents with the Save command, quite a bit of excess baggage is retained, including information about recently deleted text and graphics. PageMaker needs this data to recover the current file with its mini-save feature if you suffer a power outage or computer malfunction before you can save changes using Save or Save As. This extra data also causes PageMaker files to quickly grow to huge proportions. Eventually, you may not be able to transfer the file to a floppy disk to carry with you. If you use a modem to send files elsewhere, your telecommunications costs can soar. To counteract this unrestrained file growth, choose Save As from the File menu instead of Save. Using the Save As command as the final step in archiving a publication deletes all excess data needed for mini-saving and shrinks the file to a fraction of its previous size. After you have saved your file using Save or Save As, you don't need to rely on mini-save to recover current data. Using Save, however, doesn't delete the excess information.

Printing Your Publication

All of Chapter 9, "Printing Techniques," is devoted to the subtleties of printing your PageMaker publications. In that chapter you learn about the various print options, including alternate drivers, color printing, and using a Linotronic ImageSetter. Printing from PageMaker normally is done with the Print dialog box (choose Print from the File menu).

The PageMaker Print dialog box gives you many more options to choose from than does the standard Apple dialog box (see fig. 2.14). Some of the options you may want to use right away include selecting the number of copies to be printed, printing a specific page range, scaling your page output, and choosing a paper source (from a paper tray or manual feed). These options work the same as their counterparts in the Apple Print dialog box.

You should always check one thing before you print, especially if you are working on a network with more than one printer attached. In the lower left corner of the Print dialog box is an entry labeled `Printer type`. Make sure that this entry shows the name of the correct output device. If the name is wrong, use your Chooser desk accessory. If you have questions about using Chooser, refer to the manual that came with your Macintosh.

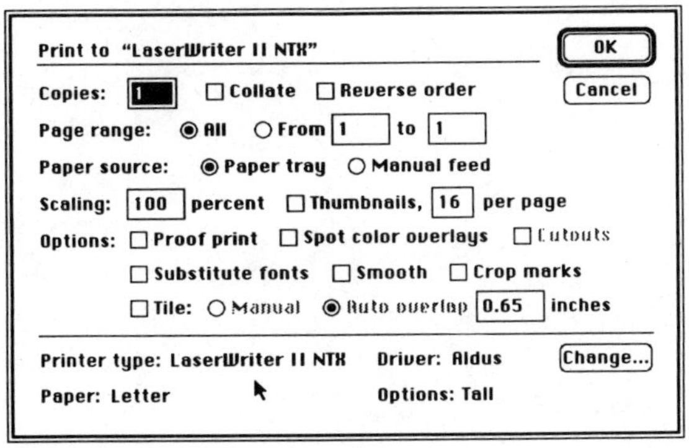

Fig. 2.14.

PageMaker's Print dialog box.

Chapter Summary

In this chapter you learned how to open new and existing documents, set the document size, adjust page orientation, assign page numbers, and configure margins.

You were introduced to PageMaker's publication window where you learned how to use the pasteboard, toolbox, rulers, and page icons. You experimented with each of PageMaker's tools to gain familiarity with them.

You also discovered an abundance of shortcuts for quickly moving about in your publications and viewing your pages. You learned how to get on-line help whenever you get stuck. Finally, you learned how to save your work and how to print with the PageMaker Print dialog box.

Now that you have covered the basics of working with PageMaker, move to Chapter 3 in which you learn how to create new documents from scratch.

Creating a Document

In this chapter, you study the most important steps to take when creating a publication. You begin by learning how to customize PageMaker's default settings to eliminate the need to configure each document. Then, you discover the effectiveness of working with master pages—a powerful, timesaving feature that enables you to create a layout once and have it repeat automatically throughout your publication.

You also learn how to develop and refine layouts using nonprinting guides to align text and graphics. You discover the secrets of using a grid to help structure documents. Finally, you learn how to use PageMaker's rulers and measuring system to position page elements.

When you finish this chapter, you will be ready to start creating publications.

Setting Document Defaults

PageMaker often is used to produce periodicals that retain the same format from issue to issue. If your company specializes in publishing tabloid-size newsletters, for example, you want to set up the program so that PageMaker defaults to a tabloid-size page when you open it. With PageMaker, you can set up this default in two ways: you can design and use a template to create publications, or you can set the program defaults ahead of time to match anticipated publishing requirements.

Templates are used best when your publication format is fixed. You learn more about working with templates in Chapter 10, "Planning Page Layouts." Setting program defaults, on the other hand, is the same as establishing a standard. The defaults give you a basis for designing publications, but don't provide the complete framework that a template provides.

If your publishing requirements are varied, you may want to set separate defaults for each document you work on. If you need to create a series of sales brochures and accompanying catalogs, for example, you may choose a two-column spread for the sales brochures and a six-column spread for the catalogs. You would not convert these column specifications into program defaults because you would have to change the settings whenever you switched layouts. To get around this problem, you can set file defaults for each publication. File defaults override PageMaker's program defaults.

Default settings are nothing more than preset choices. When you open PageMaker for the first time, you find the menu choices and dialog box options already configured for general document preparation. You can revise any or all of PageMaker's program and file defaults to reflect your publishing needs.

Changing Program Defaults

Program defaults are the global settings you expect to be in effect when you open a new document. Almost everything on-screen—and much of what you don't see immediately—is controlled by default settings and can be changed. Ruler settings, the number of columns, font sizes and styles, paragraph indents—these and dozens of other options can be preset as program defaults.

Setting program defaults is easy. When you first open PageMaker, hit any key, select any menu item, or click the mouse button to make the startup screen disappear. Don't choose New from the File menu yet: after a publication is opened, any changes you make apply only to that publication and not to the program. From the PageMaker desktop, pull down the File menu and choose Page Setup. The Page Setup dialog box appears. Enter your choices for the physical characteristics of your pages and click the OK button. Do the same for the Preferences dialog box by choosing Preferences from the Edit menu. You can continue in this way for all other dialog boxes, including Column Guides, Text Wrap, and Rounded Corners (accessible through the Options menu), and Type Specifications, Paragraph, Indents/Tabs, Define Styles, Spacing, and Alignment (accessible through the Type menu).

PageMaker enables you to convert most menu commands into default settings—even those menu items without dialog boxes. Pull down each menu and make your selections. You can, for example, set a specific line width and an object fill pattern as defaults (see fig. 3.1). You also can turn the Snap To Guides command on or off, hide or display the toolbox, and hide or display the scroll bars and page icons. Any menu commands you select or deselect from the desktop become program default settings. Some menu commands are displayed in light gray type to show that they are inaccessible—you cannot change these commands. Accessible commands are displayed in normal black type. But everything else can be preset as program defaults.

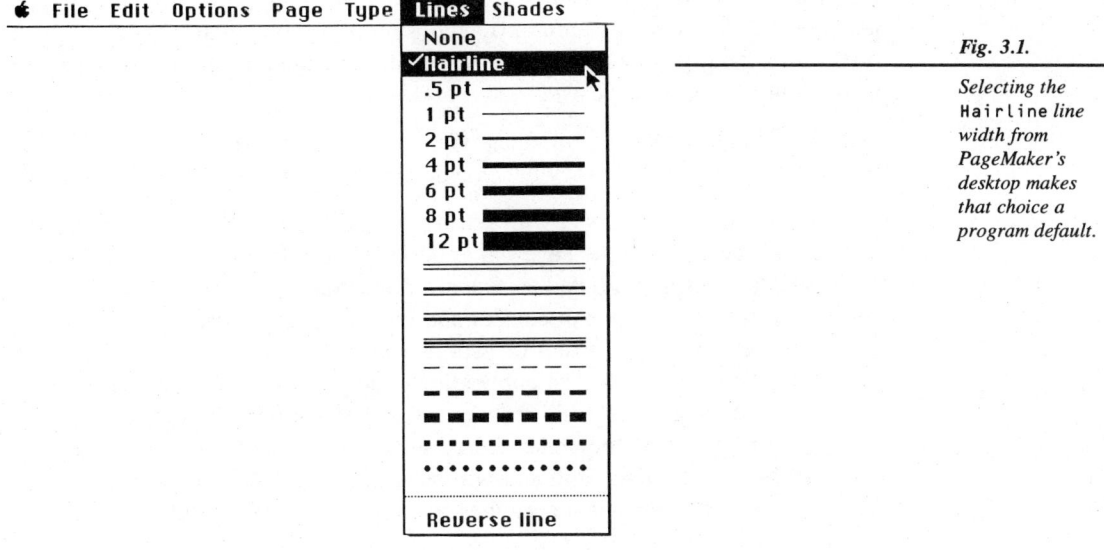

Fig. 3.1.

Selecting the Hairline *line width from PageMaker's desktop makes that choice a program default.*

You don't have to quit and restart PageMaker to change program defaults. You can close the current publication window and make changes from the PageMaker desktop before opening another document. New program defaults take effect immediately and remain active until you change them.

Changing File Defaults

File defaults are handled like program defaults, except that you set file defaults from within open publications and not from PageMaker's desktop. Generally, you choose `page-setup defaults` from the Page Setup dialog box that appears when you create a document. After a new document is opened, however, the page-setup defaults can be revised only by choosing the Page Setup command from the File menu.

When you assign text attributes, such as font type, style, and size, as new file defaults, you must be careful not to have any text selected at the time you make the changes, or the changes affect only the selected text and not the default settings. If text is selected when you change the settings, when you deselect your text, the file defaults remain the same as before—only selected text is changed. The same holds true for graphics. Any alterations you make become file defaults only if no graphic elements are selected when you change the settings.

Contrary to what the PageMaker documentation says, you don't have to use the pointer tool to set file defaults. Any tool can be used. The tool changes to a pointer when you move it out of the publication window to pull down a menu.

You also can leave various elements selected on your pages while changing defaults if those elements aren't affected directly by the changes you make. It doesn't matter if you have a graphic selected, for example, if you are changing the default setting for type size.

Default changes made to an open file are temporary until you save your publication—only then do they become a permanent part of the file.

Take a moment to experiment with setting defaults. Open PageMaker, but don't open a document. From the PageMaker desktop, pull down different menus and set a variety of program defaults. Open a document and see what results your choices produce. Close the document and repeat the experiment several times, each time setting a new group of program defaults. When you finish setting program defaults, leave the last publication open and set a group of file defaults. Save your document, close, and reopen the same document. PageMaker remembers your program and file defaults. Try setting file defaults with various tools selected. Set file defaults with and without text and graphic elements selected. The type of item selected determines whether a particular default setting is changed.

The Magic of Master Pages

Master pages are like building blueprints that help establish the framework of a publication. To access master pages, click the miniature master page icons at the lower left of the publication window—the icons with "L" and "R" represent the left and right master pages. You have one left master page (for all left-hand pages) and one right master page (for all right-hand or single-sided pages). Whatever you place on master pages repeats on all regular pages. Master pages can shorten the time it takes to create lengthy documents, especially documents requiring a consistent look. If you draw repeating elements such as rules along the tops and bottoms of your master pages, for example, the rules appear along the tops and bottoms of all pages.

Master pages are different from regular pages in several important ways. You can work on master pages like you do any other page, but master pages do not print with the publication. Although everything on these pages is duplicated on regular pages, you cannot edit or change the master text or graphics repeated on regular pages. The only place you can change a master-page element is on a master page. Working with master pages is like working with overlays that are visible but inaccessible. Master pages remain completely isolated from your regular pages.

In addition to text and graphics, you can include columns and ruler guides on master pages (see fig. 3.2). These guides also repeat throughout your publication. Unlike master text and graphic elements, however, the nonprinting guides can be repositioned at any time. Click a guide, hold down the mouse button, and drag. Nonprinting guides are never permanently anchored unless you intentionally lock them in place with the Lock Guides command from the Options menu. If you lock guides on the master page, they remain locked on all regular pages.

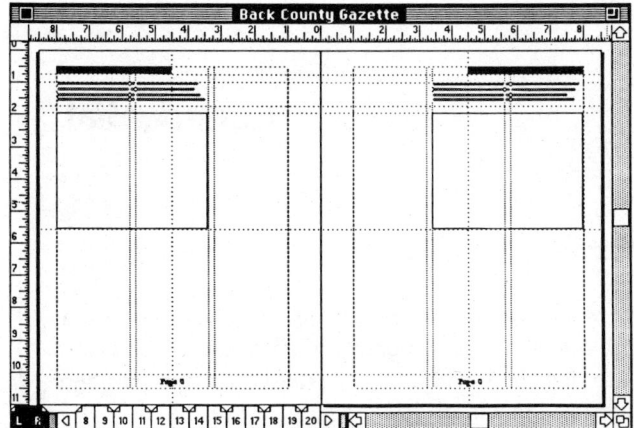

Fig. 3.2.

A pair of double-sided, facing master pages with columns, ruler guides, and placeholder text and graphics.

To place a horizontal or vertical ruler guide on your master pages (or on any page), click the appropriate ruler, hold down the mouse button, and drag the cursor onto the page. A new ruler guide appears and follows your cursor. To remove a ruler guide, drag the guide off the page back onto the ruler from which it originally came.

If you want PageMaker automatically to number the pages of your publications, on each master page drag out a text box using the text tool and press Command-Option-P. (Make sure that the Caps Lock key is not engaged, or nothing happens when you press this key combination.) Position the master-page markers (they look like zeros) where you want page numbers to appear on corresponding regular pages. If you want composite numbers like *Page 6 of 12*, type the appropriate text, replacing the changing number (6 in this example) with Command-Option-P (see fig. 3.3).

You can assign any font type, size, or style you want to the page markers on the master pages. PageMaker numbers your pages starting with the page number specified in the Page Setup dialog box. If you later add or delete pages using the Insert Pages and Remove Pages commands on the Page menu, PageMaker updates your page numbers.

Fig. 3.3.

A composite page number on a master page of a confidential document.

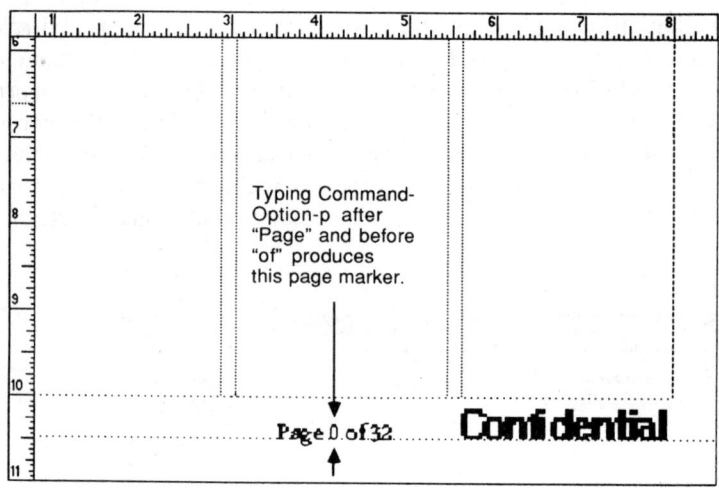

> **Note**
> If you don't want PageMaker to number every page in your publication, draw a text box and press Command-Option-P on just those pages where you do want numbers to appear. PageMaker inserts the correct numbers and updates the numbers as you add or delete pages.

Include on your master pages only those elements you want to appear on every regular page. Less frequently used text and graphics can be stored on the pasteboard and copied onto your regular pages as needed.

> **Tip**
> Use repeating ruler guides to mark areas on your pages where elements you don't want included on every page should appear. If you plan to center an illustration with a box around it in the same spot on only a few pages, for example, predefine that area on the master pages using horizontal and vertical ruler guides. When it's time to draw the boxes around the pictures on your regular pages, you can do so quickly and accurately. Similarly, if you position vertical ruler guides between adjoining columns on your master pages, you can later draw in column rules where needed.

An organized approach to setting up your master pages follows:

1. Position all nonprinting guides on both master pages, including column guides and horizontal and vertical ruler guides. Later, you can rearrange master column and ruler guides on any page without affecting other parts of your layout. If you decide to reinstate the original master guides arrangement on a page where you have moved the guides, select Copy Master Guides from the Page menu.

2. Draw any repeating rules, including rules between columns and along the tops and bottoms of pages.

3. Place repeating graphics where needed. Position company logos or other design elements on the master pages exactly where you want them to appear on all pages.

4. Add repeating text such as running heads, automatic page numbers, and classification markings.

5. Draw remaining borders and boxes.

6. To save time when creating identical master pages, do steps 2 through 5 for only one master page. Select all the elements on that page and copy the elements to the Clipboard. Paste the Clipboard contents back onto your master pages. With all the pasted elements selected, drag them as a unit onto the facing master page. Use ruler guides to reposition individual elements as necessary for perfect alignment.

To experiment with guides, create a document with several single-sided pages. Add columns, text, and graphics to the master page. Position a few horizontal and vertical ruler guides. Turn to a regular page and hide the various nonprinting guides and master elements. Make the elements reappear. Try clicking and dragging the various elements with the cursor. Note that you can move the column and ruler guides, but not the text or graphics. Without closing the document, convert it into a double-sided publication displaying facing pages and repeat the experiment. Although you cannot move separate horizontal ruler guides on each facing master page, you can move different vertical ruler and column guide arrangements.

If you want to hide the master elements on one of two regular facing pages, you normally have to deselect the `Facing pages` option in the Page Setup dialog box and revert to a single-page display. You deselect this option because the Display Master Items command on the Page menu toggles both master pages simultaneously. You can get around this constraint, however, to continue working on two pages at the same time and still hide the master elements on just one page when printing. You can use one of the following three methods:

1. To remove all master elements from one facing page, deselect the `Facing pages` option in the Page Setup dialog box. Then hide the master elements on just those pages where you don't want them to print.

   Reselect the `Facing pages` option and continue working on the publication with both pages showing. Note that the companion facing page also has the master elements hidden. If you deselect the `Facing pages` option again before printing your publication, however, the pages print correctly with the master elements hidden on the one page and not on the other. This method works because the `Facing pages` option controls only the screen display, not the actual layout.

2. To retain some, but not all, master elements on a facing page, copy the master elements you want to retain to the Clipboard, and paste them onto the publication page. With the items you pasted selected, drag them into position over the master elements already showing. (If you have already hidden the master elements, choose Display Master Items from the Page menu to see them again.) Then deselect the Display Master Items command on the Page menu. The repeating master elements disappear from both facing pages, but the elements pasted from the Clipboard remain behind. The pasted items are no longer treated as master elements.

3. To retain some, but not all, master elements on a facing page, cover any master page items you don't want to print with "electronic whiteout" by selecting the appropriate tool from the toolbox and drawing a line, oval, or box about the size needed to cover the offending element. In figure 3.4, a rectangle tool is used to draw a box around the object (see parts 1 and 2). Then, fill the box with white by choosing Paper from the Shades menu (see part 3 in fig. 3.4). Hide the borders of the line or box by choosing None from the Lines menu (see part 4 in the figure). Drag the white box into position over the master element you want obliterated. Part 5 in figure 3.4 shows the final result.

Fig. 3.4.

Eliminating a master element using "electronic whiteout."

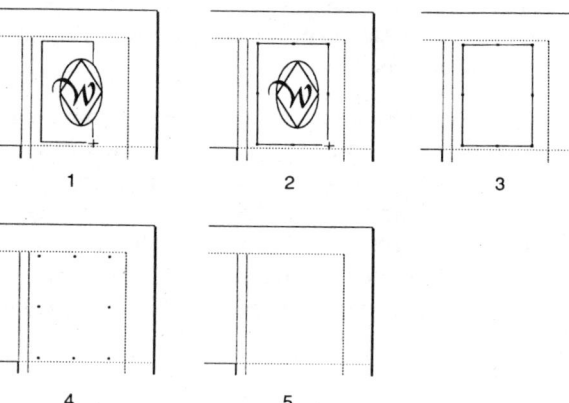

Laying a Solid Foundation

The foundation of every PageMaker publication is the layout. Layouts bring order to the way you place text and graphics on pages. With a little care in planning and executing layouts, your publications can look as professional as any seen on your local newsstand.

The Layout Grid

You can spot a poor layout as easily as a good one—often easier. Your layouts should follow certain basic design principles if you want your publications to be successful. A layout grid can make the difference. In PageMaker, a *layout grid* consists of nonprinting margin, column, and ruler guides. These guides help you place text and graphics so that they line up on the pages the way you want them to. You can think of the layout grid as the structure of your publication. Whole cities are laid out, and complex roadways built, according to predetermined grids—and so it should be with your publications. The principal is the same. The larger and more complex your publication, the more important using a grid becomes.

Traditional publishers use preprinted grid sheets to lay out publications. These grid sheets provide a ruled environment for pasteup of text and graphics, and the grid lines are light blue so that they do not reproduce during printing. Similarly, the nonprinting guides used in PageMaker become invisible during printing. On-screen, these guides are much more flexible and easier to use than a fixed grid sheet. You can drag onto your pages only the ruler guides that you need, for example, and reposition each one independently. Using just a few guides on a page gives you an unobstructed view of your work. By contrast, the many crossed lines of a fixed grid sheet clutter your screen, making it difficult to view your pages. You also have to change the entire grid spacing each time you want to adjust a small part of your display.

In addition to nonprinting guides, PageMaker provides an invisible grid that you can toggle on or off to help align page elements. This invisible grid corresponds to the intersections of imaginary lines drawn from your horizontal and vertical ruler divisions. The spacing of these divisions, or tick marks, is a function of whatever units of measure are set in the Preferences dialog box. As an example, a ruler setting of millimeters in the Fit in Window view has wider spacing between tick marks than a setting of inches or picas. When you check the Snap To Rulers command on the Options menu, PageMaker's invisible grid becomes active. When you drag text, graphics, and nonprinting column and ruler guides, they automatically snap to the invisible grid lines (see figs. 3.5 and 3.6).

Fig. 3.5.

With the Snap To Rulers command selected, the edge of the box "jumps" between ruler intervals as it's moved from right to left.

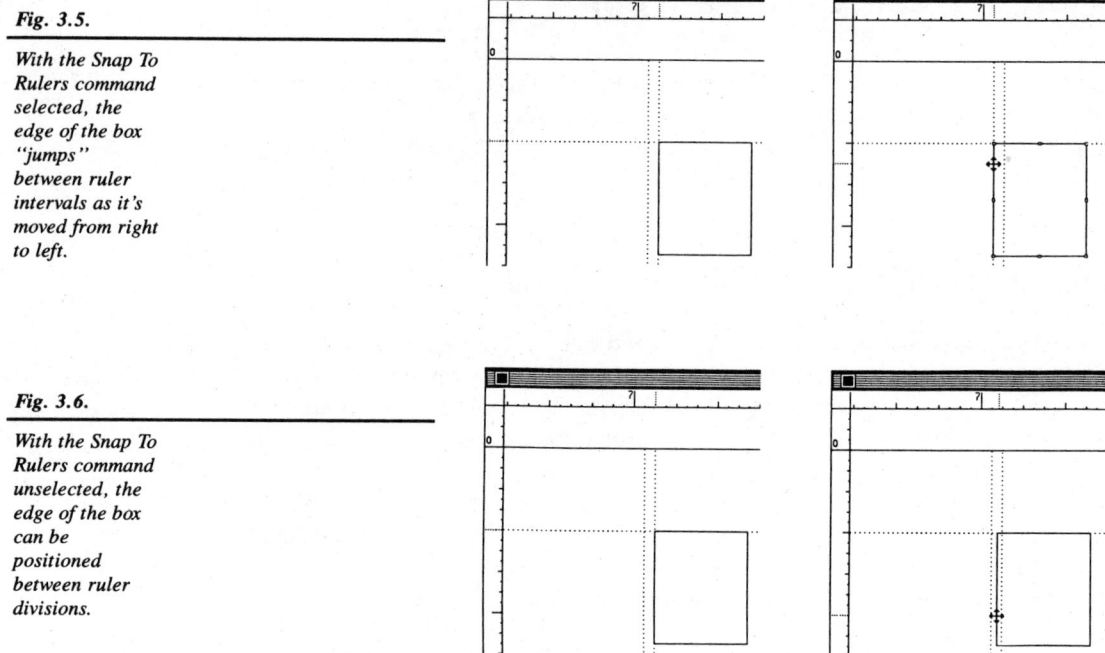

Fig. 3.6.

With the Snap To Rulers command unselected, the edge of the box can be positioned between ruler divisions.

Your layout grid provides page-to-page consistency for the placement of text and graphics. Using a layout grid doesn't mean that you have to stay within its boundaries. You may want to place page numbers, header and footer information, and design elements outside page margins. Margins define the central area of your pages where most of the layout occurs, but you can place text and graphics anywhere on the page. The only constraint is the imaging area of your output device. If, for example, you print to a Linotronic, you can *bleed* pages (run images to the very edges of the page), and the pages print fine (see fig. 3.7). On a LaserWriter, however, because of the way the internal lens aperture is constructed, you can print only to within 1/4 inch of the sides and 1/8 inch from the tops and bottoms of your pages.

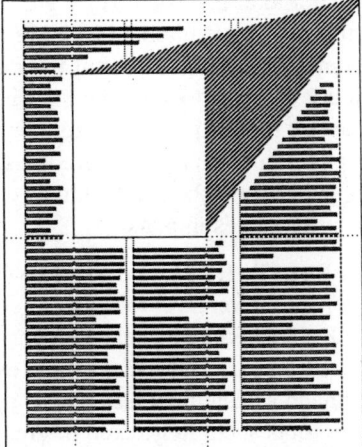

Fig. 3.7.

"Bleeding" a graphic element.

> ***Tip***
> You can get a full bleed on the top and bottom edges of an 8.5-by-11-inch page by printing on 8.5-by-14-inch legal paper and trimming the finished page down to 8.5 by 11 inches. Cut the bleed edge of your page first.

Designing a workable layout for your publication takes thought and planning. Setting up your layout grid, however, is fairly easy. The following step-by-step approach works well:

1. Verify the page size and orientation, select single-sided or double-sided pages (with or without facing pages), and set the number of pages (including the starting page number) in the Page Setup dialog box. Also make any necessary adjustments to the margin settings in this dialog box. Keep in mind that how you set the margins in this dialog box is how they appear on every page.

2. Configure the Preferences dialog box for the units of measurement you want applied to rulers. Remember that ruler settings directly affect how PageMaker's invisible grid behaves. (You learn more about setting up rulers later in this chapter under "Rulers and Measurements.")

Note: Complete as many of the following steps as possible on your master pages to eliminate repeating them for each page.

3. If your layout calls for columns of text, choose Column Guides from the Options menu and set the desired number of columns and column spacing. Your columns appear evenly spaced. Later, you can drag individual column guides as necessary to modify the spacing.

Part I: The Basics

4. Position as many horizontal and vertical ruler guides as necessary to indicate the proper placement of running heads, graphic placeholders, rules, and other design elements. Try to limit the number of ruler guides used, or you may find it difficult to sort them out later. Place the most important ruler guides on master pages and add any supplementary ruler guides to individual pages later. When you are satisfied with the arrangement of your guides, use the Lock Guides command on the Options menu to lock the guides in place.

5. Select or deselect the Snap To Rulers and Snap To Guides commands on the Options menu, depending on how you plan to work on your pages. Leaving the Snap To Rulers command selected, for example, makes it easy to align horizontally separated blocks of text evenly; leaving the Snap To Guides command selected enables you to position text, graphics, and drawing tools accurately, even in greatly reduced views. Unselecting these commands enables you to position elements freely, such as when centering text within a circle.

Changing Columns

PageMaker's Column Guides command enables you to set up to 20 equally spaced, even-width columns per page. You may think 20 is an excessive number, but many companies need to produce tabloid-size publications containing horizontal tabular data, such as phone lists, product catalogs, and financial data. In such cases, even 20 columns may be too few. You can make column assignments separately for double-sided facing pages by selecting Set left and right pages separately in the Column Guides dialog box (see fig. 3.8).

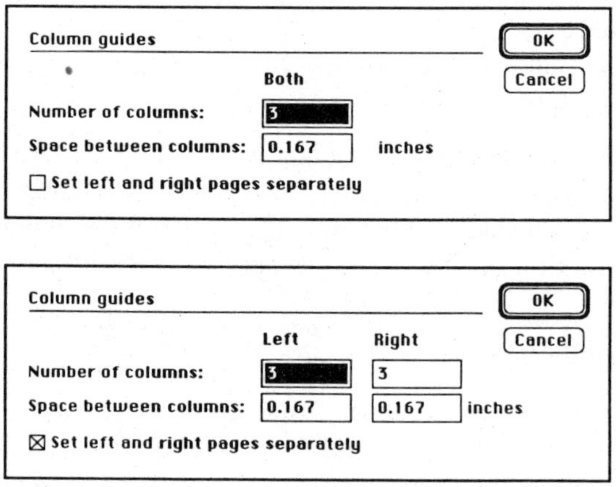

Fig. 3.8.

Using the Set left and right pages separately *box for double-sided facing pages.*

Many layout designs call for columns of variable width. After creating the desired number of columns on the page, you can drag any column guide to change the width of that column. When you drag a column guide, the value in the `Number of columns` field in the Column Guides dialog box changes from a one-digit or two-digit number to the word `Custom` to show that you made alterations to the column layout. The value in the `Space between columns` field remains constant because you did not change column spacing, only column width. PageMaker's initial default column spacing is 0.167 inch or 1 pica width, a value you can change by typing a new number in this field.

> *Note*
>
> PageMaker's *Reference Manual* states that you can change the spacing between even-width and variable-width columns by typing a new value in the `Space between columns` field in the Column Guides dialog box. This statement is true only for even-width columns, however. The spacing between columns of variable width does not change. To change the spacing of variable-width columns, choose Column Guides from the Options menu and specify the number of columns and the new column spacing you want. After you click OK, you get even-width columns with the desired spacing. To re-establish the variable-width column layout, redrag the column guides to their former locations.

> *Warning*
>
> All newly created columns are spaced to fit evenly within existing page margins. If you change the inside or outside (left or right) margin settings in the Page Setup dialog box, every column on every page in your publication is likewise spaced to fit evenly between the margins. The number of columns per page doesn't change, just the dimensions. If your publication contains custom columns, changing either side margin, even by the slightest amount, causes you to lose all the custom spacing. You immediately can select Undo Page Setup from the Edit menu to undo the damage before it becomes permanent. (The damage becomes permanent when you click the mouse anywhere in the publication window.)

You cannot drag a column guide outside a margin boundary, but you can place text outside a margin. A common use of margins is to define the "live" area on the page into which you "pour" column text. Other items of text, such as headlines and titles, then can be positioned outside the margins.

When you pour text into a column, the copy stays within the left and right column boundaries as it flows down the page. Combined with the capability to change column and margin settings at any time, flowing text into a column gives you enormous flexibility when laying out publications. Suppose that you want to create a travel brochure with two extra-wide columns containing promotional material spanning the upper one-third of the page. Across the bottom two-thirds of the same page, you want four columns where you can list benefits and booking information in smaller type (see fig. 3.9). The following is a quick way to create this brochure:

1. Pull down a ruler guide from the horizontal ruler and position the guide on the page where you want your columns to break. Make a note of the vertical placement of the ruler: you need this information when you reset the top and bottom margins.

2. Temporarily reset the bottom margin to just above where you want the page break to occur.

3. Use the Column Guides command to set the number of columns to 2. Pour the promotional text into these two columns. (You learn how to pour text in the next chapter, "Quick Start: Creating a Newsletter.") The bottom margin limits the text flow and constrains it to lie above your page break.

4. Change the bottom page margin back to the original setting. Temporarily reset the top margin to just below the page break.

5. Use the Column Guides command to change the number of columns for the bottom portion of the page to 4. The text you already have poured is not affected. Pour the benefits and booking information into these columns. The top margin now establishes the tops of the second set of columns for flowing text.

Fig. 3.9.

Creating a split-column publication in PageMaker.

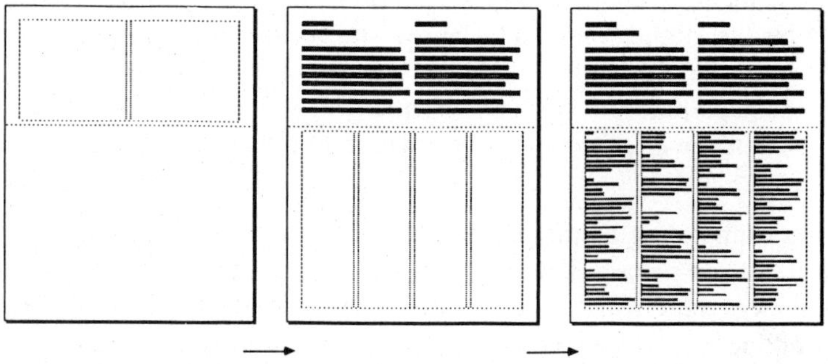

You learn more about working with columns in Chapter 6, "Formatting Text."

Using Guides

You have seen how you can use ruler guides to help determine where to set upper and lower column margins. Setting margins is only one of many creative ways that nonprinting guides can help make the preparation of your publications easier. Other techniques include adjusting page margins to create accurately sized working areas and changing the columns on a page to control text display. You learn more ways to work with nonprinting guides in later chapters.

PageMaker imposes a limit of 40 horizontal and vertical ruler guides per page, including master-page ruler guides and any guides added to regular pages. The maximum number of columns you can have on a page is 20, resulting in 22 column guides—with the two outermost column guides overlapping the side margin guides. You also are limited to a single set of top, bottom, and side page margins.

As long as you don't move or add ruler guides to regular pages, you can change the guides on the master pages, and the regular pages are updated automatically. If you adjust even one ruler guide on a regular page, however, that page becomes independent of the master page and is no longer updated. The same restriction is true for working with column guides. To update a page in your document so that the page reflects the most recent changes to the master page, choose Copy Master Guides from the Page menu. This command copies the current guide arrangement from the master page to your publication page and replaces any guides on the regular page.

You can lock or unlock column and ruler guides whenever you want by toggling the Lock Guides command on the Options menu. Because guides are easy to move accidentally when repositioning text and graphics, fixing them in place often helps. By checking the Snap To Guides and Snap To Rulers commands on the Options menu, you also can align text and graphics more easily. When these commands are checked, the column, ruler, and margin guides act like magnets and exert a pull on items near them. The guides enable you to do precision work that you cannot do otherwise except in greatly enlarged views.

Tip

When you click a column or ruler guide, the cursor changes to a double-headed arrow to show the possible directions of movement. Use this feature to distinguish between vertical and horizontal guides when trying to grab one guide in an area where several guides intersect. If you move the wrong guide, immediately choose Undo from the Edit menu to recover. If you click a side margin, you also get a double-headed arrow. This arrow, however, indicates a column guide that overlaps the margin, not a movable margin boundary. Remember that margins can be set only from the Page Setup dialog box.

> **Tip**
> If you want to see clearly the edges of elements overlapped by nonprinting guides, click the `Guides: Back` button in the Preferences dialog box. This action moves all nonprinting guides behind any elements on your pages to give you an unobstructed view of the page.

When you want to see what the completed pages look like when printed, you can hide all nonprinting guides by unselecting the Guides command on the Options menu. You can do this when working on the publication to reduce visual clutter on the pages and get a clearer idea of how your publication is taking shape. When the guides are hidden, you no longer can snap to them.

Rulers and Measurements

PageMaker's rulers extend horizontally and vertically along the top and left sides of the publication window. Each ruler can be configured independently, and the increments depend on the selections made in the Preferences dialog box. The number of increments along each ruler varies depending upon the size of your screen and your page magnification. Dotted track lines travel along both rulers to indicate the exact position of the cursor on the page. The track lines enable you to draw and resize graphic elements; position text, graphics, and nonprinting guides, and crop imported illustrations and photos to fit within designated boundaries. You can hide the rulers by deselecting the Rulers command on the Options menu.

> **Tip**
> An important use of rulers is setting variable column widths. Because variable-width column guides must be set separately for each page and because these guides cannot be copied from page to page (except through the magic of master pages), you have no automatic way to ensure that the guides mirror one another when creating identical facing pages. To get around this restriction, adjust all column widths on one facing page. Then use the rulers to set the same column widths on the other facing page.

The tick marks on PageMaker's rulers are accurate in all views to within 0.001 inch. This accuracy enables you to do precision layout work for output to a high-resolution printing device like a Linotronic. The smallest ruler increments, however, are available only at 400% Size page view, measured in decimal inches, and shown at 0.01-inch increments. For picas and points, the 200% Size and 400% Size page views display ruler divisions only at point-size intervals.

When you first open a publication, the zero point of the rulers is aligned to the upper left corner of a single page or to the center upper edge of combined facing pages. You cannot change these settings as program defaults. After a publication is open, however, the ruler zero point can be realigned anywhere on the page. This feature makes measuring the size of an object or boundary or determining the distance between two elements easy.

To reset the ruler zero point, complete the following steps:

1. Unlock the zero point by unselecting the Zero Lock command on the Options menu.
2. Click the mouse button above the crossed lines icon in the upper left corner of the publication window where the rulers intersect.
3. Press the mouse button and drag the cursor point to the desired spot on the page.
4. Release the mouse button.
5. Relock the zero point, by selecting the Zero Lock command on the Options menu, to avoid accidentally resetting it.

To practice using rulers, draw a line, a box, and a circle on a page. Taking each in turn, relocate the ruler zero point to the left end of the line, the upper left corner of the box, and the left or topmost edge of the circle. Measure the lengths and diameters of each object using horizontal and vertical rulers. After completing each measurement, double the size of each element using the rulers as a guide. Reset the zero point to the upper left corner of the page and repeat the exercise. Note how much more difficult it is to take accurate measurements when the ruler is in its default position.

The units of measure set in the Preferences dialog box apply to the entire publication, including the rulers and all dialog boxes in which you enter dimensional values. You can change the measurement settings at any time, but take care not to complicate the layout by using too many systems of measurement.

If you work in an environment in which your publication must be set up for one measurement system, but you are more comfortable working with another, you can use abbreviations when typing values into dialog box fields. Suppose that your publication is set up to measure in inches, but your background is in traditional publishing, and you are used to working with picas and points. In the dialog boxes, you can enter measurements expressed as numbers of picas, followed by a small *p* and the numbers of points (for example, *6p3*), as shown in figure 3.10. PageMaker recognizes this abbreviation and makes the conversion to inches for you. Note that a number always must precede the abbreviation, even if that number is zero. Table 3.1 lists abbreviations that can be used in this way.

Table 3.1
Measurement Abbreviations

Abbreviation	Example
i for inches	3.75i (3-3/4 inches)
m for millimeters	16.2m (16.2 millimeters)
p for picas	12p (12 picas) (Note that the *p* follows the number.)
p for pica points	0p3 (3 points) (Note that a zero precedes the *p* that precedes the number.)
p for picas and pica points	12p3 (12 picas, 3 points) (Note that the *p* lies between the numbers.)
c for ciceros	12c (12 ciceros) (Note that the *c* follows the number.)
c for cicero points	0c3 (3 points) (Note that the zero precedes the *c* which precedes the number.)
c for ciceros and cicero points	12c3 (12 ciceros, 3 points) (Note that the *c* lies between the numbers.)

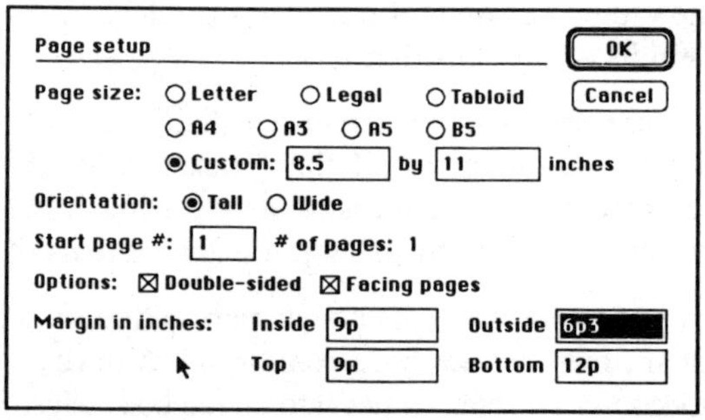

Fig. 3.10.

Pica margin values can be typed into the Page Setup dialog box set for inches.

If you use PageMaker's rulers, your layouts will go more smoothly. By custom setting your vertical ruler to read the same point size as your text, for example, you can use PageMaker's Snap To Rulers command to align the baselines of text in adjoining columns. By setting your measurement system to inches, you can use an ordinary household ruler to check existing hard-copy specs when recreating existing documents. If you produce publications for clients who supply you with pica-point or metric specifications, you can set up your measurement system in the same way so that you don't have to compute each conversion or remember to type overriding abbreviations in all the dialog boxes.

Chapter Summary

In this chapter, you added to your knowledge of PageMaker's basics. You learned how to set program and file defaults and how to tap the hidden power of PageMaker's master pages. You also acquired an understanding of grids and how to use them to produce professional-looking publications. You sharpened your skills by learning how to manipulate column and ruler guides, change measurements, and adjust ruler settings. Now you are ready to move on to the Quick Start in Chapter 4 in which you put what you have learned into practice by creating a four-page newsletter.

4

Quick Start: Creating a Newsletter

In this chapter, you create a simple four-page newsletter. First, you assemble an overall layout, then design a detailed front page. This chapter reviews what you have learned so far and briefly previews several design techniques you learn about in later chapters. Try to follow along and duplicate as many of the steps as possible. Use whatever text and graphics you have handy—you don't have to reproduce exactly what you see here to benefit from the example. When you finish this section, you should have a better understanding of how to do practical desktop publishing design and layout using PageMaker, and you will be ready to start creating your own publications.

Opening PageMaker

Your assignment is to create a four-page fictitious weekly newsletter titled *Barnyard Gossip*. The design calls for a simple, informal look that must avoid a cosmopolitan complexion if the newsletter is to appeal to a target audience of farmers.

The first step is to open PageMaker and select New from the File menu. Set the margins in the Page Setup dialog box (see fig. 4.1). The inside margins must be set large enough to allow room for archiving the newsletter in a three-ring notebook binder. Make the top margin larger than the outside and bottom margins for a more eye-pleasing effect. Select Facing pages to make creating a balanced layout easier. Click the OK button to open your new publication.

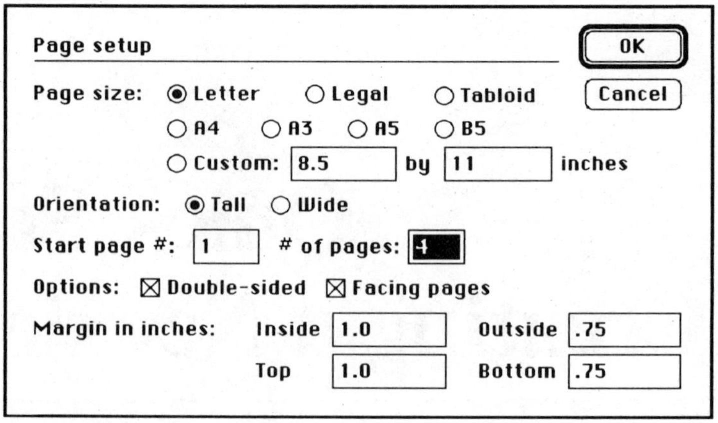

Fig. 4.1.

Setting new document specifications in the Page Setup dialog box.

Setting Up Master Pages

The next step is to set up your master pages. Click the master page icons in the lower left corner of the publication window to display your master pages. This Quick Start assumes that you already assembled text and graphics, prepared a preliminary layout sketch, and developed a clear idea of how you want your newsletter to go together. If you were publishing this newsletter on a regular basis, you would save your master page's layout as a template for later use. With a template, you don't have to start over from scratch each time you put together a new edition.

Figure 4.2 shows your initial master-page setup. You prepare the newsletter using this familiar three-column layout because the layout permits good design flexibility and easy reading. To set the desired number of columns, choose Column Guides from the Options menu and type *3*.

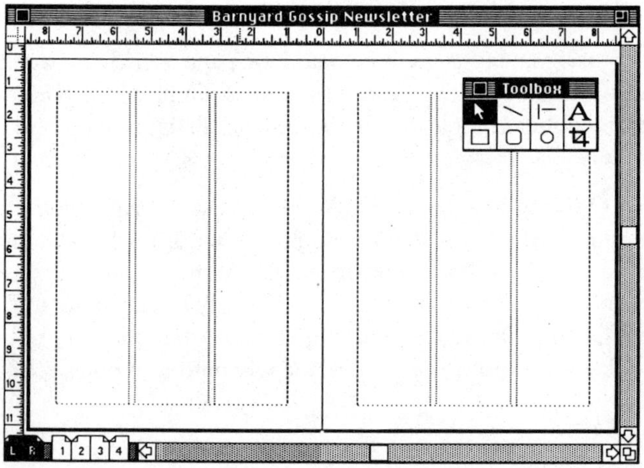

Fig. 4.2.

Left and right master pages set up in a three-column format.

Positioning the Logo

A recognized trademark of your newsletter is a rooster-chasing-a-chicken logo that appears at the bottom of each page (see fig. 4.3). Although most newsletters traditionally include the logo as part of the banner, the unique graphic design of this logo enables you to use it to encourage readers to turn the page. (On the last page, the logo is reversed to provide a gentle touch of humor and to mark the end of the newsletter.)

The infamous Barnyard Gossip logo! Note how it's used to entice the reader to keep turning pages. On the last page its reverse orientation marks the end of the publication.

Fig. 4.3.

A birds-eye view of the newsletter layout.

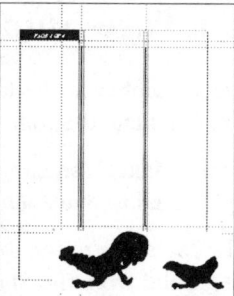

To ensure accurate logo placement, pull down two horizontal and one vertical ruler guides, and position the guides as shown on the facing master pages (see fig. 4.4). The vertical ruler guide and intersecting lower horizontal ruler guide help you place your logo accurately on each page. The upper horizontal ruler guide shows where columnar text directly above the logo must end.

You don't reproduce the logo on the left and right master pages. You want to wrap text around the logo on each page, and because master-page graphics cannot affect text wrap on regular pages, you manually place the logo on each page.

Fig. 4.4.

Marking off the area for the logo with horizontal and vertical ruler guides.

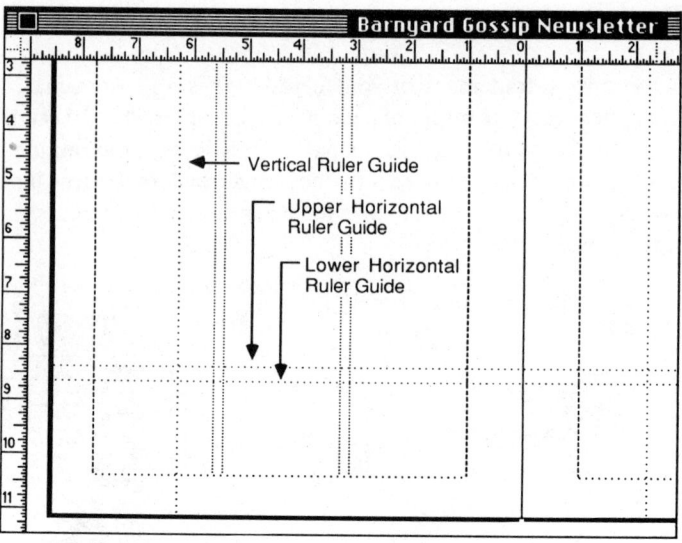

Creating a Page-Number Block

You need a page number at the top of each page. To create an attractive page-number block, complete the following steps:

1. Select PageMaker's square-corner rectangle tool and draw a horizontal rectangle equal to one column's width on the left-hand page.

2. Drag the rectangle to the top of the first column and fill in the block by choosing Solid from the Shades menu (see fig. 4.5).

Fig. 4.5.

The page-number block filled in by choosing Solid from the Shades menu.

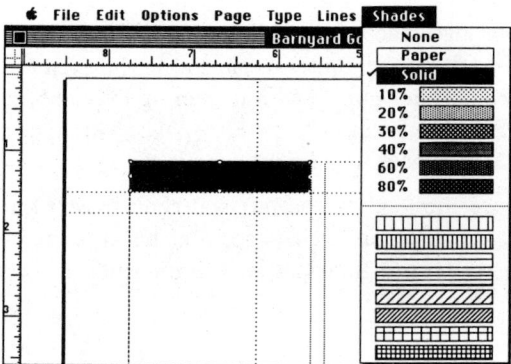

Chapter 4: Quick Start: Creating a Newsletter

3. Choose the text tool from PageMaker's toolbox and type *Page (Command-Option-p) of 4* to yield a fixed repeating text string with automatic page numbering.

4. Using the text tool to highlight what you just typed, choose Type Style from the Type menu.

5. Select Reverse from the Type Style submenu to invert and change the text to white (see fig. 4.6).

6. Using the pointer tool, drag and center the text over the black rectangle (see fig. 4.7).

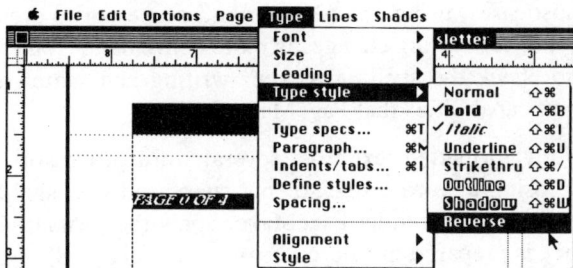

Fig. 4.6.

Reversing selected type changes the lettering from black to white.

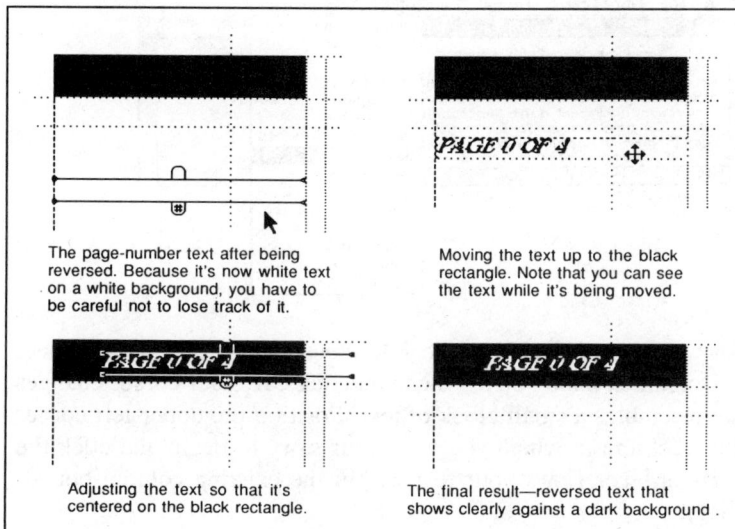

Fig. 4.7.

Placing reversed type on a dark background is a way of highlighting important text.

The page-number text after being reversed. Because it's now white text on a white background, you have to be careful not to lose track of it.

Moving the text up to the black rectangle. Note that you can see the text while it's being moved.

Adjusting the text so that it's centered on the black rectangle.

The final result—reversed text that shows clearly against a dark background.

To create an identical page-number block on the right-hand master page, do the following:

1. Select the text and rectangle and copy them to the Clipboard.

2. Repaste and drag the text and rectangle as a unit to the top of the third column on the right-hand master page.

Preparing and Loading Text

Your text can be prepared in any word processor, or you can type directly within PageMaker. In most cases, using a dedicated word processor to prepare stories and using PageMaker for editing changes is more convenient. You can use your word processor to check the spelling of your writing and search-and-replace text—two important capabilities that PageMaker lacks.

You can import fully formatted text from several word processors into Page-Maker. If you are using a word processor not supported by PageMaker, save your stories as text-only files and let PageMaker apply the formatting. For this example, each story is prepared in Microsoft Word (see fig. 4.8).

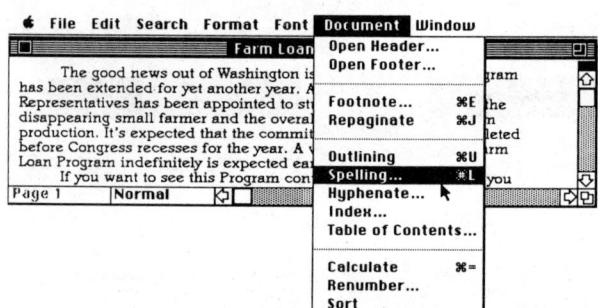

Fig. 4.8.

Creating text in Microsoft Word before importing it into PageMaker.

To import a story, choose Place from the File menu and select the document from the Place Document dialog box. When you click OK, your cursor changes into an icon that resembles a small block of text. Position the upper-left corner of this icon in the column in which you want your story to begin and click the mouse button. PageMaker flows your text within the existing column boundaries (see fig. 4.9).

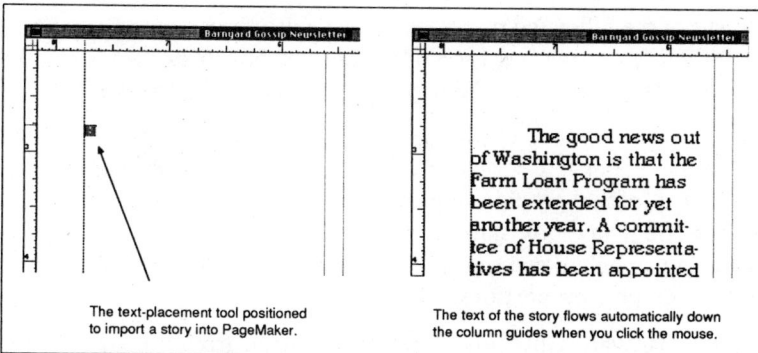

Fig. 4.9.

Placing text in a PageMaker column.

If your story is longer than one column, click the + sign on the windowshade handle at the bottom of the column to recover your text icon (see fig. 4.10). You can reclick the text icon anywhere within your publication to flow remaining text into other columns. (You learn how to autoflow text throughout a publication in Chapter 5, "Text Basics".) Continue both front-page stories on following pages by using this method. A # sign appearing on the bottom windowshade handle indicates that you have placed all the text for that story.

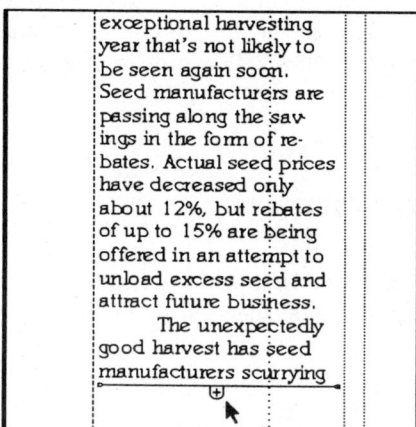

Fig. 4.10.

The + in a column windowshade handle indicates that more text is to be placed.

Preparing and Placing Graphics

PageMaker provides drawing tools for creating graphic design elements like circles, boxes, and rules. To prepare detailed artwork or illustrations you have to use a separate graphics program. You can import pictures created elsewhere by using the Place command. Depending on the graphic you select, your cursor changes into one of the following placement icons: a paintbrush for a Paint file, a pencil for a PICT file, a gray box for a TIFF file, or the letters PS for an EPS file. Each of these file formats can be imported directly by PageMaker.

To import an illustration, position the upper-left corner of the placement icon where you want the upper-left corner of the illustration to appear and click the mouse button. The entire graphic appears on the page. You can resize the graphic by selecting any box handle with the pointer tool and dragging the boundaries. If you hold down the Shift key as you drag a corner handle, you keep the original graphic proportions.

The logo for the Barnyard Gossip newsletter is scanned from a pencil tracing made from a 19th century silhouette. Zedcor's DeskPaint desk accessory, a handy commercial utility for editing black-and-white TIFF files, was used to clean up stray pixels and fill in the scanned outline. The completed graphic is imported into PageMaker using the Place command and reduced proportionally to fit within the ruler guides on the first page. The resulting image was copied to the Clipboard and pasted onto each remaining page of the newsletter. The graphic on the last page of the newsletter was copied back into DeskPaint, flipped, and repasted into PageMaker by using the Clipboard.

The text run-around was done using PageMaker's Text Wrap command from the Options menu. You learn more about how to use this feature in Chapter 8, "Formatting and Enhancing Graphics." This process enables you to reshape the text to fit the graphic.

Refining the Document

Importing text and graphics is the first step in creating a publication. Most of your time and effort probably will be spent on refining your layouts.

Working with Short Text

Short pieces of text, such as headlines, bylines, tables of contents, and column continuations, are best typed within PageMaker after you import the stories. Typing these short text items in your word processor makes little sense because headlines usually have different font type, style, and size characteristics than the main body text.

For this exercise, create each non-story text element within PageMaker. The only exception is the banner title that requires special handling. For the banner, type the text in MacDraw or another graphics program that enables you to save files in PICT format. Import the PICT file into PageMaker so that the graphic can be compressed horizontally or vertically stretched. This procedure makes fitting a headline within a designated space easy, and you can give your masthead a more striking appearance than you can with ordinary text.

To set up the formatting, pull down three horizontal ruler guides from the upper ruler. These guides mark off the banner area and a 1/4-inch space below the banner to house the newsletter's subhead, issue number, and publication date. The lower guide also separates the banner from the main body text. Type the subhead, issue number, and publication date and align them with the pointer tool (see fig. 4.11).

Fig. 4.11.

Using ruler guides enables you to place your banner and any subhead text.

Position the guides behind whatever text and graphics the guides overlap by selecting the `Back Guides` button in the Preference dialog box. Selecting `Back Guides` reduces the chances of you accidentally grabbing and moving a guide when trying to move graphic and text elements. When your layout is set, lock the guides in place by choosing Lock Guides from the Options menu.

Creating a Table of Contents

In this example, you reserve the center column on the front page for your table of contents. This design guides the reader's eye directly from the title banner to the logo at the bottom of the page. To reinforce this eye movement, create a light *sidewalk* of gray with PageMaker's square-corner rectangle tool. Execute the following steps:

1. Draw two intersecting rectangles: one horizontally around the lower part of the banner and the other one so that the rectangle completely surrounds the table of contents.

2. Move both rectangles behind the text by selecting them and choosing Send To Back from the Edit menu.

3. Choose a line width of None from the Lines menu to eliminate border lines.

4. Select a minimum 10% fill from the Shades menu so that the foreground text stands out sharply from the gray background.

Your shaded path now walks the reader's eye down the page toward the logo, and the nature of the logo subtly urges the reader to turn the page and keep reading (see fig. 4.12).

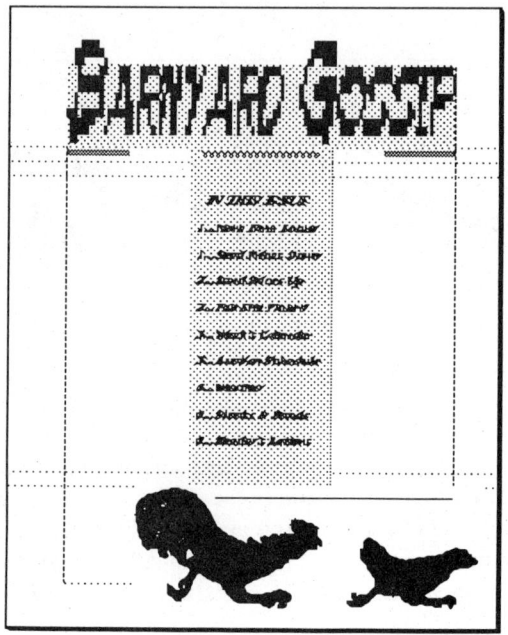

Fig. 4.12.

Using background shading as a design tool helps tie together different elements on the same page.

Using Drop Caps

Drop caps are a popular design feature for marking the beginnings of stories. Creating drop caps may seem a little tricky at first, but after you create one, the rest are easy. For this newsletter, make each drop cap a 48-point bold character using the same typeface as the body text. Use the following step-by-step procedure to create drop caps (see fig. 4.13):

1. Type the drop cap in the desired font, size, and style. Select the cap with the pointer tool, and move it into place over the existing column of 12-point text.

2. Select the column of text.

3. Using the pointer tool, grab the leftmost lower column handle and drag to resize the column so that it fits within the space to the right of the drop cap. Make sure that the number of lines of text showing match the height of the drop cap.

4. Delete the first letter the drop cap is intended to replace. In this example, delete the "T."

5. Click the + in the column windowshade handle.

6. Position the text-placement icon beneath your drop cap and click the mouse button. The remaining text reflows between the original column guides.

7. Adjust the space between the two vertical columns to be the same as the original line spacing.

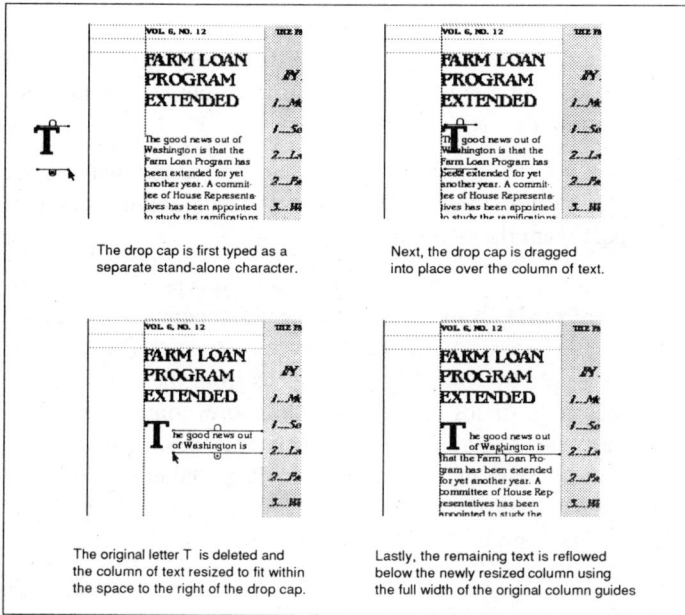

Fig. 4.13.

Creating a drop cap.

Selecting Fonts

In this example, Adobe System's ITC Benguiat bookface in 12-point size is used for the newsletter's body text because of its readability and whimsical styling. ITC Benguiat is a serif face that complements the informal tone of your newsletter. Serif fonts have small cross strokes at the characters' ascenders and descenders (see fig. 4.14). The typeface also conveys a clean, non-busy look to the reader.

Fig. 4.14.

Distinguishing between serif and non-serif type.

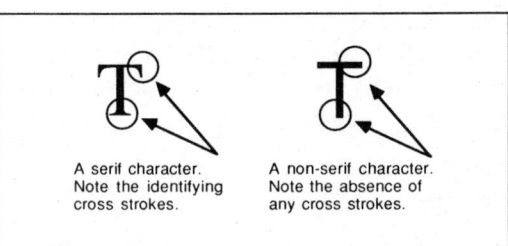

ITC Benguiat also is used for story headlines, although using a non-serif face like Helvetica for headlines is more customary. Helvetica is not used because most designers agree that you shouldn't mix more than two typeface families on the same page, and the banner is boldly set in Image Club Graphic's casual Paint Brush font. All story headlines are 22-point bold, or slightly less than twice the size of the accompanying body text.

Because the Paint Brush font used in the banner is italicized, the table of contents beneath the banner also is italicized to avoid interrupting the reader's eye movement. The table of contents is 14-point bold and double-spaced to set the list apart from the main body text.

The issue number, banner subtitle, publication date, and story continuations are 10-point type. The story continuations at the bottom of each column also are italicized to set them apart from the main body text.

As you design future publications, you have to make similar type-style choices. Most of your selections are made from the hierarchical submenus under Page-Maker's Type menu. Others are set with the Type Specifications dialog box shown in figure 4.15 (accessible by choosing Type Specs from the Type menu). Using the Type Specifications dialog box gives you more control over text formatting. For example, the 22-point size used for this newsletter's story headlines is not one of the commonly listed sizes in PageMaker's Type Size menu. This type size is set separately by choosing Type Specs from the Type menu and entering the desired value.

Fig. 4.15.

PageMaker's Type Specifications dialog box.

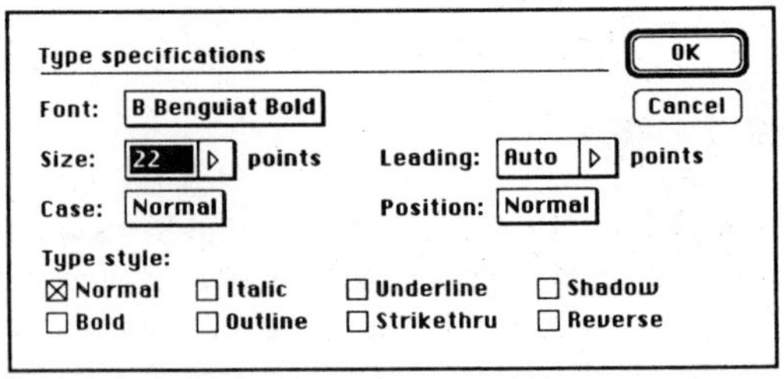

Using Rules and Snap To Guides

To help separate your columns, draw vertical rules on both master pages. Eliminate the repeating vertical rules on the first page of your newsletter because the gray backdrop for the center column already provides a natural column separation. To eliminate the vertical rules on the first page, deselect the Display Master Items command on the Page menu.

Place a horizontal rule above the logo on each page except the last to separate the logo from the preceding columns. Leave the horizontal rule off the last page to allow text wrapping of the first two columns around the reversed logo.

To create perfectly placed vertical column rules, drag vertical ruler guides to the spaces between the adjoining columns on your master pages. Use PageMaker's 90-degree line tool to draw your rules. Drawing rules along a ruler guide with Snap To Rulers selected on the Options menu lays the rules exactly on top of the guide (see fig. 4.16). The same technique can be used to draw the horizontal rules.

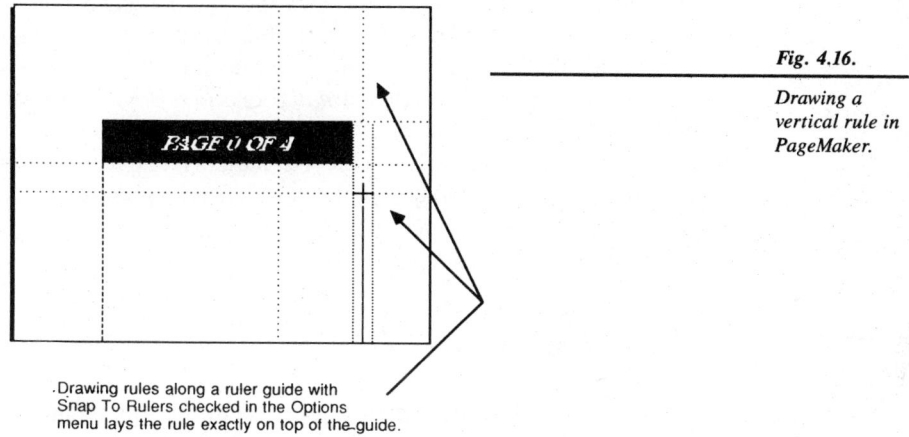

Fig. 4.16.

Drawing a vertical rule in PageMaker.

Editing Your Work

You can edit text easily with PageMaker's Type menu commands and text tool. To change font types, sizes, or styles, select the text to be edited and choose the appropriate menu commands. Remember that if you choose the menu commands first, only newly typed text is affected. To manipulate body copy, use the text tool as you would within your favorite word processor. To insert new text into an existing story, click your text cursor at any point and start typing.

Making changes and corrections by zooming in on your documents is sometimes convenient. Zooming in on a small section of a page enables you to work on tiny details. Zooming out again enables you to see how your overall layout is shaping up. Choose the appropriate commands for the page size you want from the Page menu or use the keyboard shortcuts presented in Chapter 2 (see "Viewing Your Publication").

Saving and Backing Up

Saving your publication should not be left for last. Save your work at periodic intervals to avoid losing everything accomplished up to that point. A PageMaker mini-save (see "Saving Your Work" in Chapter 2) is executed when you add or delete pages, change page setup specifications, or turn to a new page in your publication. Do not count on automatic mini-saving, however, to recover work.

Assign your publication a name and save the publication to your hard disk as soon as you set the initial specifications in the Page Setup dialog box (by choosing Save from the File menu). Immediately save a duplicate copy to a floppy disk by choosing Save As from the File menu. *Save your work at least every 10 or 15 minutes to your hard disk and to a floppy.* This process keeps you from losing more than 10 or 15 minutes of changes, and the floppy serves as a backup if you have a problem with your hard drive. Creating a running backup is a wise move that someday may keep you from having to rebuild a publication you thought was safely archived.

Printing Your Work

To print your publication, choose Print from the File menu. You are presented with a Print dialog box containing several choices. For this exercise, use the existing settings. Click the OK button to produce the final output (see fig. 4.17). You learn more about printing in Chapter 9, "Printing Techniques."

Chapter 4: Quick Start: Creating a Newsletter   93

Fig. 4.17.

The completed front page as printed on an Apple LaserWriter.

Chapter Summary

In this chapter, you learned how to produce a sample four-page newsletter using the concepts and techniques covered in earlier chapters. If you are unclear about something you studied, take time to do a quick review before going on to the next chapter. Now that you have a solid foundation on which to build, the remainder of this book helps you acquire the skills you need to become proficient at designing and laying out your own publications.

II
Working with Text

Includes

Text Basics

Formatting Text

Text Basics   5

In this chapter you begin working with text. You learn how to import text so that it flows throughout a publication and how to edit and manipulate text afterward. You also discover how to create whatever additional text you need in PageMaker, using PageMaker's own text tool and Type-menu commands.

To format your text, you learn how to set different type specifications and manipulate special characters. As you explore PageMaker's text-handling capabilities, you see how you can improve the readability of your publications by kerning type (to *kern type* means to adjust the space between adjoining characters for a better fit; for example, tucking the little *o* under the overhang of the capital letter *T* in the word *To*). You also learn how to export text back out of PageMaker, to update your original word processing files or to use elsewhere.

This chapter is your introduction into the detailed mechanics of using PageMaker. The discussion is aimed at helping you master the fundamental hands-on skills needed to produce professional-looking publications on your own. As with earlier chapters, you should follow along and do each lesson on your Macintosh. Learning by doing is the best way to gain proficiency.

Importing and Copying Text into PageMaker

Most of the time you want to create and format your text using one of the many popular Macintosh word processors. A dedicated word processor lets you do the kind of power word processing that a page-layout program is not designed to do. Word processors generally come with many built-in keyboard shortcuts and other convenience features to help make preparing documents easier. They're your best choice to quickly prepare text for your publications.

You can import text into PageMaker using the Place command (under the File menu); alternatively, you can copy and paste text into your publications using the Clipboard. When importing text into PageMaker, however, not all the original formatting always come through intact. The formatting retained depends greatly on the word processor you use. Except for a few special characteristics, such as double underlining, headers, footers, and hidden text, PageMaker fully supports the Microsoft Works, Microsoft Word, WriteNow, and MacWrite word processors. Built-in translation filters enable PageMaker to accurately import formatted files created with these programs.

To import formatted files from other word processors, you first must install the appropriate import filters. PageMaker comes with a Filter Installer utility that makes installing filters easy. You use the utility program in the same way as Apple's Font/DA Mover utility. As new import filters become available, they can be obtained from the publisher of your word processing program or directly from Aldus.

You also can import data from any application—word processor, spreadsheet, or database—that enables you to save documents in text-only (ASCII) format. *Text-only* means that a file carries no assigned style or formatting attributes beyond simple carriage returns, spaces, and tabs. PageMaker automatically applies the current default type specifications to imported text-only files.

Preparing Text

Importing text into PageMaker is fairly straightforward. Problems can occur, however, if you include formatting in your documents that PageMaker doesn't recognize or handle well. Because PageMaker doesn't contain all the sophisticated features found in many of today's dedicated word processors, you occasionally may run into minor program incompatibilities when readying text for importing into PageMaker.

PageMaker handles most general type specifications without difficulty, including font types, styles, and sizes. Note, however, that fonts are imported in whole-point sizes only (PageMaker automatically rounds any half-point sizes up to the next whole-point size). Superscripts, subscripts, single underlines, and strikethroughs also are supported. Unique word processing features like double underlines, hidden text, and automatically typeset formulas, however, are not supported.

> ***Note***
> A useful rule of thumb is that if PageMaker can produce a particular format, the program can import that format as it exists in your word processor.

Sometimes PageMaker can recognize a particular word processor format, but must modify the format slightly. Imported superscripts and subscripts, for example, are restructured by PageMaker according to the following formulas:

Imported superscript and subscript sizes = 7/12 * normal type size.

Superscript and subscript character placement = $\pm 1/3$* normal type size.

Using this approach, superscripted text in 24-point type in your word processor is brought into PageMaker as 14-point type raised 8 points above the baseline. You can change these assigned values later using PageMaker's Type Specifications dialog box (choose Type Specs under the Type menu).

> ***Note***
> If you select superscripted or subscripted text with the text tool and look at PageMaker's Size menu or Type Specifications dialog box, you see the original type size, not the scaled-down size. Don't be deceived. No matter what size you select for superscripted or subscripted type, you get that size scaled by 7/12, not the size indicated in the menus or dialog box.

Paragraph formatting generally is preserved when importing text into PageMaker. You can set tabs and indents, line and paragraph spacing, and left, right, or center justification in your word processor any way you like. If you use nested indents (automatically assigned sets of indents in which one group of indented paragraphs sits within another group of indented paragraphs, as in an outline) to indent successive paragraphs, however, PageMaker changes the nested paragraphs into regular paragraphs. The paragraph formatting is preserved, but the nested indents become normal left and right indents. The indents can be changed only by individually resetting them with the Indents/Tabs command in the Type menu. (You learn to work with indents and tabs in Chapter 6 under "Formatting Paragraphs.")

PageMaker sometimes has difficulty handling first-line indents. Regular indents (indented normally to the right) and hanging indents (extended to the left, away from the body of a paragraph) can yield unpredictable results if the indent is wider than the column. An overly wide regular first-line indent, for example, may cause the first word of your indented paragraph to be squashed against the right column guide. The squashed type you see displayed on-screen prints the same way on your laser printer (see fig. 5.1). Make sure that your first-line indents are narrower than the columns into which you place them. If you ever run into this problem, you can reset the first-line indent marker without reflowing your text. You learn how to handle indents in Chapter 6, "Formatting Text."

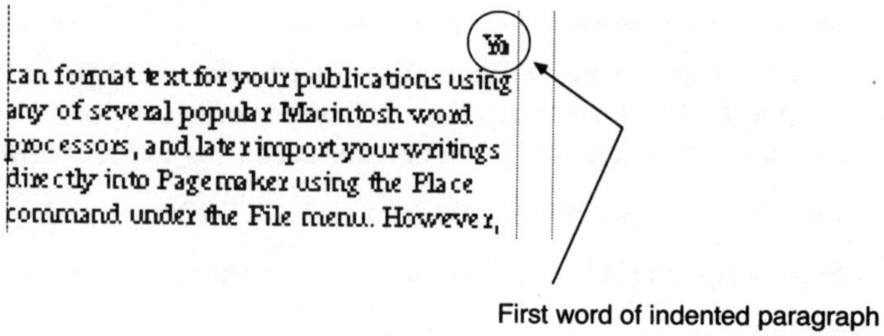

Fig. 5.1.

The result of importing a paragraph with a first-line indent set wider than the column.

can format text for your publications using any of several popular Macintosh word processors, and later import your writings directly into Pagemaker using the Place command under the File menu. However,

First word of indented paragraph

Left, right, center, leader, and decimal tabs are recognized easily by Page-Maker. You can set these tabs in your word processor to create complex tables that retain their formatting when imported into PageMaker. As with indents, however, be sure to set tab spacing to fit within your columns.

PageMaker does not preserve headers, footers, auto page numbering, right margins, or columns when importing formatted text. PageMaker can preserve footnotes, but they are collected and appended to the ends of files.

Styles (preconfigured text-formatting that can be applied on command) can be imported directly from some word processors—most notably Microsoft Word. The amount of formatting that carries over is determined by the import filter used and the degree of compatibility with PageMaker's own style sheets. To copy applied styles with your document into PageMaker, be sure that the `Retain format` button is checked in the Place Document dialog box, accessed from the File menu. (You learn to import style sheets in Chapter 6 under "Using Style Sheets.")

PageMaker can import embedded graphics along with your word processing documents. After the graphics are in PageMaker, you can manipulate them like any other graphic element. The graphics are not constrained to a particular line of text as they are in some word processors.

When PageMaker imports text-only files, the program applies the currently assigned type-specification defaults. If you import your text as text-only files, be sure to preconfigure PageMaker's default settings to avoid reworking your publication afterward.

> ***Tip***
> If you prepare your documents as text-only files, you can use a much wider range of add-on utilities, such as grammar and spelling checkers, that may not otherwise be able to decipher your word processor's proprietary file structures. Use these utilities to check your stories before importing them into PageMaker.

You can import fully formatted spreadsheet or database documents into PageMaker by first saving them as text-only files. Open the text-only files into a PageMaker-compatible word processor to reassign, as closely as possible, the original style formatting. Then import the files into PageMaker using the File menu's Place command.

> ***Tip***
> When saved as text-only files, most spreadsheet applications delineate columns with tabs and rows with carriage returns. Similarly, most database applications use tabs to separate fields. This formatting is retained when the files are imported into PageMaker. For spreadsheet and database applications that substitute commas instead of tabs, use your word processor to search out the commas and replace them with tabs. After you import the newly formatted documents into PageMaker, you can adjust the tab spacing with the Indents/Tabs command under the Type menu.

Importing Text

The first step before importing text, of course, is to prepare your layout. Set up your columns before you begin and identify how you want the text arranged. Use ruler guides to mark where you want major blocks of text to appear. Don't start placing text until you complete at least these steps, or you end up wasting time later readjusting your layout to make everything fit.

You can import text into PageMaker in two ways. You can use the Place command under the File menu to bring in a whole text file at once, or you can cut and paste selected text with the Clipboard. Whatever you choose, PageMaker enables you to control fully the text placement on your pages.

The easiest way to import text is to use PageMaker's Place command to flow an entire story at once. When you choose Place from the File menu, a dialog box appears listing the documents PageMaker recognizes. Because the Place command is used to import text and graphics files, both kinds of documents are listed in the scrollable window of the Place Document dialog box.

> **Tip**
> If in doubt about a document when placing it, click the file name in the scrollable listing in the Place Document dialog box. The first placement option to the right of the scroll bar reads `As new story` or `As new graphic`, depending on the nature of the file. Use PageMaker to help you decide whether the document is a story or an illustration.

All your stories and headlines should be housed in separate text blocks for easy handling. A *text block* is an invisible boundary that defines where text sits on a page. A text block can contain as little as a single character or as much as a full page of text (see fig. 5.2). The boundaries of the text block become visible when you click the text block with the pointer tool, draw a selection rectangle around the block with the pointer tool, or choose the Select All command from the Edit menu.

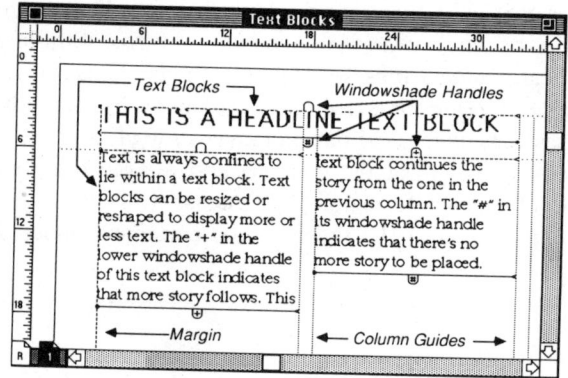

Fig. 5.2.

Text blocks can be different sizes and shapes and can stand alone or be invisibly linked for story continuity.

Text blocks can be any size and shape. When you import a story into PageMaker, many separate blocks may be required to hold all the text. Text blocks for long stories are linked invisibly, or *threaded*, with one another to provide story continuity. Additions or deletions made to text in a linked text block produce a ripple effect through all remaining text blocks.

Using Text Placement Options

The placement options in the Place Document dialog box enable you to import a file as a new story and thread the file independently through your publication (see fig. 5.3). You also can use the placement options to replace an existing story or story selection or insert new text within an existing story. Click the title of the document you want to import from the Place Document dialog box and click the appropriate button for the option you want to implement.

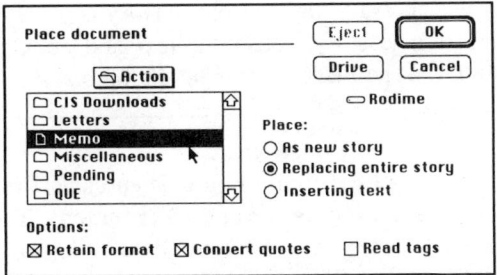

Fig. 5.3.

The Place Document dialog box.

To place a new story, make sure that the `As new story` button is highlighted before you click OK. After the arrow cursor changes to the text-placement icon, click the page where you want to begin flowing the imported text. If you click in a column, PageMaker flows the text to lie entirely within the column boundaries. If you click anywhere on the pasteboard, PageMaker creates a new text block the size of the available image area to hold your story. If you want to define a new text block on the page or pasteboard to hold the imported text, continue holding down the mouse button after you click and drag out a rectangular boundary the desired size and shape (see fig. 5.4). When you release the mouse button, PageMaker fills the block with the text being imported. If a story does not fully fit, a + appears in the longer column windowshade handle to indicate that more text remains to be placed.

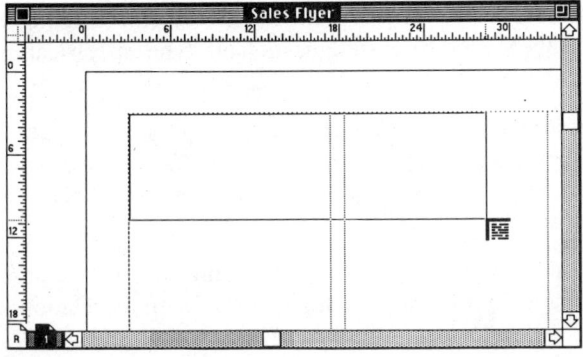

Fig. 5.4.

Dragging a text block across column boundaries with the text-placement icon.

To replace an existing story with a new one, click the text tool anywhere in the existing story before choosing Place from the File menu. In the Place Document dialog box, click the `Replacing entire story` button before clicking OK. PageMaker deletes the original story and replaces it with the new one. The arrangement of your story text blocks remains the same, but replacing a long story with a short one deletes any excess text blocks. Similarly, replacing a short story with a long one extends the last text block down the page to hold the extra text. (If `Autoflow` is selected in the Options menu, text blocks and pages are added automatically as necessary until the entire story is placed.) If you want to replace a range of text in a story, select the text and click the `Replacing selected text` button in the Place Document dialog box.

> *Note*
> PageMaker has a self-imposed limit of 64K when using the `Replacing entire story` or `Replacing selected text` buttons. You are limited in the amount of text you can replace at one time. Files larger than 64K must be broken into smaller files if they are to be used as replacements. The file-size limit does not apply to files placed as original stories.

To insert new text in an existing story, first create an insertion point by clicking the text tool at the desired location in the text. You also can highlight any text you want to replace with new text. Create the insertion point or highlight the desired text before choosing Place from the File menu. In the Place Document dialog box, click the `Inserting text` button and then click OK. PageMaker threads the new text in the existing story, starting at the insertion point. If you highlighted some text, PageMaker replaces the highlighted text with the imported text.

Along the bottom of the Place Document dialog box are three additional options buttons. The `Retain format` button keeps intact the original formatting of the documents when you import them into PageMaker. This button also enables the import of any assigned style sheets with the document. Leaving this button unselected tells PageMaker to assign its default type specifications to your imported text.

The `Convert quotes` option changes straight quotation marks (" ") and straight apostrophes (') into curly ones (" ")('). Use this option with care, because ending up with a backward quotation mark or apostrophe is easy if your document formatting isn't perfect.

The `Read tags` option tells PageMaker to read embedded style name tags and use them to automatically format paragraphs. (You learn more about using style tags in Chapter 6 under "Importing Styles.")

Using Text Flow Options

When you import text into PageMaker, you have three placement flow choices: manual, automatic, and semiautomatic (see fig. 5.5). Distinct advantages and disadvantages to each are listed in the following sections.

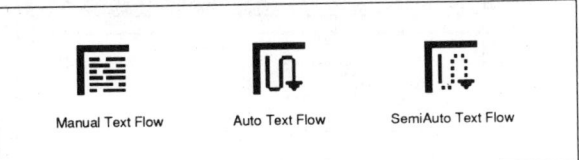

Fig. 5.5.

The text-placement icons for manual, automatic, and semiautomatic text flow.

Manual Flow

Manual flow is the easiest type of document placement to control. When you select a file to import using the Place command, the manual text-placement icon is the one you are already familiar with: the icon looks like a miniature page of text. When you click a page, text flows down existing column guides until reaching the bottom of the page. To continue flowing remaining text, click the + symbol in the windowshade handle at the bottom of the current text block (see the first portion of fig. 5.6). This action gives you another text-placement icon that you can click elsewhere to continue your story. Click the + symbol as often as necessary to place the entire story. In the second screen display in figure 5.6, the continuation text has flowed into the adjoining column. Note the + in the upper windowshade handle. This sign tells you that linked text precedes this text block. The + in the lower handle indicates that more text is to come. When the # symbol appears in the windowshade handle, no text is left to place.

You can start placing a story on one page of your publication and continue the story on another page. You also can define specific column widths in which to flow text during story placement; hold down the mouse button as you drag out the desired boundaries with the text-placement icon. When you release the mouse button, the text flows into the defined boundaries.

Tip

If you have enough computer memory, you can place several stories at once and have PageMaker keep track of the unplaced text as you work. Suppose that you have several articles that you want to continue through a lengthy newsletter, and all the articles start on the front page. Instead of working your way through the publication several times to place each story separately, start all your stories together at the same time. Use the Place command to flow text from each separate story file into the appropriate text blocks on the first page. Proceed through the remainder of the newsletter, page by page, to place the remaining text. Each time you click the + symbol in a windowshade handle, PageMaker picks up where it left off with that story file and continues placing that story's text. If you use this approach, you only have to work through a lengthy publication once to place all your stories.

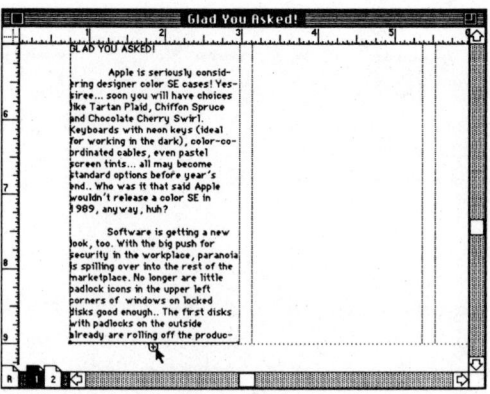

Fig. 5.6.

When you place a story in PageMaker, each text block becomes a separate link in a continuous chain.

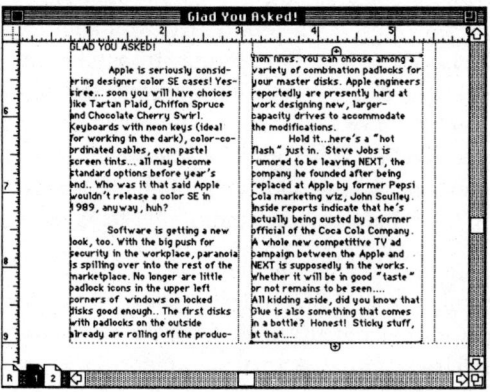

Automatic Flow

You can use PageMaker's Autoflow command to automatically thread text through a publication. The Autoflow command is especially useful when importing stories for books, catalogs, and other lengthy documents. To use PageMaker's Autoflow feature, choose Autoflow from the Options menu. Then select the story to be placed using the File menu's Place command. Notice that when you use Autoflow, the text-placement icon changes to an arrow with a snaked tail. This icon reminds you that the text will flow down one column and then down the next. After you click the icon where you want to start flowing text, PageMaker continues filling successive columns, adding pages as necessary, until you have no more text to place or until the 128-page limit is reached.

Autoflow works on publication pages, not on the pasteboard (the feature also works on master pages). If you click the autoflow text-placement icon on the pasteboard, a single column of text forms, and you have to click the + symbol in the windowshade handle of this column to continue flowing text elsewhere.

> ***Warning***
> Be sure to click within column boundaries when autoflowing text. If you make the mistake of clicking in the narrow space between adjoining columns, PageMaker first fills the available image area without regard for column boundaries. Then the program looks for the first open column space anywhere on that page, even if the open area comes before the start of your story. This process can produce text blocks that read out of sequence.

You can stop autoflowing text at any time by clicking the mouse. To resume Autoflow, click the + symbol in the windowshade handle. The autoflow text-placement icon returns. Click the location on the page where you want to start flowing text again.

When PageMaker autoflows text, the program runs over, skips over, or wraps around any graphics encountered. PageMaker's approach to text and graphics depends on how you have configured each graphic with the Text Wrap command on the Options menu. If PageMaker encounters a graphic that completely fills a column and Text Wrap is set so that the story skips over the image, PageMaker places an empty text block at the top of the column as a placeholder. (The empty text block has upper and lower windowshades pressed together—no text can fit in the empty text block until it expands.) If you later move or resize the graphic, the empty text block automatically expands downward to fill the open space. You learn how to configure graphics for text wrap in Chapter 8, "Formatting and Enhancing Graphics."

When PageMaker runs into another block of text while autoflowing, the text being flowed starts at the top of the next open column instead of jumping over the existing text. The usefulness of autoflow, therefore, is limited in documents where multiple blocks of text are arranged on each page. To overcome this limitation, PageMaker enables you to flow text semiautomatically.

Figure 5.7 shows how PageMaker flows text automatically in some typical situations. Part A shows the screen as you get ready to autoflow a story onto a page with a graphic at the top of the second column and an overlooked text block overlapping the first column. Part B shows that as the story flows down the first column, the stray text block forces a jump to the top of the second column. Because that column is filled with a graphic, PageMaker places an empty text block and skips to the top of the third column. After filling that column, the program continues autoflowing text, adding new pages as needed, until the entire story is placed. Part C shows that deleting the stray text block and pulling down the lower windowshade handle of the text block directly above fills the remainder of the first column with text. Part D shows that cropping the graphic to delete the uppermost image causes the empty text block above the graphic to expand downward and fills the open space with text.

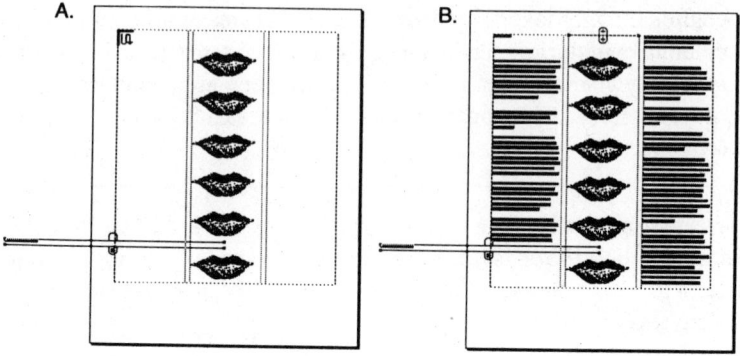

Fig. 5.7.

Autoflowing text in a typical publication layout.

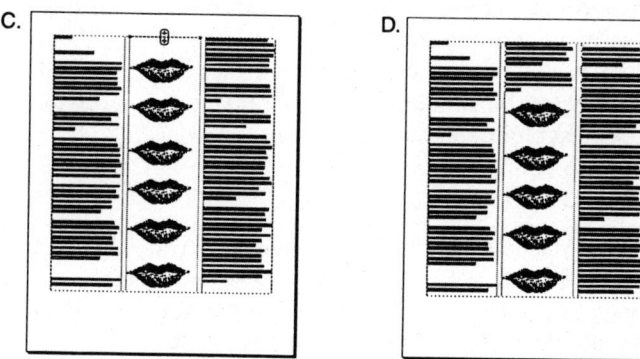

Semiautomatic Flow

Semiautomatic flow works much like manual flow in that text stops at the bottom of each column. Unlike manual flow, however, you don't have to click the + symbol in the windowshade to recover the text-placement icon. When flow stops in one column, the text-placement icon reappears, ready to continue placing text in another column, giving you more control over text placement than autoflow allows. You can continue flowing stories past other text blocks in the same column, for example, without skipping automatically to the top of the next open column. Flowing text semiautomatically is not as fast as autoflowing, but is much less tedious than manually flowing text.

Changing Text-Flow Modes

You can switch quickly between text-flow modes at any time during story placement using special combination keystrokes. The only way to flow text semiautomatically is to hold down the Shift key while clicking a text-placement icon. Holding down the Shift key changes the autoflow and manual flow icons into the semiautomatic flow icon. The semiautomatic flow icon looks similar to the autoflow icon, except that the curved tail of the arrow is a dotted line instead of a solid line.

You also can change text-flow modes from automatic to manual and from manual to automatic, by holding the Command key while clicking the text-placement icon. This key sequence works whether or not the Autoflow command is checked on the Options menu. Note that you must stop autoflowing text by clicking the mouse before you can change the mode from automatic to semiautomatic or manual.

Tip
If you have already clicked OK in the Place Document dialog box, but decide not to flow text, click the pointer tool to cancel the operation.

Using the Clipboard

When you import text using the Clipboard, you get different results depending on where the text originates. If you copy text from another application, the text is reassigned PageMaker's default type specifications when you paste it into PageMaker. If you copy and paste text from another PageMaker document or from your current PageMaker publication, the text retains the existing type specifications, even if the text is pasted into the middle of a block with different styles.

If you highlight a selection with the text tool and copy the text to the Clipboard, the text automatically wraps to fit within column boundaries when pasted back into the document. If you use PageMaker's pointer tool to select and copy a block of text, the block of text retains the original dimensions when pasted back onto your pages. If you click the text tool in an existing block of text to create an insertion point before pasting, the text you paste is threaded continuously into that story.

> ***Tip***
> You can use the Clipboard to create composite text from multiple text blocks. If you select a group of text blocks, copy them together as a unit to the Clipboard, and then paste them back into PageMaker, they normally reappear as separate text blocks. If you first click the text tool in the document to create an insertion point before pasting, however, or click-drag to define a column boundary, the separate text blocks reappear as one continuous block of text. Use this technique to meld multiple text blocks continuously into an existing block of text—just click within the existing text block where you want the composite text to appear and paste. When you combine multiple text blocks this way, the composite text reads in the same order as the blocks originally appeared on your pages.

Creating and Editing Text

You can use PageMaker's text tool to type new text or edit old text. Select the text tool from the toolbox and click anywhere on your page to get started.

If you click in an existing text block, the text you type becomes part of that story and takes on the same formatting as the surrounding text. Text that comes after the insertion point is pushed forward to accommodate the new material. The text blocks don't change size or shape; the exception is the last text block in the story, which expands to handle any overflow.

If you click the text tool outside an existing text block, anything you type takes on PageMaker's default type specifications. The new block assumes different shapes depending on where you click, however. Click anywhere within a column, and the insertion point appears at the left-column guide. The text you type starts there and wraps to fit at the right-column guide. Click the page margins or pasteboard, and whatever text you type may run off the screen as it fills the width of the available image area before wrapping. Click and drag to create a bounding box, and your words wrap to lie within the defined area, even if that area starts between or extends across existing column boundaries.

> **Tip**
> The click-drag technique is a powerful way to control the placement of text. Use this technique to create large text blocks to hold items like headlines and pull quotes spanning multiple columns or to create small text blocks to hold narrow items like picture captions and page numbers. To create text blocks of an exact width, drag two vertical ruler guides onto your page, then click and drag the cursor or text-placement icon between them. Make sure that the Snap To Guides command in the Options menu is toggled on.

As you continue typing in a column, your text extends down the page. You find that the text blocks lengthen as necessary to hold the text you type. If the bottom of your text block bumps into a nonwrapping graphic, touches the lower edge of the page, or reaches the edge of the pasteboard, however, you get an error message telling you that PageMaker can no longer show the insertion point (see fig. 5.8). If you receive this message, drag a corner handle to resize your text block or click the + symbol in the windowshade handle to create another text block and resume typing.

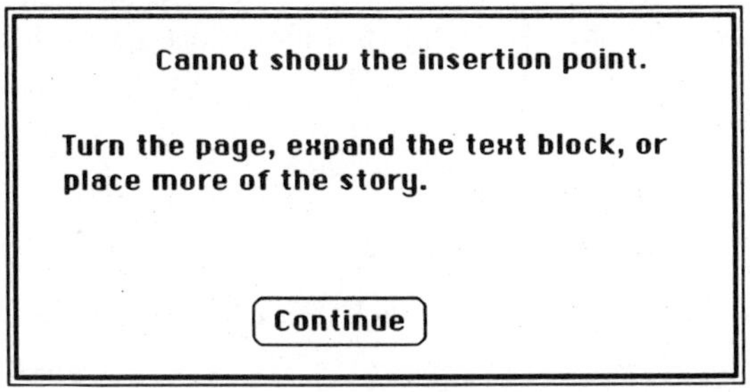

```
Cannot show the insertion point.

Turn the page, expand the text block, or
place more of the story.

        [ Continue ]
```

Fig. 5.8.

PageMaker must display the text cursor when you enter new text.

> **Tip**
> When you create a new text block in a page margin or on the pasteboard, its width is the same as the available image area—which sometimes can be quite large. If a text-block boundary is left to invisibly extend beyond your columns after being dragged onto your pages, the boundary blocks automatic flow of newly placed text. The text block also may overlap other elements in the same vicinity, making selecting these elements with the pointer tool difficult. The easiest way to control the width of text blocks is to click-drag with the text tool to define specific text-wrap boundaries before typing or before importing text. In any case, you always can adjust the width of a text block later by selecting the block and dragging a corner handle.

To edit existing text, click the text tool to create an insertion point, backspace to delete individual characters, and immediately type any new replacement text. You also can highlight a selection by dragging across the selection with the text tool and typing new text to effect an instant replacement. The familiar Edit menu Cut, Copy, Paste, and Clear commands also can be used to effect changes to selected text (for details on how these commands work, consult the manual that came with your Macintosh).

> *Tip*
> To select a particularly lengthy passage of text, create an insertion point at the start of your selection, then hold down the Shift key while clicking to mark the end of your selection. Everything between the clicks is highlighted for editing. This technique works anywhere in the same story, even if the start and the end of your selection lie on different pages.

With PageMaker, you can use the keyboard cursor (arrow) keys as a shortcut to move a text insertion point up, down, left, or right, one character or line at a time. If you hold down these keys, the movement is repeated. You also can use the numeric keypad to do the same thing. The 8, 2, 4, and 6 number keys on the numeric keypad correspond respectively to the up, down, left, and right cursor keys. If you hold down the Shift key while pressing these keys, all the intervening text is selected.

Fonts and Type Styles

A *typeface* consists of a family of fonts. Each *font* is a distinct style variation on the basic typeface. Times and Helvetica, for example, are *typefaces*, but Times 12-point Italic, and Helvetica 24-point Bold are *fonts*. Typefaces may be proportional or nonproportional. Proportional faces, like Times and Helvetica, use variable character spacing to produce a more pleasing typeset appearance. Nonproportional or monospaced typefaces, like Courier, closely resemble typewriter text, with each character equally spaced. Monospaced typefaces give text a slightly uneven appearance. Nonproportional type is used rarely today unless needed to simulate the informal appearance of typewritten copy (see fig. 5.9).

One common mistake desktop publishing beginners make is to use the wrong kinds of fonts in their publications. You may be tempted to use monospaced fonts like Courier because you're comfortable with typewritten copy. That's okay if your readers expect typewritten copy, but not if they expect a typeset look. At other times you may mistakenly use the more difficult-to-read sans serif faces, or even totally unreadable decorative faces, for body text. Stick to serif bookfaces for body copy.

> This is Times. It's a proportional, serif face. Each of its characters enjoys a slightly different spacing for a better fit with its neighbors. This gives Times an almost typeset, business look.
>
> ```
> This is Courier. It's a non-
> proportional, serif face. Each
> of its characters is equally
> spaced. This gives Courier
> an informal "typewritten" look.
> ```

Fig. 5.9.

These typefaces are the same size and style, yet they look completely different because of their character spacing.

For headlines, avoid small serif fonts that seem nearly indistinguishable from the text of your stories. Don't mix multiple typefaces that include bold, outlined, shadowed, and italic styles on the same page. Although PageMaker enables you to use a wide variety of font types, sizes, and styles in your documents, remember that using all this typesetting power for every publishing task is not necessary.

In PageMaker, you choose the fonts and type styles you want to apply to selected text from the Type menu or Type Specifications dialog box (select Type Specs from the Type menu). You also can preset font and type style choices as program and file defaults.

PageMaker's Type menu contains three hierarchical submenus specifically used for assigning type attributes to text. The Font submenu lists your system's installed fonts, and the Size and Type Style submenus each offer a generous selection of popular font sizes and styles. The right-pointing arrowheads on the Type menu indicate that the submenus pop up to the right of the main menu. Drag the pointer into a submenu to assign a particular font attribute to selected text or to set a program or file default.

PageMaker's Type submenus list the most popular font attributes. A wider selection of choices is available using the Type Specifications dialog box (choose Type Specs from the Type menu). The primary advantage of using the Type Specifications dialog box is that you can set several attributes at the same time. When you use the hierarchical Type submenus, you have to pull down the menus repeatedly and set each type attribute separately.

The Type Specifications dialog box also uses pop-up submenus (see fig. 5.10). The submenus are displayed when you click a font attribute. Make your selections by dragging the pointer tool through the menus, just as you do when using a normal drop-down menu.

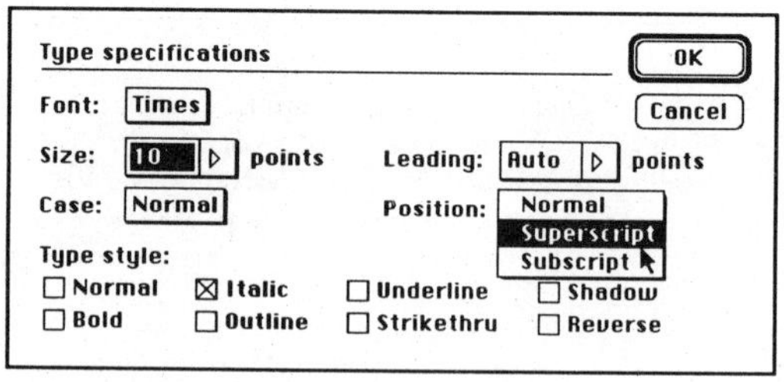

Fig. 5.10.

PageMaker's Type Specifications dialog box with the pop-up Position menu displayed.

Using the Type Specifications dialog box, you gain access to two pop-up submenus not immediately available from the Type menu. These menus are Case (with the options `Normal`, `All caps`, and `Small caps`) and Position (with the options `Normal`, `Superscript`, and `Subscript`). Using the Type Specification dialog box also provides the capacity to specify less commonly used type sizes and leading values by entering them directly from the keyboard. (Although you can assign leading to selected text with the Type menu or Type Specifications dialog box, leading is often considered a paragraph or story specification. You learn more about leading in Chapter 6, "Formatting Text.")

Font Types

PageMaker normally lists in the Font menu and Type Specifications dialog box the fonts currently installed in your system. If you open a PageMaker document created with fonts not on your system, however, PageMaker also displays the names of these fonts in the pop-up menus, but grays out the names to indicate that they are not installed. You cannot select a grayed-out menu listing.

Tip

If you want to find out the fonts, sizes, and style attributes used in a document created on someone else's system, select some of the text in question and choose Type Specs from the Type menu to bring up the Type Specifications dialog box. The correct type specifications for that text are displayed, even when those fonts are missing from your system (the names of all the missing fonts used in the document are shown grayed out in the pop-up Font menus). After you identify the missing fonts, use Apple's Font/DA Mover to install the fonts on your system before printing the document. (See the manual that came with your Macintosh to learn how to use Apple's Font/DA Mover.)

Font Sizes

PageMaker's hierarchical Type Size menu enables you to apply a limited selection of point sizes (6, 8, 9, 10, 12, 14, 18, 24, 30, 34, 48, 60, and 72 points), to your text. If you need more choices, however, use the Type Specifications dialog box to assign sizes from 4 to 127 points. To assign a type size, select a range of text with the text tool, and type the desired size in the Type Specifications dialog box.

Tip

A quick way to change font sizes without accessing a menu or dialog box is to use the keyboard shortcuts Option-Command-Shift-> and Option-Command-Shift-<. Each time you press one of these combinations, the highlighted text becomes one point-size larger or smaller respectively. If you press Command-Shift-> or Command-Shift-<, your text increases or decreases in the increments listed in the Type Size menu.

Tip

The largest font size that PageMaker can produce is 127 points. To create and use larger font sizes, you must type the text in a program that enables you to save files in PICT or EPS format. You then must import these files into PageMaker as graphic images. Because the text is a graphic image, you can stretch text to any desired size. The oversized graphic fonts still print smoothly because the PICT and EPS file structures retain the necessary font coding information for downloading to your laser printer.

Type Styles

You can assign type styles individually using the Type Styles menu or collectively by checking options in the Type Specifications dialog box. A type style consists of attributes, such as Bold, Italic, or Underlined, that you assign to a selection of text to differentiate it from surrounding text. You can combine multiple type styles for a given text selection. A common example is a headline assigned both bold and italic styles at the same time. PageMaker provides the following type styles from which you can choose:

Normal
Bold
Italic
Outline
Underline
Strikethru
Shadow
Reverse

Type styles are best applied sparingly. Outline, shadow, and reverse (white type that can be viewed only if set against a dark background) styles should be used strictly for special effect. Underlined type should rarely be used—bold or italic styles are more effective for creating emphasis (underlining is a holdover from the typewriter days when bold and italic were not available as options).

Position and Case

The Position menu in the Type Specifications dialog box gives you three choices for arranging text: `Normal`, `Superscript`, and `Subscript`. Normal text is what you are used to working with: text positioned directly on the character baseline. Both superscripted and subscripted text are smaller than normal text. In PageMaker, superscripted and subscripted text is set to 7/12 of the selected point size, and raised or lowered from the baseline by a distance equal to 1/3 of the selected point size. Superscript and subscript text generally is used for typesetting mathematical formulas, scientific notation, footnote markers, and special characters, including trademark, registration, and copyright symbols.

PageMaker's Case menu in the Type Specification dialog box also provides three choices: `Normal case`, `All caps`, and `Small caps`. When you choose `Normal case`, the text looks just as you originally typed it, generally a mixture of uppercase and lowercase letters. When you choose `All caps`, however, the selected text is converted to all uppercase letters. The `Small caps` option affects lowercase letters, changing them to small caps (70 percent of full size). Use the `All caps` and `Small caps` options sparingly. Text consisting of all caps, even a mixture of full-size and small caps, is more difficult to read than text consisting of both uppercase and lowercase letters.

> ***Tip***
> The Case and Position menu options have keyboard equivalents that you can use to make type style assignments without bringing up the Type Specifications dialog box. The keyboard shortcuts are listed in the following chart.
>
> | *Option* | *Keyboard Shortcut* |
> |---|---|
> | Small caps | Command-Shift-H |
> | All caps | Command-Shift-K |
> | Subscript | Command-Shift- − (minus) |
> | Superscript | Command-Shift- + (plus) |
>
> To revert to your original format settings (those you originally assigned to the text) after applying these shortcuts, or any other type-style changes, select the text and press Command-Shift-space bar.

Typing Special Characters

Almost all fonts come with a complement of built-in special characters, including curly quotation marks and apostrophes, trademark and copyright symbols, bullets, paragraph markers, and so on. You can use the Apple Key Caps desk accessory, supplied with your system software, to identify the locations of these characters on your keyboard (refer to the manual that came with your Macintosh computer for details on using the Apple Key Caps desk accessory).

PageMaker provides additional special characters of its own that are useful for formatting your text. The most important of these characters are the page-number marker (Command-Option-P), which you learned about in Chapter 3 under "The Magic of Master Pages," four nonbreaking spaces, and a nonbreaking hyphen.

Nonbreaking spaces are inserted between words or characters to ensure that adjoining text stays together on the line. PageMaker's four nonbreaking spaces are as follows:

- ❑ Em space (Command-Shift-M): equal to the selected point size (also equal to the width of a capital M in most fonts)

- ❑ En space (Command-Shift-N): equal to 1/2 the selected point size

- ❑ Thin space (Command-Shift-T): equal to 1/4 the selected point size

- ❑ Fixed space (Option-space bar): varies according to the selected font type

> **Tip**
> Because the fixed space is font dependent, the space may not always be available. If you find that you cannot type a fixed space in a particular font, select another font from the Type menu. Type the fixed space in that font and then select the original font to continue typing. The fixed space is roughly the same size as a thin space.

Type the *nonbreaking hyphen* by pressing Option-- (hyphen). The nonbreaking hyphen enables you to keep hyphenated text, including numbers with minus signs in front of them, together on the same line (see fig. 5.11).

Fig. 5.11.

Use a nonbreaking hyphen whenever you want to keep a hyphenated word from breaking at the end of a line.

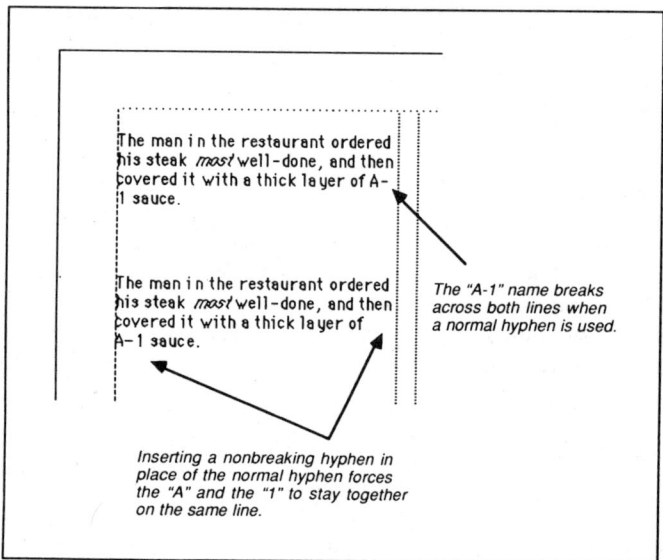

Another special character worthy of mention is the *discretionary hyphen*. The discretionary hyphen is a hyphen inserted manually to tell PageMaker where to break a word at the end of a line if that word is not contained in PageMaker's hyphenation dictionary. To add a discretionary hyphen, press Command-- (hyphen) at the point where you want the word to break at the end of a line. The discretionary hyphen isn't displayed until hyphenation occurs. (You learn more about discretionary hyphenation in Chapter 6 under "Discretionary Hyphenation.")

Kerning Type

To *kern* type is to adjust the space between adjoining characters to obtain a more pleasing fit. Kerning has little noticeable effect on small type sizes: most type is designed to look good at 12 points or less. Kerning becomes important when typesetting headlines and other large text. At larger point sizes, inequitable spacing between adjoining characters quickly becomes noticeable. To eliminate unsightly gaps, you can let PageMaker automatically pair-kern the text. (Pair-kerning is done by PageMaker based on specific character pair information. For example, the character pair consisting of a capital T and a lowercase o is stored in the installed fonts.) You also can manually refine individual character spacing.

Automatic Kerning

To let PageMaker pair-kern automatically, choose the Paragraph command from the Type menu to display the Paragraph Specifications dialog box. Click the `Pair Kerning: Auto` button and type a point size above which you want type to be kerned automatically. Be sure that you set a point size large enough so that only headlines and other text to which you want kerning applied are affected. PageMaker does not kern type smaller than the value you specify. Because automatic pair-kerning causes your screen display to refresh slowly, the less type you kern, the quicker you can work. To help speed production, you may want to wait to apply pair-kerning until your publication is nearly completed.

To automatically pair-kern an existing paragraph, insert the cursor anywhere in the paragraph before turning on pair-kerning. To pair-kern a group of paragraphs, select them first with the text tool. PageMaker pair-kerns whole paragraphs, even if only parts of the paragraph are selected. If you later delete one character of a kerned pair, the other character reverts to its normal spacing without affecting other kerned pairs. If you turn off automatic pair-kerning for a paragraph, all the text reverts to normal spacing.

Automatic kerning works only with fonts having built-in pair-kerning information. You cannot tell by looking at a font, however, if it has built-in kerning information, but you can see the effects of kerning on-screen when using large type sizes. If pair-kerning doesn't work for a particular font, you still can manually kern the type. You also can manually kern type that has been automatically kerned.

Manual Kerning

Manually kerning type gives you the most control over the final appearance of your publications. Although the built-in spacing of many fonts is satisfactory, some jobs call for highly refined character spacing. For example, headline type may call for refined spacing because overly wide spacing can detract from the appearance of your pages. At times, you may want to selectively widen the space between characters for emphasis. PageMaker's manual kerning enables you to subtract and add space easily.

To kern type manually, do the following:

1. Using the text tool, place the insertion point between the two characters you want to kern.

2. Press Command-backspace to remove space and tighten character spacing.

3. Press Command-Shift-backspace to add space and widen character spacing.

Press the appropriate keys for each bit of space you want to add or remove. Each press of the key sequence kerns type in amounts equal to 1/48 of an em space (an em space has the same dimensions as the selected point size). Kerning 24-point headline type, for example, adds or removes space in increments of 24/48, or 1/2 a point. The larger the type, the larger the increment of change. Figure 5.12 shows the process of manually kerning type.

When you kern type smaller than 48 points, the kerning increments are always less than 1 point in size. Because the pixels that make up your screen display also are 1 point in size, you may not be able to see the effects of kerning smaller type, especially if you work in PageMaker's Actual Size view. To better evaluate the effects of kerning, manually kern type only when working in an enlarged view of your page.

Tip

If the exact size of the screen font you are kerning is not installed in your system, the screen display is grossly inaccurate, making precise manual kerning nearly impossible. The screen display is inaccurate because your computer uses a scaled approximation, based on an installed font size, to reconstruct missing font sizes. If you don't want to kern by trial and error, and have to repeatedly run test prints to fine-tune your work, install a separate screen font using Apple's Font/DA Mover for each type size you use. Even with exact screen sizes installed, however, you still may have to do an occasional test print to verify the appearance of minor kerning changes.

Fig. 5.12.

Manual kerning can greatly improve the appearance of headline type.

Exporting Text

An exciting feature in PageMaker is its capability to export text back out of your publications to update the original word processed documents. You can create stories externally using your favorite word processor, import them into PageMaker, make any necessary corrections or editing changes, and update the original files with the changes without ever leaving PageMaker. You also can save exported text as a separate file to use elsewhere and preserve your original document unaltered.

Export filters, similar to the import filters PageMaker uses to import formatted text, enable you to export formatted text back to your word processors. The only limitation is that PageMaker cannot export formatting that the program doesn't support, even if the formatting was recognized during importing. Although PageMaker recognizes and imports superscripts from Microsoft Word, for example, PageMaker modifies the formatting to match its own superscripting (7/12 of the selected type size raised 1/3 the point size above the baseline). A 12-point superscript raised 3 points above the baseline imported from Microsoft Word, for example, becomes a 7-point character raised 4 points above the baseline in PageMaker. If you export the superscript back to Microsoft Word, the character retains PageMaker's formatting.

PageMaker enables you to export selected (highlighted) text or complete stories. Unlinked text blocks must be exported separately. To set up text for exporting, click an insertion point in a linked text block, or select a specific range of text, and choose Export from the File menu. In the Export Document dialog box, click the appropriate `Export` button (`Entire story` or `Selected text only`), pick the appropriate `File format`, and assign a name to the export file to be created. If you want to update your original word processor file, type the file name and storage location of the original file. PageMaker currently exports in text-only Microsoft Word 3.0 and WriteNow formats, but you can install other export filters as they become available just as you install import filters.

Chapter Summary

In this chapter you learned many of the basic skills needed to work with text in PageMaker. You saw how to prepare and import text into your publications and how to export the text back to its original program format. You discovered that, in most instances, you can preserve much of the original formatting when importing or exporting. You learned how to control the flow of text onto your pages and how to create new text wherever needed.

You also learned how to edit text, change type specifications, and kern type to improve the content and appearance of your pages. Now you're ready to move on to Chapter 6, "Formatting Text," where you acquire even more text-handling skills.

Formatting Text   6

In this chapter you continue to explore PageMaker's text-handling capabilities. You start with simple layout tasks like adjusting guides and reshaping text blocks, and then move on to more complex formatting using indents and tabs, adjustable leading, and hyphenation. You learn how to align text, and you discover how paragraph formatting interacts with word spacing to help control the general appearance of your pages. Finally, you learn how to use style sheets to save production time and speed up document preparation.

Performing Simple Layout Tasks

Whenever you create a publication, you usually go through several layout revisions. Along the way, you may want to experiment with different column formats, add or delete whole pages, resize or reshape text blocks, or use guides to help position text and graphics elements accurately. You also may find that you want to store items on the pasteboard so that they are accessible whenever you need them. All of these layout tasks are easy to do in PageMaker.

Creating Columns

PageMaker's columns are made up of nonprinting guides that help you define text placement. Choose Column Guides from the Options menu to specify the number of columns you want displayed on a page. The columns PageMaker creates have equally spaced left and right guides. These column guides can be moved to change column widths, but the spacing between the columns themselves remains fixed unless you enter a new value in the Column Guides dialog box. You can move the far left and right column guides (that overlap the page-margin boundaries) independently; all other column guides move together in fixed pairs.

> **Tip**
> You cannot set variable spacing between columns on the same page. If this restriction limits your layout designs, create more columns than you need. Adjust the extra column guides to create the desired spacing between your main columns. Then skip over the extra columns as you pour your text.

Column guides are used primarily to control line widths when placing text. As you flow text into a column, the text wraps to fit within the column boundaries as it flows down the page. Each line is broken automatically, regardless of the original margin settings of the word processor used to create the text. Other paragraph formatting set in your word processor (such as indents and tabs), however, is retained.

After you have placed your text, you can move the column guides and use them elsewhere without affecting the text blocks you have created. Similarly, you can change the number of columns on a page using the Column Guides command without affecting text already on that page. In this way you can use different column layouts on different parts of the same page.

PageMaker enables you to create from 1 to 20 columns per page. If you use many columns on a single page, your page margins and column spacing must be set narrow enough to allow a column width of at least one pica (1/6 inch). You can specify the spacing between columns, the number of columns per page, and the page-margin boundaries between which your columns lie. But you cannot specify column width—PageMaker specifies the width. The only way to have PageMaker set up exact column widths is to precalculate the other variables ahead of time and enter them for PageMaker to use. Adjusting column guides is easier after you create the number you want. Use PageMaker's horizontal ruler to accurately reposition each column-guide pair.

If you plan to use the same column structure throughout a publication, set up the column guides on your master pages so that they repeat on all regular pages. You can still adjust any column guide on any regular page by dragging the guides with the pointer tool. Whenever you work with facing pages, the Column Guides dialog box enables you to specify column setups separately for each page.

Inserting and Removing Pages

After you define the number of pages for a new publication in the Page Setup dialog box and click the OK button, you cannot go back and change that number. As long as you don't exceed PageMaker's 128-page limit, however, you can add or remove pages by choosing Insert Pages or Remove Pages from the Page menu.

The Insert Pages dialog box enables you to add new pages to your publication. You can tell PageMaker how many pages to add and where to insert them: `Before current page`, `After current page`, or `Between current pages`. In this instance, *current page* means the single page (or facing pages) being viewed at the time of menu selection. `Between current pages` applies only to facing pages.

Each page you add is configured according to existing Page Setup dialog box settings, and all pages following any inserted pages are renumbered. New pages also display any existing master page elements. When you insert new pages between pages that contain linked text blocks, the stories they contain remain linked.

> *Warning*
> Inserting an odd number of pages into a double-sided, facing-pages publication forces PageMaker to reorder all following pages. Not only do previously facing pages no longer face one other, but if your publication's inner and outer margins differ, PageMaker repositions text and graphics to lie within the readjusted margin boundaries. This repositioning can destroy a carefully composed layout, but PageMaker gives you no warning on-screen.

The Remove Pages command enables you to remove existing pages from a publication. You tell PageMaker what pages to delete by specifying beginning and ending page numbers (to remove a single page, make both numbers the same). PageMaker discards those pages and any pages between. All text and graphics on those pages also are discarded. If you want to save items, you must transfer them elsewhere or drag them onto the pasteboard. Items residing on the pasteboard are unaffected by page deletions. Note that the same warning about inserting an odd number of pages into a double-sided, facing-pages publication also applies when removing pages.

Be careful not to remove pages containing text from the middle of a story. Text blocks on earlier and later pages remain linked, but any text on deleted pages is missing. The only way to recover is to reflow your story again. To prevent missing text, use the windowshade handles to close up all the text blocks on the pages you plan to delete. Moving text-block top and bottom windowshade handles together forces story content to flow out of those text blocks and into any follow-on text blocks.

If you make a mistake while adding or deleting pages, immediately choose Undo from the Edit menu to restore your publication.

Rearranging Text Elements

PageMaker enables you to grab text blocks with the pointer tool and move the blocks anywhere on your pages in the same way that you would pick up a news clipping and move it to another spot on your desk.

Whenever you click a text block and hold down the mouse button for a moment, your pointer tool changes into a four-headed cursor arrow. If you begin dragging immediately after clicking, you see a solid box outline showing the boundaries of your text block (see fig. 6.1). Because this outline follows your cursor, you can use the outline as a guide to placement. The original text or graphic remains behind until you release the mouse button. Only then does the text or graphic jump to its new location on the page.

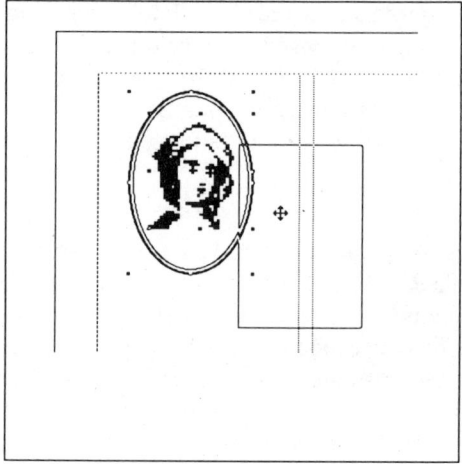

Fig. 6.1.

Dragging a combined selection immediately after clicking on it.

If you wait a second or two before dragging, you see a transparent, ghost-like image of your text surrounded by a dotted boundary box. This ghost image also moves with your cursor so that you can position the image exactly. When you have placed the text block, release the mouse button. The text is redrawn in its new location. If you are not satisfied with the placement, choose Undo from the Edit menu or grab and drag the text block again.

You can move text blocks to different areas of your page, or drag them onto the pasteboard for temporary storage. Column and ruler guides help you align them properly. If you choose the Snap To Guides command on the Options menu before you start dragging, your text blocks are attracted to the guides like metal shavings to a magnet. If you also choose the Snap To Rulers command, your text blocks move in increments equal to the intervals between ruler tick marks.

Adjusting Guides

Margin, ruler, and column guides are nonprinting visual elements that you can use to help structure your pages. Margin guides are dashed lines, ruler guides are dotted lines with the dots widely spaced, and column guides are dotted lines with the dots finely spaced. If you use a color monitor, all these guides show on-screen as solid lines. Margin guides are pink, ruler guides green, and column guides light blue.

PageMaker normally places guides in the foreground where the guides lie in front of text and graphics. This placement can sometimes be a problem when working with a color monitor because the solid guidelines tend to obscure whatever lies behind them. You can move your guides behind other elements by clicking the `Back Guides` option in the Preferences dialog box (choose Preferences from the Edit menu). Moving guides to the rear makes selecting text and graphics easier without accidentally grabbing and moving a guide instead. After you have all your guides arranged the way you want them, you can set them in place to prevent any further movement by choosing Lock Guides from the Options menu.

> *Tip*
> If you are using many guides and rearranging them frequently, leave them in the foreground so that they are easy to get at. If you move them to the rear, you are not able to click them when they are covered by text or graphics. If you try to select text or graphics in the background, and you snag an overlapping guide instead, hold down the Command key as you click to select whatever lies beneath the guide, and not the guide itself.

Occasionally you may want to adjust your page margins to meet changing layout requirements. Enter the new margin values in the Page Setup dialog box (choose Page Setup from the File menu) and click OK. The new margin boundaries are displayed on all pages (see fig. 6.2). PageMaker respaces all column guides throughout your publication (but not the text within them) to fit equally within the new margin boundaries. If you used column guides to set variable-width columns on some of your pages, that column formatting is lost.

The column and ruler guides on the master pages repeat on all regular pages. Unlike other master-page elements, however, you can move the guides to meet changing layout requirements. To adjust a column or ruler guide, click the guide with the pointer tool and drag. Your pointer tool changes to a two-headed arrow to show the possible directions of movement. As you drag the guide, a dotted marker in the opposing ruler follows along to indicate exact position on the page.

Fig. 6.2.

Adjusting page margins has no affect on existing text blocks.

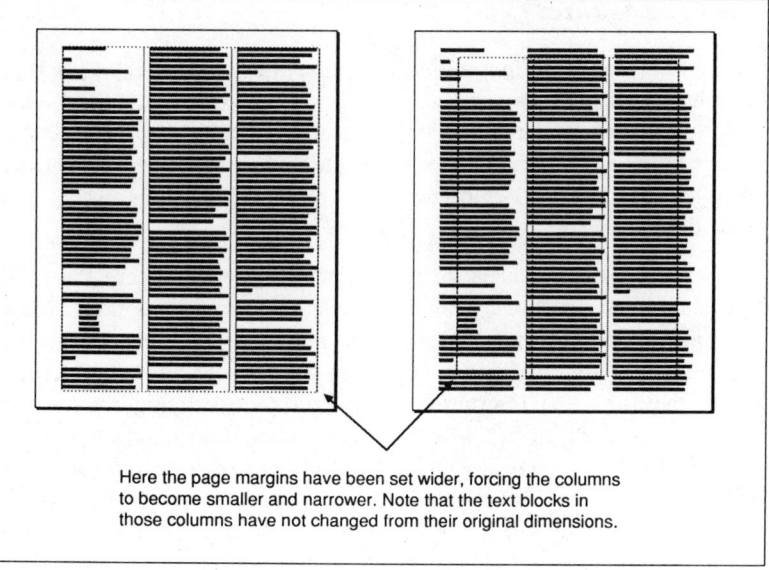

Here the page margins have been set wider, forcing the columns to become smaller and narrower. Note that the text blocks in those columns have not changed from their original dimensions.

If you need additional ruler guides, click the appropriate ruler to drag them, one at a time, onto your pages. To remove a ruler guide, drag the guide off your layout and back onto the ruler from which it came. If you need to change the number of column guides on a page, you must change the number of columns first (choose Column Guides from the Options menu). You cannot drag column guides onto or off a page. Although column and ruler guides are visible only on your pages, column guides are further restricted to lie within only the page margins. You cannot use column or ruler guides on the pasteboard.

If you want to see how your pages look when printed, deselect the Guides command from the Options menu to hide all the margin, column, and ruler guides.

Resizing Text Blocks

Resizing text blocks enables you to reformat your layout to meet changing needs. Suppose, for example, that you want to insert a graphic into the middle of a column. You must shorten the text block that already fills the column, add the graphic, then create a continuation text block of the correct size to fill the empty space. This process is easy in PageMaker.

You have two ways to resize a text block. The first is to drag the top or bottom windowshade handles. Click in the loop of a windowshade handle with the pointer tool, press the mouse button, and drag up or down (see fig. 6.3). The text block lengthens or shortens, depending on which way you drag.

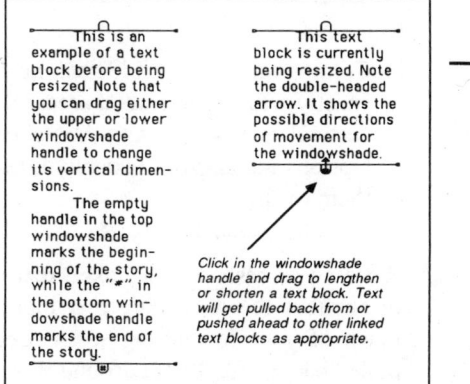

Fig. 6.3.

You can resize a text block within a column by dragging a windowshade handle.

If you lengthen a text block, threaded text flows backward from later text blocks to fill the newly expanded space. If you have no follow-on text, the windowshade handle marks the end of the story with a # sign to indicate that no text is left to place. If you shorten a text block, the text is pushed forward. If no follow-on blocks exist to hold the overflow, a plus sign (+) appears in the windowshade handle to indicate that more story needs to be placed.

The second way to resize a text block is to drag a corner handle (see fig. 6.4). Dragging a corner handle enables you to reshape a text block without regard for column boundaries. You can reshape a text block so that the block spans multiple columns, bleeds text across facing pages, or fills an arbitrary area. The text rewraps to fit in the new text-block boundaries.

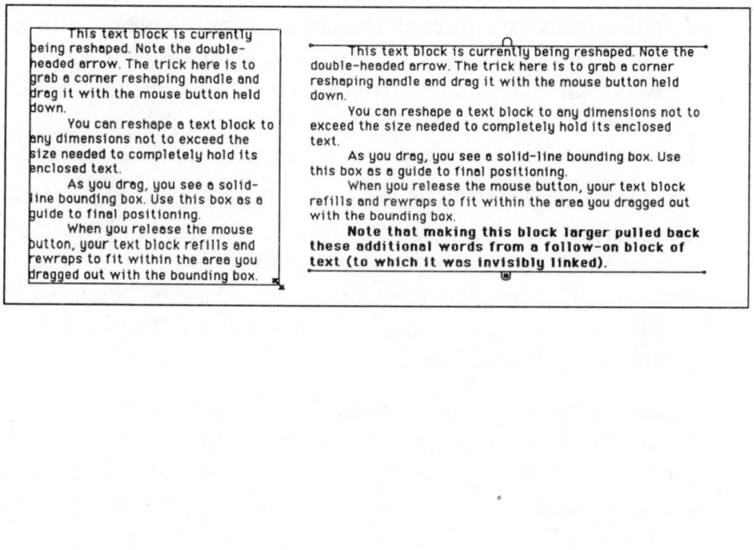

Fig. 6.4.

You can reshape a text block by dragging a corner handle.

> ***Tip***
> Column and ruler guides can help you accurately shape text blocks to lie exactly within designated areas. If you mark each area with horizontal and vertical ruler guides and then choose the Snap To Guides command in the Options menu, your text-block borders snap to the guides as you reshape them to fit.

Resizing or reshaping a linked text block produces an immediate ripple effect throughout the remaining text blocks of a story. This ripple effect can undo much of your formatting work, because threaded text is pushed forward or pulled backward. To get around this problem, PageMaker enables you to isolate text blocks from one another.

To unlink or isolate a text block, select the block with the pointer tool and move the text to the Clipboard with the Cut command in the Edit menu. Paste the block back onto your page and drag the block to its original position. The text in that block looks the same as before, except that the text is unthreaded from the rest of the story. The text is unaffected by any changes you make to other text blocks. To rethread the text into your story, cut the block, use the text tool to create an insertion point at the end of the previous text block or at the beginning of the next, and repaste the block.

> ***Warning***
> When you unlink a text block, the invisible threading of your story isn't broken. It still exists for all the remaining text blocks. If you make any editing or formatting changes to your story, your text is pushed forward or pulled backward through the chain, skipping over the isolated block and eventually knocking your text out of sequence. To avoid this problem, isolate all blocks of text from a story at the same time you isolate one text block.

To break a single text block into several smaller text blocks, shorten the original block, then click the + in the windowshade handle. Flow the continuation text into a new block. Repeat for as many blocks as you need. Each time you create a new block this way, you push the text ahead as you compress the copy, and then pull the text back to fill the newly created block. The text is threaded throughout all the newly created blocks.

To consolidate two or more blocks into one block, completely close up one of the blocks by dragging the windowshade handles together (see fig. 6.5). Text is pushed ahead, and the empty block is deleted. Enlarge the preceding or following text block to fill the empty space, and the text you pushed ahead flows backward to fill the expansion.

Chapter 6: Formatting Text

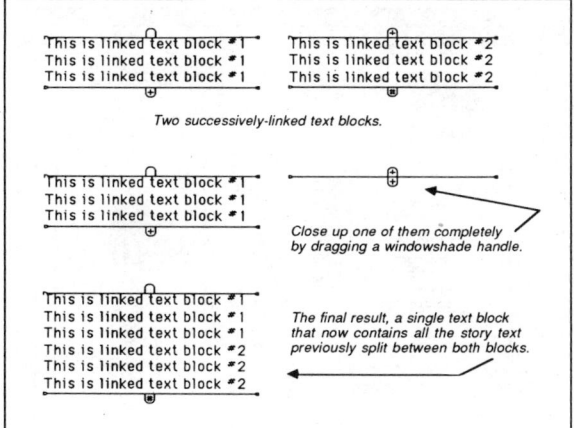

Fig. 6.5.

Consolidate multiple text blocks by using windowshade handles to close up one of the blocks.

To delete a text block, select the block with the pointer tool and press the Backspace key, or choose Clear from the edit menu.

> **Tip**
> Just as clicking in the bottom windowshade handle of a selected text block enables you to continue flowing text into a new, follow-on text block, clicking in the top windowshade handle enables you to reflow text from that block into a new, preceding text block.

Using the Pasteboard

The pasteboard is a convenient work and storage area that completely surrounds the page display (see fig. 6.6). You can see the whole pasteboard by holding down the Shift key as you choose Fit In Window from the Page menu. The pasteboard is a handy place for creating new text, such as headlines and picture captions. The pasteboard also is convenient for storing text and graphics that you intend to use later in your publication.

You can drag any element onto the pasteboard, and whatever you have stored on the pasteboard can be dragged or copied and pasted back onto your pages at any time. Because the pasteboard gets carried along whenever you turn pages, what you store on the pasteboard is always immediately available for use. Be sure, however, that when you store an item on the pasteboard, no part of the item touches your pages. Otherwise, the item remains behind with the page it touches as you turn to a new page.

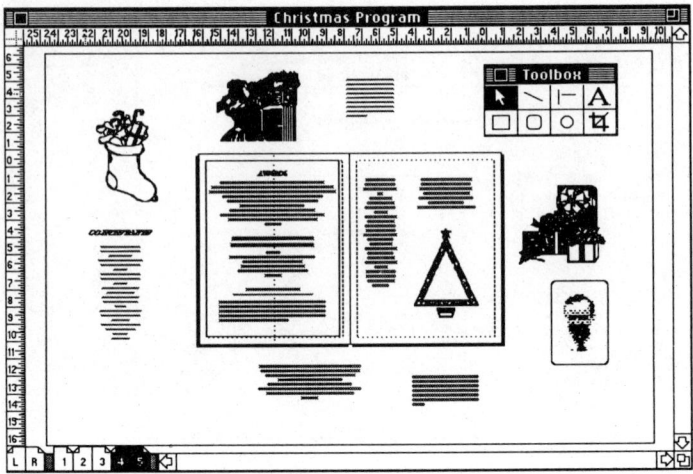

Fig. 6.6.

The pasteboard can be used to store text and graphics.

If you leave an item on the pasteboard and quit PageMaker, the item is still on the pasteboard the next time you open your publication. Because nothing you store on the pasteboard is printed, you don't have to worry about removing items before printing.

Use the pasteboard to archive text and graphics temporarily as you experiment with different layouts. You also can use the pasteboard to store rules, boxes, and other design elements so that you don't have to switch between pages to copy them from one to another.

Tip

If you don't have enough text items formatted the same to warrant creating a separate style sheet (see "Using Style Sheets" later in this chapter), prepare a text place holder and store the holder on the pasteboard. A place holder is a sample block of text that is already formatted. Whenever you want to enter formatted text on a page, first copy and paste the place holder, then select and replace the text by typing your own words. Your newly typed text assumes the place holder's formatting. This method eliminates the need to repeatedly reassign the same type specifications.

Formatting Paragraphs

In PageMaker, as with most word processors, paragraphs are separated by carriage returns. Two sequential carriage returns separated by text tells PageMaker that the intervening text is a paragraph. Paragraphs are not the same as text blocks, however. A text block can contain part of a long paragraph, or many short paragraphs.

Paragraphs can be formatted independently of one another, and the formatting style of one paragraph can be saved and later applied to other paragraphs. PageMaker gives you complete control over how your paragraphs look when printed.

In addition to normal type specifications that apply only to selected text, PageMaker enables you to assign other specifications to paragraphs and stories. These specifications include leading (pronounced ledd-ing), indents and tabs (to help structure your text), hyphens (to help break lines properly for orderly word wrap), and alignment (to left-, right-, or center-justify text within columns).

Leading

Leading refers to the vertical space between successive lines of text (see fig. 6.7). This space is measured in points and can be set manually to incremental half-point sizes or automatically as an overall percentage of type size (PageMaker internally rounds these percentages to the nearest half-point size).

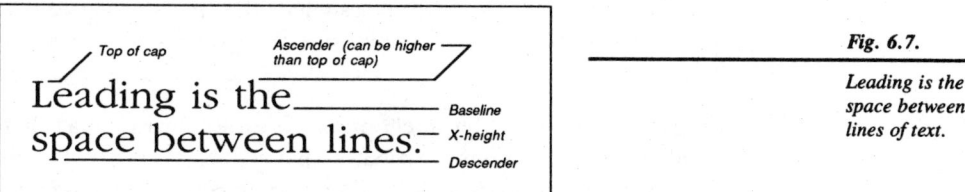

Fig. 6.7.

Leading is the space between lines of text.

Although you can assign different leading values for successive lines of text, different leading values yield uneven line spacing and detract from legibility. You should apply a particular leading only to whole paragraphs or entire stories. Your goal should be to format your documents so that the text is easy to read and understand. Often legibility can be improved vastly by making only minor adjustments in leading.

PageMaker computes leading at 120 percent of type size. For example, 10-point type is spaced using 12 points of leading, or the equivalent of two points of empty space between vertical characters. You can assign different leading values to increase or decrease line spacing in two ways:

1. Select the text you want changed and pick a point size from the Leading menu (under the Type menu). PageMaker displays a group of values close to the selected type size. If no text is selected, PageMaker displays a set of commonly used leading values to pick from.

2. Choose Type Specs from the Type menu to display the Type Specifications dialog box. Pick a point size or enter a new value from *0* to *127* points for `Leading`.

You also can change the percentage that PageMaker uses. Make sure that you have created an insertion point and that you have selected Auto in the Leading menu. Then choose Spacing from the Type menu. In the Spacing Attributes dialog box, enter a new percentage into the `Auto leading` field. When you click OK, PageMaker applies the new leading to your entire story.

If you manually assign leading to a story and choose Auto from the Leading menu with some text selected or if an insertion point exists anywhere within that story, the entire story is reformatted. To apply auto leading to only newly typed text, make sure that no previous text is selected and that no insertion point exists when you choose Auto from the Leading menu.

Tip

If you increase the point size of even a single character and Auto Leading is in effect, the leading for that line changes, but not the leading of other lines. To avoid this problem, choose a leading for the whole paragraph in which you plan to make the change. If you manually set leading equal to the same value PageMaker assigned, the line spacing remains constant whenever you change the point size of any character or word.

PageMaker enables you to choose between `Proportional` and `Top of caps` leading in the Spacing Attributes dialog box. You usually use proportional leading. With proportional leading, two thirds of the assigned line-space lies above and one third lies below the baseline. For example, 24-point leading allows 16 points of leading above the baseline, and 8 points below the baseline. This leading enables you to mix disparate font types on the same baseline and still keep overall vertical line spacing uniform (fonts from different publishers can produce different size characters, even if assigned the same type size). Top of caps leading sets line spacing without regard to the baseline.

Tip

To start a paragraph with an oversized capital letter without disrupting subsequent line spacing, assign the capital the same leading value as the rest of the paragraph. Make sure that you also have chosen `Proportional` for the `Leading method` in the Spacing Attributes dialog box.

> *Tip*
> If you regularly use an odd type size and leading combination, for example, 10-point type over 11 1/2-point leading, set your vertical ruler divisions in the Preferences dialog box to equal the assigned leading—in this case, 11 1/2 points. With the Snap To Rulers command from the Options menu toggled on, aligning adjoining text blocks or other page elements along a baseline is easy. This method is an effective way to lay out tables quickly using data from multiple text blocks.

Spacing

By enabling you to specify the exact spacing between paragraphs, PageMaker makes double-spacing after carriage returns to insert extra space between paragraphs unnecessary. You can have PageMaker insert space before or after a paragraph (you also can do both at the same time). Paragraph spacing combines with assigned line leading, and is inserted each time you press the Return key.

To change paragraph spacing, select the paragraphs you want to adjust, then choose the Paragraph command from the Type menu to display the Paragraph Specifications dialog box. Enter a new value for `Spacing Before` or `Spacing After`. The paragraph spacing is revised immediately after you click the OK button.

> *Tip*
> Set paragraph spacing by using the Paragraph Specifications dialog box. Inserting extra carriage returns can lead to alignment problems if they are styled differently from surrounding text. Although carriage returns are distinct characters to which style attributes can be individually applied, they are invisible on-screen, which can make them hard to detect.

Indents and Tabs

Indents and tabs enable you to control the internal formatting of your paragraphs. After you understand how they work, assembling and formatting complex documents is much easier.

Setting Indents

PageMaker's left and right indents determine how far your text is set in from the left and right page margins or the left and right column guides. You also can use nested indents to create paragraphs set in from the main body of text. You set left and right indents by selecting the paragraphs you want to apply them to and choosing the Paragraph command from the Type menu to access the Paragraph Specifications dialog box. Enter the desired values into the Indents Left and Indents Right fields.

You might prefer to choose Indents/Tabs from the Type menu for a ruler that gives a visual display (see fig. 6.8). On the ruler, the left indent is represented by the small triangle toward the left end of the scale; the right indent is represented by the large triangle at the right end of the scale. You can move these indent markers to any position along the ruler by clicking and dragging them with your pointer tool. You also can drag the ruler window on the page, and you can scroll the ruler left or right using the small hollow arrows at either end, which can help you align the ruler tick marks for accurate indent and tab placement. The zero tick mark on the ruler indicates the left page margin or column guide, not the left edge of the page.

PageMaker's first-line indent determines how far the first line of text in a paragraph is indented. If the indentation is set in toward the right, it is called a normal indent. If the indentation is set out toward the left (away from the body of a paragraph), it is called a hanging indent. As with PageMaker's left and right indents, you can set the first-line indent value in the Paragraph Specifications dialog box or set the value with the Indents/Tabs ruler. On the ruler, the first line indent is represented by the small triangle toward the left end of the ruler. Drag the triangle to any spot along the ruler to make a change.

To set a hanging indent, enter a negative value for Indents First in the Paragraph Specifications dialog box. Be sure to enter a larger positive value for Indents Left, or PageMaker does not accept your numbers. You must have room for the hanging indent to exist within the left page margin or column boundary. Set a hanging indent using the Indents/Tabs ruler. First, drag the left indent marker to the right to make room for the hanging indent. The first-line indent moves with the left indent to hold its position with respect to the left edge of the paragraph. When you have enough space, move the first-line indent marker back to the left to create the hanging indent.

When you drag an indent or tab marker along the ruler, you see a numerical value displayed just below the Clear and to the left of the Cancel buttons. This digital number gives the exact position of the marker. Use the number as a guide to precise marker placement.

Chapter 6: Formatting Text — 137

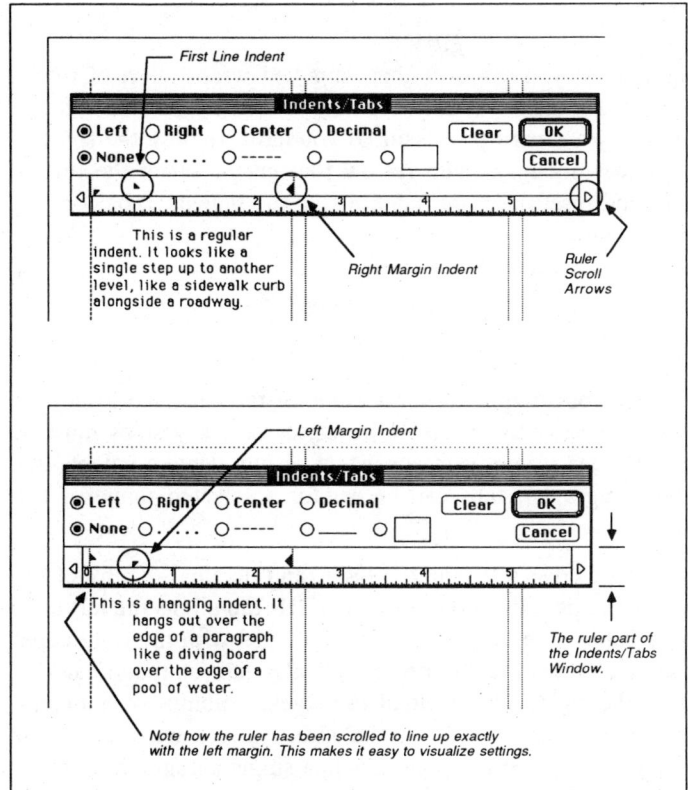

Fig. 6.8.

The Indents/Tabs ruler.

Tip
If you are working in a 400% Size page view (by holding the Shift key and selecting 200% Size from the Page menu) and your publication's units of measure are set to picas, the Indents/Tabs ruler displays ruler tick marks at one-point intervals. These marks make setting indents and tabs in one-point increments easy. Use the digital number display to check your work.

You can set indents to lie only within existing page margins or column guides, and any settings you make apply to only selected paragraphs. If you create a paragraph without making changes, PageMaker assumes the preceding paragraph's formatting. Similarly, new text inserted into an existing paragraph assumes the host paragraph's formatting.

> ***Tip***
> If, when placing a story, you discover that your text wraps short of the right column boundary, check to make sure that you haven't set the right indent in too far with your word processor. If you have, remove the right indent in your original document and reflow the text or select the text within PageMaker and reset the right indent using the Indents/Tabs command on the Type menu.

Setting Tabs

PageMaker also enables you to apply several kinds of tabs and tab leaders to your documents. Tabs are easy to set up; however, certain key steps must be performed in strict sequence if you want consistent results. Unlike indents that apply to only whole paragraphs, tabs can be set for a selected range of text within a paragraph.

You can use four kinds of tabs: left, right, center, and decimal. Think of tab stops as invisible wires running down the page. The left tab aligns the left edge of your text to this invisible wire. The right tab aligns text with the right edge. The center tab causes each line of text to be split equally, half on the left side of the wire, and half on the right. The decimal tab stacks columns of numbers, aligning their decimal points vertically along the wire. All tabs are set using the Indents/Tabs ruler, and you can set up to 20 tabs in a single paragraph.

> ***Tip***
> Use tabs instead of spaces to format tables and lists of data. Most fonts are proportional, and the space surrounding individual characters varies. If you space your data with the space bar, the alignment is uneven when you print your document, even if the text looks good on-screen. If you use tabs, the alignment is exact.

Each tab marker is an icon shaped like an arrow. The left-tab marker has a bent tail that points to the right, toward the aligned text. The right-tab marker has a bent tail that points to the left. The center-tab marker has a straight tail to indicate that text moves away from the marker in both directions. The decimal-tab marker has a small decimal mark next to its tail (see fig. 6.9).

When you set tabs in PageMaker, you also can set accompanying tab leaders. Tab leaders are repeating characters—usually dots, dashes, or lines—that precede indented text.

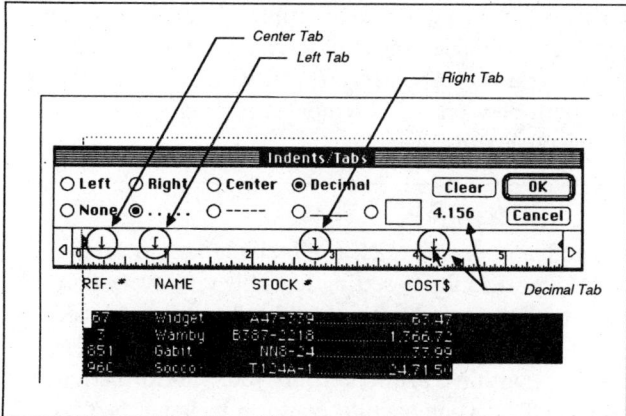

Fig. 6.9.

Adjusting tabs using the Indents/Tabs ruler.

Set your tab stops and leader styles using the following procedure:

1. Unless you want to use the existing tabs as displayed, click the Clear button to remove them from the ruler. Otherwise adjust the tabs individually by dragging or remove them one at a time.

2. Choose the kind of tab you want (left, right, center, or decimal).

3. Choose the kind of leader style you want (dots, dashes, solid line, a character of your own choosing, or none). If you want to create your own tab leader, click the last button, and enter one or two repeating characters into the leader style box.

Note

The tab leader you specify during this step becomes an inseparable part of the tab stop you create in the next step. If you don't do this step first in the sequence, no tab leader is assigned.

Tip

To create a leader composed of dots less tightly spaced than they are in the style provided, in the leader style box, enter a period followed by a space.

---

4. Click the lower or upper half of the ruler (not the ruler window) to make the tab marker appear.

5. Drag the marker to the desired location along the ruler. Each tab marker aligns to a different ruler tick mark. You can drag any marker over any other. Use the digital number display to check placement accuracy.

Be sure that you follow this exact sequence every time. Even if you have assigned a tab leader that you later decide you want to change, you must again repeat all the steps. First, remove the tab marker(s) to which that leader is assigned, then replace them with new ones. To remove a tab marker, drag the marker up or down until it disappears off the ruler.

> ### *Warning*
> If you assign several tabs and later decide to clear all tab markers from the ruler and start over, PageMaker defaults to setting invisible tabs every half inch. After you enter a tab character with the Tab key, PageMaker remembers the tab from then on. Because you have no way to search for and strip tab characters from within PageMaker, all your tab-formatted text instantly reorganizes itself on your page to conform to PageMaker's invisible default tab settings. This reorganization usually turns formatted text and tables into screen garbage. Any new tabs that you add eliminate the invisible half-inch default markers to the left of the tab you added so that you get proper spacing when you press the Tab key. But PageMaker's invisible tabs always exist to the right of the last tab marker placed.

If you remove a single tab marker, the text aligned with that marker shifts to the left to align with the preceding tab stop. If you have no preceding tab stops, your text aligns with the left indent, first-line indent, or column guide. If you remove the last tab marker from the ruler, your text aligns itself with the next invisible default tab stop to the left.

To use tabs you created when typing new text, press the Tab key to move your text insertion point to the next tab stop. If the tab has an associated tab leader, the leader appears when you type the first character. To tab existing text, create an insertion point and press the Tab key. Your text reformats at the next tab stop according to the type of tab alignment specified. If your tab has an associated tab leader, you see the leader when you press the Tab key.

When you import a document, PageMaker normally assigns tabs and indents to match the formatting created in your word processor.

As with PageMaker's horizontal and vertical page rulers, the tick marks on the Indents/Tabs ruler change their spacing as you switch between different page views or assign different units of measure using the Preferences dialog box. Because each indent and tab marker must align exactly with a ruler tick mark, you may want to try different window views and units of measure when placing indents and tab stops. Generally, positioning indent and tab markers is easier when you work in an enlarged page view.

Hyphenation

PageMaker hyphenates text to wrap it evenly within column boundaries. If a word at the end of a line is too long to fit in column boundaries and PageMaker cannot hyphenate the word, the whole word is moved to the beginning of the next line. This process can leave unsightly gaps of white space that detract from the appearance of your publication. To correct this problem, you can have PageMaker hyphenate your text. You also can have PageMaker prompt you whenever the program encounters a word it doesn't know how to hyphenate. You also can use the special discretionary hyphens that you insert manually, or you can turn off all hyphenation.

PageMaker comes with two dictionaries for checking hyphenation—a built-in 110,000-word Houghton Mifflin dictionary and a separate user dictionary that can be configured to hold up to 1,300 additional hyphenation specimens. Whenever PageMaker hyphenates a publication, the program checks the text against both hyphenation dictionaries beginning with the supplementary user dictionary.

Automatic Hyphenation

To turn on automatic hyphenation, choose Paragraph from the Type menu, and choose Hyphenation Auto in the Paragraph Specifications dialog box. Page-Maker hyphenates all newly typed or imported text and any text selected at the time auto-hyphenation is turned on. Normally you want to leave auto-hyphenation on as you work. PageMaker rehyphenates your stories as you resize or reshape text blocks, or insert or remove text.

Prompted Hyphenation

If you want more control over PageMaker's hyphenation, select the text you want to hyphenate and choose Hyphenation Prompted in the Paragraph Specifications dialog box. As PageMaker attempts to hyphenate the selected text, the program stops on any word that doesn't fit at the end of a line. You are shown the word, along with preceding and following text, in a dialog box on the lower part of your screen. If Hyphenation Auto is on, the word is displayed with the dictionary-applied hyphens already inserted. You also are shown any discretionary hyphens previously added. A blinking cursor marks the last character that can fit on the line.

Click the word (to the left of the blinking cursor) wherever you want PageMaker to create a break. If you don't want PageMaker to hyphenate the word, click to create a hyphen at the beginning of the word. Choose Add Word to Diction-

ary if you want to add that word and its new hyphenation to the supplementary user dictionary. Note that, for this option to be available, auto-hyphenation also must be turned on.

The supplementary user dictionary is a simple text document that you can open and edit using your word processor. Each word in the dictionary is on a different line and is separated by a carriage return. Each word contains regular hyphens to tell PageMaker where the word can be broken. You can add or delete hyphens to suit your preferences. Because the supplementary user dictionary is an ordinary text file, you can customize the user dictionary easily. Use the supplementary dictionary to indicate the desired hyphenation of proper names, technical jargon, and other words you use frequently but are not contained in PageMaker's built-in dictionary. If you don't want a particular word ever to be hyphenated, also include that word, but without any hyphens.

Tip

You can edit the supplementary user dictionary quickly at any time without having to leave PageMaker or close your current publication. Choose the Place command from the File menu and select the user dictionary. Click the text-placement icon to flow text anywhere on the page or pasteboard where you have room to work. Make your changes, then select and export the text back to the same folder. Save the text as a text-only file under the same name. Your updated version replaces the original file.

Discretionary Hyphenation

Discretionary hyphenation is a quick way of telling PageMaker how to hyphenate words the program cannot find in the dictionaries. Unlike ordinary hyphens, you don't see discretionary hyphens until PageMaker uses them to break words at the ends of lines. Discretionary hyphens apply to only the document in which they are entered.

To insert discretionary hyphens, press the Command key and type a hyphen wherever you want the words to be broken. Follow this procedure for already hyphenated words if you want to change the hyphenation for a better column fit. For example, entering a discretionary hyphen in the first word of a line breaks that word and moves part of the word up to fill the hole at the end of the previous line; entering a discretionary hyphen in front of the last word in a line, even if it's already auto-hyphenated, moves that whole word down to the beginning of the next line.

To remove a discretionary hyphen, insert the cursor immediately after the hyphen and backspace over the hyphen. To remove a discretionary hyphen from a word in the middle of a line (where the hyphen isn't displayed), select and replace the word by typing over it.

> *Tip*
> Always use discretionary (soft) hyphens in preference to regular (hard) hyphens. When you reformat your layout by resizing or reshaping text blocks, discretionary hyphens within words that move to the middle of lines no longer display. Regular hyphens, however, display no matter where their words appear on the page.

Aligning Text

PageMaker's Alignment command (from the Type menu) gives you several choices for aligning text within columns (see fig. 6.10). You can align text evenly along the left edge (Align Left), its right edge (Align Right), or left and right edges (Align Justify). You also can center your text (Align Center). These commands should not be confused with tab stops. Tab stops apply to only tabbed text; the alignment commands apply to columnar text. For example, if you choose Align Right, your selected text reformats so that the right edges of all lines lie flush against the right column guide.

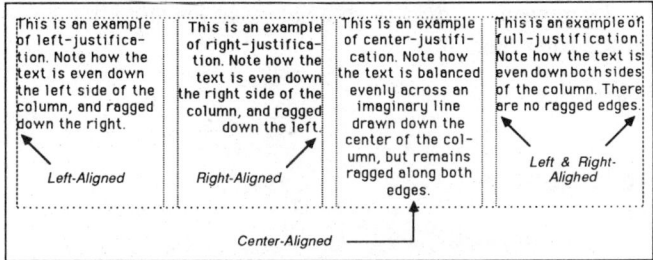

Fig. 6.10.

In PageMaker you can left-, right-, center-, or fully justify text.

Text is often left-aligned (sometimes called ragged-right justification), because this layout is the easiest kind to read. The next easiest-to-read alignment is fully justified text, also called left-right justified. PageMaker's Align Justify command formats text so that each line is of equal length, often to the detriment of word or letter spacing. Right-aligned or right-justified text is generally used in only special instances, such as a list of items confined to the right side of a page. Right-justified text is difficult to read unless confined to narrow columns. Center-aligned (center-justified) text is often used for design emphasis or to focus reader attention. Because long center-justified passages can be difficult to read, use this kind of formatting sparingly.

> **Tip**
> Justifying columns can create uneven spacing between bullets and the text that follows them. To ensure even spacing, insert a tab to mark the beginning of your text and tab over to the text after you type each bullet. You also can enter a fixed Space (press Option-space bar) if the fixed-space character is supported by the font you're using.

After you have aligned the text in the columns, align your text blocks. To align text blocks vertically, place a vertical ruler guide where you want to stack them, select the Snap To Rulers command on the Options menu, and drag each text block so that the block lies against the ruler guide. To align text blocks horizontally, use a horizontal ruler guide to align adjoining baselines. If you want to stack two unlinked text blocks vertically so that the text they contain reads continuously and has the same line spacing where they join, use the following procedure:

1. Align both text blocks vertically using a vertical ruler guide. Position one block in its final position. This block is the anchor block. The other text block is the move block.

2. Select the anchor block with the pointer tool so that its windowshade handles show. Pull down a horizontal ruler guide, and place the guide on top of the handle nearest the move block.

3. Select the move block and, while holding down the Shift key to vertically constrain its movement, drag the block so that the adjoining boundary overlaps the ruler guide.

4. Delete any extra blank lines.

Adjusting Word Spacing

When PageMaker justifies text, the program sacrifices word and letter spacing to achieve equal line widths. This process can sometimes lead to unsightly "rivers" of white space that snake down a column. To help compensate, you can use the Type menu's Spacing command to specify the desired spacing for words and letters and to set an acceptable range of maximum and minimum spacing values. You set these values in the Spacing Attributes dialog box (see fig. 6.11). Spacing attributes apply to entire stories, not just to selected text.

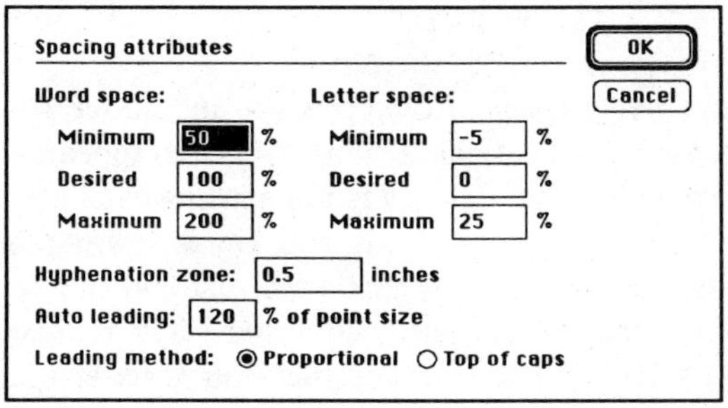

Fig. 6.11.

The Spacing Attributes dialog box.

Although this method often helps, formatting justified text requires a mixture of skill and patience. Variables such as word and character spacing, hyphenation, and text-block size come into play. You may go through much trial-and-error formatting before you approach ideal results. However, don't be discouraged. PageMaker generally does a credible job of justifying text, and you can improve spacing with little extra effort.

To adjust word or letter spacing, enter an insertion point in your story, then choose Spacing from the Type menu. The values you enter for `Word space` and `Letter space` take effect immediately after you click OK. To add more space between words and letters, increase the range values by entering a smaller number in the minimum field and a larger number in the maximum field. (Do just the opposite to subtract space.) Keep in mind that increased range values tend to create more rivers in your columns; decreased range values help eliminate rivers.

The allowable range of values you can enter for `Word space` is 0 percent to 500 percent. For `Letter space`, you can enter -200 percent to 0 percent for `Minimum`, and 0 percent to 200 percent for `Maximum`. However, all you really need to know is that if you enter 100 percent for `Word space: Desired` and 0 percent for `Letter space: Desired`, PageMaker uses the selected font's built-in spacing.

You can adjust the `Maximum` and `Minimum` field percentages as necessary to achieve optimal column justification (make sure that you also have hyphenation turned on to get the best results). Values greater than 100 percent entered into the `Word space` fields expand the space between words; values less than 100 percent contract the space between words. Similarly, values greater than 0 percent entered into the `Letter space` fields expand the space between letters; values less than 0 contract the space between letters.

> **Tip**
> Most fonts can benefit from tighter word and letter spacing. Tighter spacing gives your publications a more finished appearance and makes them easier to read (see fig. 6.12). Tighter spacing can be more difficult to edit on-screen, however. Wait until you finish editing before you set spacing to a lesser value. Depending on the font and size you use, you get different results for different assigned values. Try reducing the desired word spacing by 20 to 30 percent and the desired letter spacing by 3 to 6 percent. Set the minimum letter spacing only slightly less than or equal to the desired letter spacing for best results when using justified columns.

Fig. 6.12.

Improve the appearance of your text by tightening word and letter spacing.

> This text is set in 12-point Times. The word and letter spacing are those assigned by the font designer.
>
> This is the same font, but the word and letter spacing have been tightened 20% and 3% respectively.

> **Tip**
> Use PageMaker's Spacing command to adjust the word and letter spacing of your headlines. Headlines residing in their own text blocks are considered by PageMaker to be complete stories, and they can benefit directly from this feature.

Although tighter word and letter spacing applied to justified columns, especially narrow ones, helps to eliminate unsightly gaps, tighter spacing also increases the amount of hyphenation required. You should adjust your spacing attributes to limit to two the number of successively hyphenated lines—three lines at most. Note that you also can use prompted hyphenation to help specify words you don't want hyphenated.

Use the Spacing Attributes dialog box to specify the size of the hyphenation zone. This zone is an arbitrary region at the end of a line where hyphenation is allowed to occur for unjustified text. If the zone is set too wide, your unjustified columns may turn out excessively ragged.

> **Tip**
> You may not always be able to see the full effects of adjusting word and letter spacing on-screen. Most screen resolutions are limited to 72 dots per inch. Whenever you assign new spacing attributes to your text, do a test print to evaluate the results.

Using Style Sheets

Style sheets are sets of predefined paragraph specifications called styles (not to be confused with everyday type styles like bold and italic). You use styles to make global formatting changes to your publications. Each PageMaker publication has a style sheet that can contain any number of styles. Suppose that you created a style and used that style to set all your subheads to 12-point Helvetica bold type. You decide that 14-point bold italic type is more appropriate. You can call up the subhead style from your style sheet and make the necessary editing changes using the Type Specifications dialog box. When you click OK, PageMaker updates every subhead throughout your entire publication.

Style sheets are great time-savers, and they are useful for giving a consistent look to your publications. Style sheets, however, can be tricky to work with at times. The problem stems from making ordinary menu style changes—made by using PageMaker's menus and Type Specifications dialog box—within paragraphs that have style-sheet formatting applied. If you later change the style that was used, or another style upon which that one was based, or apply a new style to those same paragraphs, you may lose whatever other ordinary style changes you have made.

Use caution with style sheets. Start by formatting just one or two items, and, as you gain experience, gradually work up to applying styles throughout your publications. After you master the basics, you will discover many exciting ways to use style sheets.

Style Sheet Basics

Style sheets enable you to assign type, paragraph, indent/tab, and even color specifications globally to selected paragraphs. (Remember that a paragraph within a range of text is bounded by two carriage returns. A single headline in its own text block also is a paragraph.) Applying styles is a fast way to do extensive formatting. You can select a group of paragraphs or a whole story, and, with a single click, change completely the way it looks.

Style sheets are publication-dependent. When you create a style, the style sheet is saved with your publication or template. If you send that file to be printed, your built-in styles accompany the file. Each new PageMaker publication opens with a set of built-in styles that you can modify to match your own formatting needs.

> **Tip**
> Create a Master Styles publication template. After that, whenever you begin a new publication, start by opening a copy of the template. All your styles are available to you, and you don't have to import the style attributes selectively from other publications.

Styles can be added to your publications by creating them anew, basing them on pre-existing styles, copying them from other PageMaker publications, or importing them along with your word processor documents. Styles you create are listed in and readily accessible from:

- ❏ The Styles Palette (choose Style Palette from the Options menu)
- ❏ The Define Styles dialog box (choose Define Styles from the Type menu)
- ❏ The Styles menu (under the Type menu)

Generally, you want to set up different styles for different paragraphs in a publication—headings, subheads, picture captions, credit lines, footnotes, body text, and so on.

Defining and Editing Styles

To define a new style, choose Define Styles from the Type menu. Choose `New` and, in the Edit Style dialog box, type the name of your new style (see fig. 6.13). If you are basing your new style on an existing style, type the name of that style on the `Based on` line. Then choose `Type`, `Para`, `Tabs`, and `Color` one at a time. Each option brings up a different dialog box in which you can assign desired formatting specifications.

Fig. 6.13.

The Edit Style dialog box.

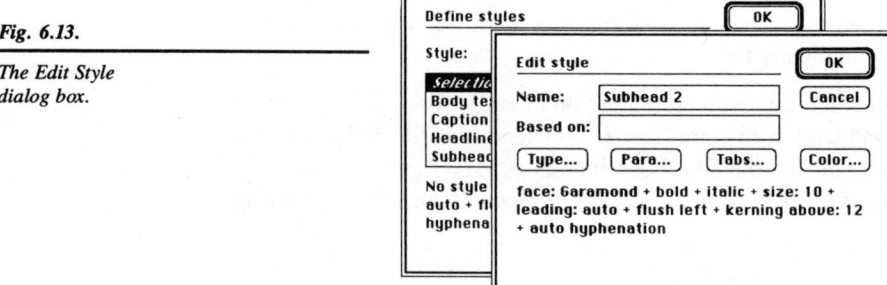

> **Tip**
> If you click on a style listed in the Define Styles dialog box before selecting `New`, that style name appears on the `Based on` line in the Edit Style dialog box; you don't have to enter the name each time.

You also can create a style based on existing text that has been formatted using only menu commands (no style assigned). Select the text you want to base your style on, or click an insertion point somewhere within the text. You see the style attributes for that text listed in the lower half of the Define Styles and Edit Style dialog boxes. Make any additional modifications as desired.

When you are finished, click `Close` or OK to save your style to your publication's style sheet. `Close` saves your style without applying the attributes. If the paragraph has an insertion point, or if text in one or more paragraphs is highlighted, clicking OK applies the new style.

> **Note**
> If you base new styles on existing styles, they become linked permanently into a style chain. If you later edit any style upon which others are based, all the other styles update to reflect the changes made, and all the paragraphs throughout your publication to which those styles have been applied also are updated.

To edit an existing style, follow the same general procedure as for defining a new style. But, in the Define Styles dialog box, click on the style that you want to edit, and then click `Edit` to bring up the Edit Styles dialog box with your chosen style ready for editing. A shortcut to the Edit Styles dialog box is to hold down the Command key as you click on a style in the Styles Palette. You then can edit that style directly. Click on `No Style` to create a new style. When you edit a style, your changes are applied to every paragraph previously assigned that style.

To copy styles from another PageMaker publication, click on the `Copy` button in the Define Styles dialog box. Choose the publication containing the styles you want to copy. When you click OK, PageMaker copies that publication's styles (all of them) into your current document. You then can modify any of those styles to meet your specific needs.

To remove a style from a style sheet, select the style name from the Define Styles dialog box and click `Remove`. This option does not remove any formatting you previously applied to your publication using that style (be sure to click `Close` as you exit the Define Styles dialog box).

Importing Styles

To import styles created by your word processor, they must have been used to format the documents being imported. When you import those documents, make sure that the `Retain format` option in the Place Document dialog box is selected. When PageMaker imports a document, any assigned styles found also are imported (when the styles are compatible) and added to your publication's style sheet. These styles are listed in the Styles palette and Styles menu and are followed by an asterisk to distinguish them from styles you have defined within PageMaker. Imported styles are applied directly to the imported text. If any imported styles have names that match the names in PageMaker's style sheet, PageMaker uses its own styles instead.

PageMaker also can import and apply styles included as name tags within word-processed documents. Each name tag must be set at the beginning of the paragraph to which the tag applies and enclosed in angle brackets, such as <caption>. However, no tags are needed for a following paragraph that is formatted the same as a previous tagged paragraph.

If the name tag caption, for example, exists as a style in your publication style sheet, PageMaker applies its own specifications to the imported text. If PageMaker doesn't find a matching style name in the style sheet, the program creates a new style name the same as the name tag. You can edit the new style to apply the desired formatting. In both cases, the name tags and enclosing brackets are deleted from the text. To import styles as name tags, make sure that the `Read tags` option is selected in the Place Document dialog box.

Assigning Styles

To assign a style, select a range of paragraphs using the text tool and click the name of the style in the Styles Palette, or choose the name from the Style menu. Your choice takes effect immediately. You also can select a style name listed in the Define Styles dialog box. Click OK to apply the style attributes to your text. Generally, applying body styling to the entire story first and then applying additional styles is easiest. To move quickly through a story, use the Styles Palette to make your style assignments. Click an insertion point in each paragraph to be styled, then click the style you want to assign in the Styles Palette.

> **Warning**
> Exercise caution when applying styles. You cannot undo the changes you make using the Edit menu's Undo command. The only way to recover your original paragraph formatting is to choose Revert from the File menu, which restores the last-saved version of your publication, or apply another style having the same formatting specifications as the original text.

Overriding Styles

You can always use the Type menu's commands to apply specific type attributes to selected text, even within paragraphs to which a style has been applied. For example, after applying a style based on italic type to a paragraph, you might select a word or phrase and make the selection bold for added emphasis. When you modify an applied style this way, a plus sign (+) is placed after that style's name in the Style Palette and Style menu to indicate that the style has been overridden. You see the plus sign only when you select the text that has been overridden.

You can create permanent or temporary overrides. Permanent overrides apply conventional type style attributes, like bold or italic, to your text. They're considered permanent because they're the kind of changes you generally want to be permanent. If you later apply a new style to a paragraph that contains a permanent override, the override itself remains unaffected. The only exception is when the new style applies the same attribute as you used to create the override. In that case, the override toggles to maintain its distinguishing characteristics. If, for example, you apply a style using bold type to a paragraph containing words or phrases set to bold for emphasis, those words or phrases toggle back to normal type; therefore, they keep their emphasis.

Temporary overrides are created by applying any of the nonstyle type attributes to your styled text, including point size, hyphenation, leading, tabs, and indents. These overrides are called temporary because, if you later apply a new style having the same attributes, you can wipe out all your changes. For example, if you changed some text to 12-point to make an idea stand out in a 10-point paragraph and then you applied a new 12-point style to that paragraph, your text no longer stands out because all the text is in 12-point type.

Sometimes deciding whether to apply a new style or to use menu commands as overrides is difficult. If you use many different type attributes interchangeably, your list of styles might become unmanageable. On the other hand, if your documents are complex, and you inadvertently apply a new style to a paragraph containing overrides, you could lose all your carefully planned formatting. The best approach is to use the power of style-sheet formatting to streamline your work, but keep a list of overrides to check just before your publication goes to print.

> ***Tip***
> To keep temporary overrides intact while you apply a new style, hold down the Shift key and click the new style in the Style Palette or choose the style from the Style menu. Your paragraphs are updated to reflect the new style attributes, but your temporary overrides remain unchanged. Note that this tip doesn't work if you use the Define Styles dialog box to apply your new style.

Chapter Summary

In this chapter you learned how to manage text to format and restructure your documents. You learned how to vary the number of columns on a page and how to adjust the number of pages in a publication. You also learned how to rearrange text blocks and align them accurately with other page elements. You discovered that you can resize and reshape text blocks to create more interesting layouts, and you found that PageMaker's pasteboard can serve as a supplemental work area.

You learned how to use indents, tabs, and leading, and you found that you can control hyphenation to improve column fit. You acquired new insights into word and letter spacing, and you saw how subtle changes in both can dramatically affect the appearance of your pages.

Finally, you gained an appreciation for the hidden power of style sheets, and you learned how to apply them to your publishing tasks. Next, in Chapter 7, "Graphics Basics," you learn about PageMaker's graphics-handling and printing capabilities.

III
Graphics and Printing Techniques

Includes

Graphics Basics

Formatting and Enhancing Graphics

Printing Techniques

Graphics Basics

7

With PageMaker, you can import, resize, reshape, and crop many different kinds of graphics, ranging from simple bit-mapped pictures to highly refined Encapsulated PostScript drawings. PageMaker also provides several basic drawing tools for enhancing your pages with graphic design elements. Because PageMaker is a page-layout program, however, its focus is on page assembly, not the creation of original artwork. Most of the pictures and illustrations you use are created in separate drawing programs and later imported into PageMaker.

In this chapter you get to know each of the different graphic formats PageMaker supports. You learn how to import, modify, and even export illustrations. You also learn how to use PageMaker's own drawing tools to produce simple design elements like rules, boxes, and circles.

Graphics Supported by PageMaker

PageMaker supports four kinds of graphics formats for imported images: Paint for bit-mapped illustrations, PICT for object-oriented drawings, EPS for high-resolution Encapsulated PostScript images, and TIFF for scanned line art and photographs. Each of these formats is described in the following sections.

Using Paint Images

Paint images are bit-mapped images composed of dots, or pixels (72 pixels per inch). The Paint format became popular shortly after Apple introduced the Macintosh. In the beginning, Apple bundled MacPaint, a primitive bit-mapped graphics program, with every Macintosh sold. The popularity of the Macintosh led to MacPaint's file format becoming a standard for the interchange of bit-mapped graphics. Today, nearly all Macintosh software that handles bit-mapped graphics supports this format.

The dots that make up Paint images are the same size as Macintosh screen pixels. Because pixels are square instead of round, Paint images tend to look ragged around the edges. Raggedness restricts the usefulness of Paint images to applications where high-resolution printing isn't critical (see fig. 7.1). Dots always print as dots, and 72-dpi images always look slightly jagged, even with the `Smooth` option applied (a LaserWriter option in the Print dialog box), no matter how high the resolution of the output device.

Fig. 7.1.

The more you enlarge a Paint image, the more apparent the raggedness becomes.

Paint graphics can be unusually rich in detail. The tools found in most Paint programs closely simulate traditional artist's tools, and the ability to edit an image down to the single-pixel level gives the electronic artist complete control over the final appearance of a bit-mapped image. Although you cannot edit Paint images in PageMaker, you can modify them by changing their brightness and contrast and applying different screen patterns. You learn more about modifying images in Chapter 8, "Formatting and Enhancing Graphics."

Using PICT Images

Draw-type graphics are object oriented, with each object outline, or shape, described by mathematical vector notation. Objects can float above and overlap one another as if stacked in layers. This approach to graphics enables you to move and rearrange images to produce composite groupings. The line widths and fill patterns of objects also are changed easily. Because of their geometric nature, draw-type graphics are ideally suited for precision work, such as engineering or architectural drawings.

In a Paint program, each pixel represents a unique data point, and its individual page coordinates are stored separately in memory. When you draw a shape using a Paint tool, the shape consists of hundreds of independent pixels. Describing a shape, or object, in a drawing program takes much less information. A rectangle, for example, needs only enough code space to identify the object type (a rectangle), the location of the object on the page (the coordinates of a single corner point will do), and the object's dimensions (the angle and length of an invisible diagonal from the origin to the opposite corner of the rectangle). The advantage of this method is that changing the dimensions of an object, in this case the rectangle, requires only that you change its mathematical description. Because objects are described mathematically, they can be reproduced at any size or resolution without distortion.

Apple's MacDraw was the first object-oriented drawing program for the Macintosh. With this program, you can save drawings as MacDraw files (a proprietary format) or as PICT files (now a primary standard for transferring object-oriented files between applications). Since MacDraw was released, the original PICT format has been modified slightly to accommodate new features and special effects, such as rotated text and graduated shading, contained in some of the newer drawing programs. PageMaker can import files saved in the original PICT format and later variations.

Using EPS Images

The Encapsulated PostScript (EPS) file format is a graphics file-interchange standard based on Adobe Systems' high-level PostScript page-description language. EPS drawing programs, such as Adobe Illustrator and Aldus Freehand, give you exceptional control over the creative process and let you assign your artwork an enormous range of special graphics effects, including curved and filled text, graduated shadings, and shape transformations (see fig. 7.2). EPS files have a distinct advantage over their Draw-type counterparts in that line widths can be optionally scaled for finer, high-resolution output.

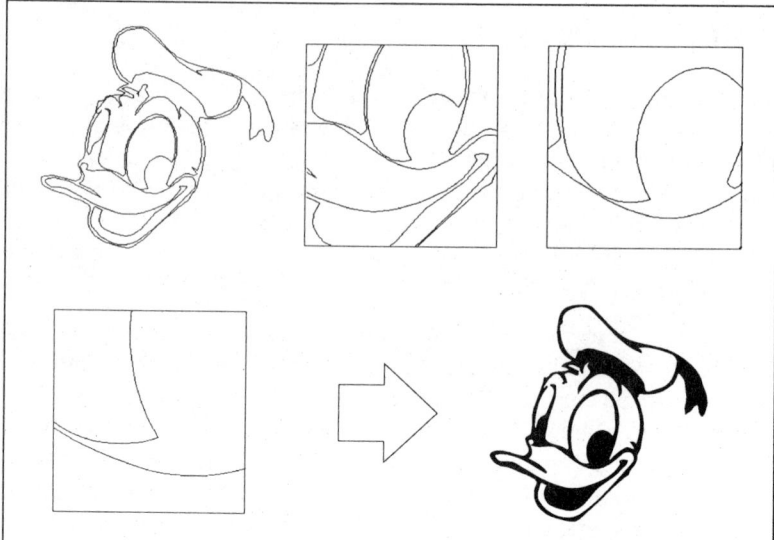

Fig. 7.2.

EPS graphics can be effectively scaled to any size without image distortion.

The Adobe PostScript interpreter built into most laser printers for the Macintosh converts EPS files directly into printed copy. The output resolution is limited only by the printing device itself. For this reason, EPS graphics are often referred to as *device independent*. Most laser printers reproduce images at 300 dpi, and some can handle 400 dpi or 600 dpi. A high-resolution ImageSetter like the Linotronic L300, for example, outputs images at 2,540 dpi (resolutions above 1,100 to 1,200 dpi are considered magazine-quality printing). No matter which device you use to print an EPS image, the image prints in the maximum resolution of that device.

PostScript images are stored as text files. If you know how to program in the PostScript language, you can create or edit PostScript files using an ordinary word processor and import the files into PageMaker for printing. You also can create the files in PageMaker, add the correct header information, export them as text files, and then reimport them into your publications.

EPS files differ from ordinary PostScript files because EPS files allow a PICT image to be attached to the pure PostScript file coding. In PageMaker, such an EPS file provides a screen image that you can use to adjust image size, shape, or placement. Although many graphics and special effects programs fully support the EPS format, a few still fail to take advantage of the screen-display capabilities of EPS files. When you import files produced by such programs into PageMaker, you see only a gray bounding box. This box is used to control image placement. You can resize, reshape, and move the box like any ordinary graphic, but you must print a test sheet to gauge the effects of your work.

Using Scanned Images

Scanners digitize artwork and photographs for use in your publications. You can edit and manipulate scanned images using a variety of drawing and image-enhancement programs and later import them directly into PageMaker.

Scanning black-and-white line art produces high-density bit-mapped pictures ranging in resolution from 75 dpi to 300 dpi. Such bit-mapped images are excellent for use as general-purpose illustrations and can be edited using almost any Paint program.

Scanning photographs is much more complex. To understand how to reproduce a typical glossy photograph as an electronically scanned, digitized image, you first should know something about how photographs are normally handled by commercial printers.

Photographs are continuous-tone images consisting of varying shades of gray. To reproduce the gray tones on traditional printing presses requires that images first be broken into a series of discontinuous, or discrete, halftone dots. Printing presses then apply ink to printing plates wherever the dots appear. If the images were continuous tones instead of discrete dots, the application of ink also would be continuous, and shades of gray would appear as solid black (much the same thing can be seen when trying to photocopy a glossy photograph on an office copier machine—all the subtle gray shading is lost).

To divide photographs into dots, commercial printers first recopy the image using a camera and a halftone screen. A halftone screen is actually a piece of film made up of a fine array of opaque dots. When a halftone screen is laid over the film in the camera, the tiny dots break up the exposed image coming in through the camera lens. The result on the film is a pattern of dots that vary in size, depending on the intensity of the light reflected from the photograph. The finer the screen used, the more dots produced per inch, and the higher the quality of the final print.

When an offset printing plate is prepared from the exposed negative, instead of a continuous image being formed, a pattern of evenly spaced halftone dots of varying sizes is produced. The ink from the press is applied to each individual dot, and the composite collection of dots creates an image that is then transferred back onto paper. Because the dots are different sizes, they effectively simulate the original grays in the photograph. Smaller dots that appear more widely spaced yield a lighter shade of gray; larger dots that look closer together produce a darker shade of gray. Take a magnifying glass and look at any photograph in any newspaper or magazine—the photograph is composed of nothing but thousands of tiny halftone dots.

Scanning photographs and outputting them directly to a laser printer effectively bypasses the whole traditional printing cycle. Although electronic reproduction of photos is adequate for many desktop publishing endeavors, scanned images generally yield softer, fuzzier output than the images a commercial printer strips in by hand—even when using a Linotronic ImageSetter to generate output directly to film. The time it takes to print finely digitized images on a Linotronic also can be excessive, resulting in increased production costs.

Most scanners produce digital halftones or gray-scale images. Digital halftones are normal bit-mapped images with the dots arranged in pseudo-random patterns to simulate the distribution of gray tones. These halftone simulations are produced during the scan itself, and their quality depends greatly on the scanning software used. Because the resultant images are bit maps, with each dot having the same fixed size, scaling or reshaping digital halftones usually causes distortion.

Gray-scale scanners, on the other hand, assign varying levels of gray to each area of the interpreted image, but leave the halftone simulation to the output device. Because the printer handles the final halftone conversion, output quality is improved greatly. Most importantly, this approach enables you to resize and reshape gray-scale images without distortion.

To reproduce gray-scale images, your laser printer builds halftone cells, or matrices, to hold gray-scale information. A 4-by-4 cell, for example, can display 16 different gray values, plus white. With all the dots in the cell filled in, the cell is black. With none of the dots filled in, the cell is white. That leaves 15 in-between gray values that can be simulated by turning on different numbers of dots within each cell. In the same fashion, a 16-by-16 cell can display up to 256 gray shades. Note, however, that the larger the cell's dimensions, the fewer cells can be crowded into a given area. Different combinations of settings, therefore, entail significant printing tradeoffs. The issue is one of numbers of gray values versus lines-per-inch resolution (see fig. 7.3). You learn more about these tradeoffs in Chapter 9, "Printing Techniques."

Because the standard Paint format is fixed at 72 dpi and cannot handle gray-scale or color information, another file format is needed for photographs. This format is known as TIFF, or Tag Image File Format, and is used to store scanned data and transfer the data between applications. PageMaker recognizes files saved in black-and-white and gray-scale TIFF (up to 256 shades), but not color TIFF. Aldus has announced a new Open Prepress Interface (OPI) standard, however, that allows the handling of color TIFF files by PageMaker when used with the new Aldus PageMaker Color Extension for the Macintosh.

A 150 dpi digital-halftone scan, printed on an Apple LaserWriter.

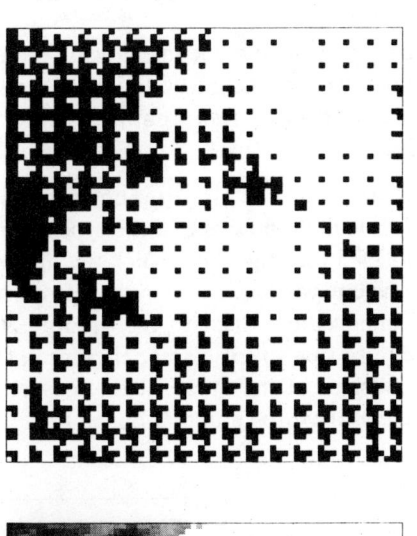

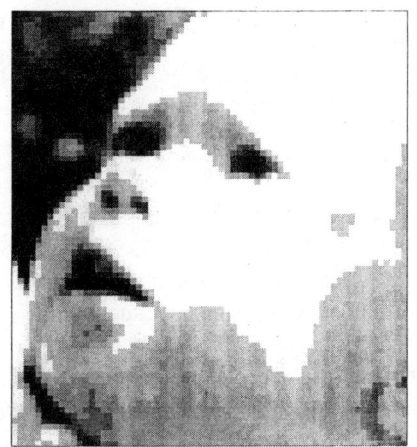

A 150 dpi gray-scale scan with 16 shades of gray, printed on an Apple LaserWriter.

Fig. 7.3.

Viewing an enlarged detail shows the differences between digital-halftone and gray-scale scans.

Importing Graphics

You can import graphics into PageMaker directly by using the File menu's Place command or indirectly through the Clipboard by using the Edit menu's Paste command. The Place command gives you more control over image placement, but using the Clipboard is sometimes more convenient, especially when working in MultiFinder. To learn more about MultiFinder, consult the manual that came with your Macintosh.

Using the Place Command

To place a graphic in a document using the Place command from the File menu, choose the name of the image file from the scrollable list in the Place Document dialog box. Select As new graphic or Replace entire graphic, and then click OK.

If you choose the As new graphic option, PageMaker displays a graphic-placement icon in the shape of the type of graphic being imported: Paint, PICT, TIFF, or EPS (see fig. 7.4). Click the upper left corner of the icon on the page exactly where you want the upper left corner of the graphic to appear. Page-Maker imports and displays the graphic at its original size. If you want the graphic to fit in a specific area, click-drag the graphic-placement icon to define the boundaries of the area. When you release the mouse button, PageMaker draws the graphic to fit in that boundary.

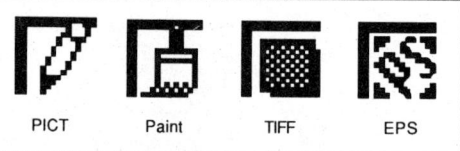

Fig. 7.4.

PageMaker's graphic-placement icons.

Tip

You can create text in another application and save the text as a PICT or EPS file. When you import such a file into PageMaker, you can stretch and shape the file like any other graphic and still have the text print at the same high resolution as the original. To fit the "graphic text" exactly in a predefined area on your page, click-drag the graphic-placement icon during placement. Use this technique to create giant headlines or prominent advertising copy.

If you choose the Replace entire graphic option, PageMaker substitutes the imported graphic in place of the existing graphic you selected, regardless of format. The newly imported graphic occupies the same bounding-box area as the old one. If, after placement, you want to restore the new graphic to its original proportions, select the graphic with the pointer tool, click any handle, and hold down the mouse button while pressing the Shift key.

If the graphic you replace has text-wrap attributes assigned, the new graphic assumes the same attributes, even if these attributes include a customized standoff boundary (you learn about PageMaker's Text Wrap command in Chapter 8, under "Flowing Text around Graphics"). Imported graphics and graphics created in PageMaker can be replaced with the File menu's Place command and the Replace entire graphic option. You can create a publication template using graphic placeholders (shaded boxes) to mark where illustrations should go, and later substitute imported artwork or photographs (see fig. 7.5).

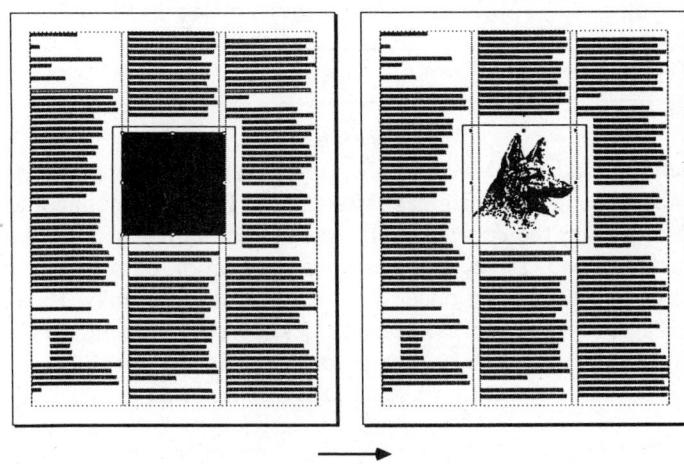

Fig. 7.5.

Replacing a graphic placeholder with an imported illustration using PageMaker's Replace entire graphic *option.*

Most graphics imported into PageMaker are saved with your publication. Because TIFF files are typically large (usually several hundred kilobytes), however, these files receive special treatment. When a TIFF file size exceeds 64K (most of the time), PageMaker substitutes a low-resolution bit-map image as a temporary screen display. You can manipulate this temporary image as if PageMaker had imported the original graphic, and any changes you make to the graphic are reflected in your final printout. The screen display remains linked to the original graphic so that, whenever you print your publication, the original high-resolution bit map is sent to your printer.

PageMaker looks for linked files when you first open your publication. If the files are not in the same folder as when you first placed the originals in your document, PageMaker asks for help in locating them (see fig. 7.6). After you locate the file, click on the Link button to re-establish the connection between the graphic and your publication. After you re-establish the links and save changes to your document, PageMaker remembers the new locations of the graphics.

Fig. 7.6.

If PageMaker cannot find a linked TIFF graphic when opening a publication, the program asks for help.

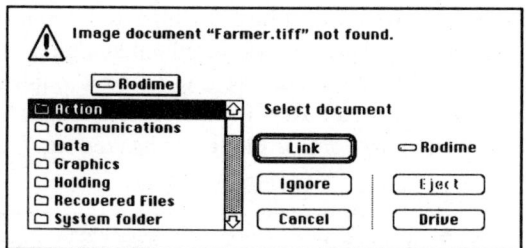

> ### Warning
> Whenever you send PageMaker publications to a service bureau for printing, be sure to include all original TIFF files. If PageMaker cannot locate a linked TIFF file, the corresponding low-resolution bit-map screen display is used instead. If you transfer your publication on a floppy disk, open the document at least once to re-establish the file links, then save changes. PageMaker then prints the graphics correctly without the service bureau operator having to take time to locate each one.

> ### Tip
> If the imported TIFF files are larger than 64K, you can replace them with new ones without opening your publication for editing. You can replace TIFF files without opening the publication because of the following considerations:
>
> - ☐ Changes made to an original graphic after placing the graphic in PageMaker aren't updated on-screen—PageMaker continues to use and display the original low-resolution bit-map image created when you first imported the graphic.
>
> - ☐ When you print your publication, PageMaker looks for the original graphic by file name and type. If you modified the graphic after importing it and saved the graphic with the same file name, the revised version is downloaded and printed. Similarly, if you replace the original graphic with another one having the same file name, the new graphic is downloaded and printed.
>
> This capability means that, to quickly update editions of recurring publications like catalogs, shopper's guides, yearbooks, and so on, you can replace existing TIFF files with new ones having identical names. If you set up an orderly numbering system for naming graphics, managing the substitution is easy, even for large publications.

The Place command also can be used to import the entire contents of your Scrapbook (for information on how to use the Scrapbook desk accessory, consult the manual that came with your Macintosh). When you select the Scrapbook file from the Place Document dialog box, the cursor changes into a special icon showing the number of items to be placed. You can import all the items at once by repeatedly clicking with the placement icon. Each time you click, PageMaker places a graphic and subtracts one number from the remaining total. To cancel the placement of additional Scrapbook items, click the pointer tool in the toolbox. To delete any items you don't want from your pages, select them and press the backspace key or choose Clear from the Edit menu.

> *Tip*
> If you frequently use an assortment of graphics when preparing publications, store them in separate custom Scrapbooks. Load a selection of graphics into the main Scrapbook, rename the file (select the Scrapbook icon in the Finder and type a new name) to identify the data stored in that file. If you store a bunch of design elements, for example, you may rename your Scrapbook *Design Stuff*. Create as many supplementary Scrapbooks as you like and tuck them away in a folder somewhere on your hard disk. Later, whenever you need a particular collection of images, open the appropriate Scrapbook using the Place command.

Using the Clipboard

The Clipboard is a communications bridge between applications. You can copy a graphic to the Clipboard when working in one program and later paste the graphic into another program. Each time you copy something to the Clipboard, the new image replaces whatever was there.

You can use the Clipboard to copy and paste Paint and PICT graphics into PageMaker without difficulty. The Clipboard is limited in its ability to handle more complex graphic formats, however. If you try to copy and paste a TIFF or EPS image from outside PageMaker, the image comes through as a low-resolution bit map and prints that way. For this reason, TIFF and EPS files should always be imported using the Place command. You can convert an EPS graphic into a PICT image, however, by copying the graphic to the Clipboard while holding down the Option key. You can paste the PICT version into PageMaker and print the file at high resolution.

When you paste a graphic into PageMaker, the graphic appears in the center of your display window ready for you to drag or manipulate.

> *Tip*
> If you import a PICT image using the Place command, it may come into PageMaker as an opaque object obscuring anything in the background. The same image copied to the Clipboard and pasted into PageMaker likely comes in as a transparent object, so that where you have surrounding empty space, background objects show through. With Print images, the opposite is true: the Place command brings Print images in as transparent objects; the Paste command brings them in as opaque objects. For the type of file being imported, choose the method that best satisfies your particular design requirements.

Using PageMaker's Drawing Tools

PageMaker's toolbox contains a minimum assortment of drawing tools that you can use to create rules, boxes, circles, and rounded-corner rectangles. Although the tools are few, you can use them in many different and combined ways to enhance your publications. See Chapter 2, "PageMaker Basics," for more details about what each tool does.

To use any drawing tool, click the tool in the toolbox and move the cursor over the page. The tool changes into a crosshair. Click and drag with the crosshair to create a graphic element. The center of the crosshair is the point from which all lines and shapes are drawn.

For precise work, set PageMaker's rulers to the required dimensions and drag ruler guides onto your pages to mark drawing boundaries. Turn on the Snap To Guides and Snap To Rulers commands on the Options menu so that object edges and corners align easily. Choose an enlarged page view for detailed work, but choose a reduced page view for drawing large objects. If you work in a reduced page view, continue to use the guides and snap-to commands to improve drawing accuracy.

> *Tip*
> PageMaker includes a set of keyboard shortcuts to quickly select any tool. These shortcuts are handy if you work with a large-screen monitor where the toolbox is some distance away from where you're drawing. The shortcuts also are handy if the toolbox is hidden (you don't have to choose Toolbox from the Options menu to display the toolbox before selecting another tool). The keyboard shortcuts are Control-Shift-F1 through Control-Shift-F8. To remember which function key goes with which tool,

count the tools across the rows of the toolbox from left to right to determine corresponding numbers. Table 7.1 lists the keyboard shortcuts.

**Table 7.1
Keyboard Shortcuts**

Key Combinations	Toolbox Selection
Control-Shift-F1	Pointer tool
Control-Shift-F2	Diagonal-line tool
Control-Shift-F3	Perpendicular-line tool
Control-Shift-F4	Text tool
Control-Shift-F5	Square-corner rectangle tool
Control-Shift-F6	Rounded-corner rectangle tool
Control-Shift-F7	Circle tool
Control-Shift-F8	Cropping tool

Drawing Lines

PageMaker's toolbox contains two types of line tools: a diagonal-line tool and a perpendicular-line tool. You can draw straight lines in any direction with the diagonal-line tool; you can draw straight lines horizontally, vertically, and at other multiples of 45 degrees with the perpendicular-line tool. You can constrain the diagonal-line tool to move the same as the perpendicular-line tool by holding down the Shift key while drawing.

Any time you draw a horizontal or vertical line using one of these tools, you can adjust the line to lie on either side of the crosshair by dragging slightly across the drawing axis with the cursor. The line flips from one side to the other of the center point. This capability is especially useful when drawing thick lines that you want to line up on a particular side of a nonprinting guide.

To adjust the length or angle of a line, drag one of the end handles. The other end handle remains anchored. To move the entire line without changing its length or orientation, click anywhere between the handles and drag.

> **Warning**
> A line drawn with the perpendicular-line tool "forgets" which tool was used to create it after the line is deselected. If you later drag an end handle to change its length, the line may shift slightly off center and no longer be perfectly aligned along the original axis. To prevent the line from shifting, hold down the Shift key as you drag.

You can assign different line widths and styles to selected lines and to the outlines of selected objects. The Lines menu contains eight line thicknesses ranging from hairline (0.25 point) to 12-point. The menu also contains four double-line and triple-line patterns (for creating frames and borders) and five dashed-line patterns (see fig. 7.7). You can make only one menu selection at a time.

Fig. 7.7.

PageMaker's Lines menu.

The Lines menu also has a None command useful for creating objects with fill patterns but no borders or for a Reverse Line command assigned the color Paper (Paper is normally set to white, but can be assigned a different color with the Define Colors menu). The Reverse Line command is a powerful design tool that can be used in combination with any of the other Line-menu choices to produce special graphic effects. You also can use the Reverse Line command as "electronic whiteout" to touch up imported graphics.

Drawing Boxes and Circles

PageMaker's toolbox contains three types of tools for drawing boxes and circles. The square-corner and rounded-corner rectangle tools enable you to draw rectangles of varying dimensions. To produce perfect squares, hold down the Shift key while drawing with these tools. Choose Rounded Corners from the Options menu to assign any of six different corner shapes to boxes. The circle tool lets you draw ovals. Hold down the Shift key while drawing to produce perfect circles.

To reshape existing rectangles and circles, drag a side or corner handle. Dragging a side handle changes object dimensions in one direction, horizontally or vertically. Dragging a corner handle enables you to change object dimensions in both directions at once.

Press the Shift key at the same time that you drag a handle to make the objects reshape proportionally.

Applying Shades and Patterns

PageMaker's Shades menu enables you to apply an assortment of commonly used shades and fill patterns to objects (but not to lines). Figure 7.8 shows the shades and fill patterns available. You can choose from eight shades ranging from None (0% or transparent) to Solid (100% or black). The Paper shade is simply the color of your paper, usually white. You also can choose from eight fill patterns made up of vertical, horizontal, diagonal, and crosshatched lines. The patterns are reproduced without distortion when the objects are resized.

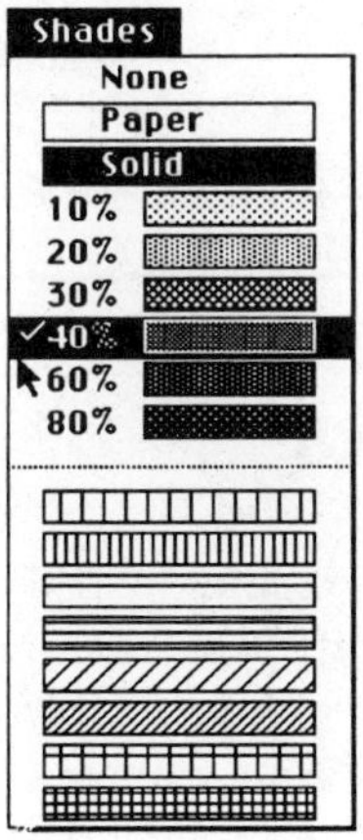

Fig. 7.8.

PageMaker's Shades menu.

To apply a shade or pattern to an object, select the object by clicking it with the pointer tool and make the desired Shades-menu choice. To select an object filled with the None shade, click its boundary. Because the object has no assigned fill, clicking within the boundary is the same as clicking the empty page.

The printed quality of shades and patterns depends entirely on the resolution of your output device. You get much finer output from a Linotronic ImageSetter than from a 300-dpi laser printer.

Figure 7.9 shows an image created with PageMaker in just minutes using the line, rectangle, and oval tools. Two ovals were drawn, one on top of the other, and filled with 20% and 40% fill shades. The bottom half was covered with a rectangle filled with a shade of Paper and assigned a line width of None. The 6-point radial lines were created using the diagonal line tool. All lines were reversed after being drawn in place. A small oval filled with a shade of Paper and assigned a line width of None was used to cover the area where the lines intersect. *Fly East* was typed in MacDraw, saved as a PICT file, and imported into PageMaker as a graphic where it was structured to its current size. *And Meet The Orient* was typed in PageMaker. This example shows the imaginative and powerful uses to which PageMaker's tools can be put.

Fig. 7.9.

An example of what can be done in PageMaker using the line, rectangle, and oval drawing tools.

Modifying Graphics

With PageMaker, you can modify graphics by resizing, reshaping, and cropping them. You also can move them to different locations in your documents. As you resize images, you can scale them proportionally or nonproportionally. If you distort them by too much stretching or compressing, you can return them to their original proportions with a click of the mouse. Any excess image area can be eliminated by cropping.

You also can adjust the contrast and brightness of Paint and TIFF files for improved printing and apply different halftone screens to them to create special visual effects. Individual gray levels of gray-scale TIFF files can be modified, too (you learn to make these adjustments in Chapter 8, under "Working with Scanned Images").

Resizing and Reshaping Images

As you enlarge or stretch Paint images in PageMaker, the number of dots in the image remains the same, but each dot expands in size. Stretching a Paint image increases overall image coarseness. On the other hand, shrinking a Paint image doesn't shrink the dots. Instead, shrinking produces less-detailed images that become muddy-looking as individual pixels squeeze together and begin to "drop out." To resize or reshape a Paint image, drag any bounding-box handle. To keep the original proportions of the image, hold down the Shift key as you drag.

> *Tip*
> Whenever you drag a corner or side handle of a selected graphic, you normally see only the dimensions of the image's bounding box change. The image remains unaffected until you release the mouse button; then the image is redrawn to its new size and shape. If you pause while dragging, however, PageMaker redraws the image at the interim size so that you can gauge the effect of your work. If you like what you see, release the mouse button to preserve the display. If not, continue dragging.

Some image distortion generally results if a complex Paint graphic is resized to an inexact multiple of its original dimensions because fractional pixels cannot be accurately substituted for whole pixels to preserve image integrity. The image distortion can yield undesirable Moiré patterns when patterned or shaded images are resized. With PageMaker, you can compensate for this distortion by resizing bit-mapped graphics in discrete steps to match the output resolution of your printer (see fig. 7.10).

To use PageMaker's resizing feature, hold down the Command key whenever you resize or reshape a Paint image. The on-screen object bounding box is resized incrementally according to PageMaker's calculated sizes as you drag a handle. If you later change printers, select the new printer type in the Print dialog box and use the Command key to resize the image for that printer. Note that PageMaker has more incremental sizes for higher-resolution printers. Hold down the Shift key at the same time you drag to proportionally resize an image.

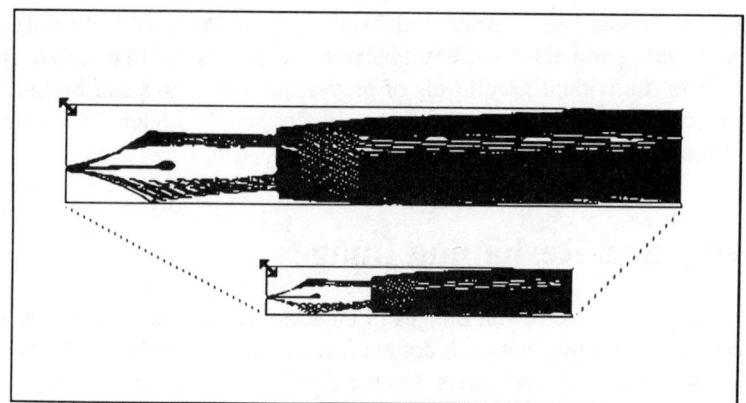

Fig. 7.10.

Incrementally resizing a TIFF graphic in PageMaker to prevent the introduction of Moiré patterns.

> ***Note***
> For Command-key resizing to work, the graphic must be imported directly with the Place command. If the graphic is imported from the Clipboard using the Paste command, the Command key has no effect, and you cannot adjust the image to match the output resolution of your printer.

Often you can improve the appearance of bit-mapped Paint images by printing them with PageMaker's `Smooth` option turned on in the Print dialog box. The `Smooth` option uses rounding calculations to help reduce raggedness. Sometimes smoothing can detract from the flavor of your images, however, especially when trying to capture a bit-mapped look for special effect.

All the comments made here about Paint graphics apply equally to black-and-white TIFF graphics. A black-and-white TIFF graphic is simply a Paint graphic with finer resolution. TIFF and Paint graphics are composed of fixed dots. You encounter less-pronounced distortion when modifying TIFF files only because the larger number of dots means that the adverse effects of scaling are less apparent. PICT and EPS graphics always can be scaled without distortion.

Any graphic scaled nonproportionally can be restored to its original aspect ratio (not necessarily its original size) by clicking any of the handles with the pointer tool while holding down the Shift key (see fig. 7.11). Hold down the mouse button while PageMaker does the required calculations, and the graphic boundaries reshape themselves. Hold down the Command key at the same time to adjust the graphic's size for optimal printing.

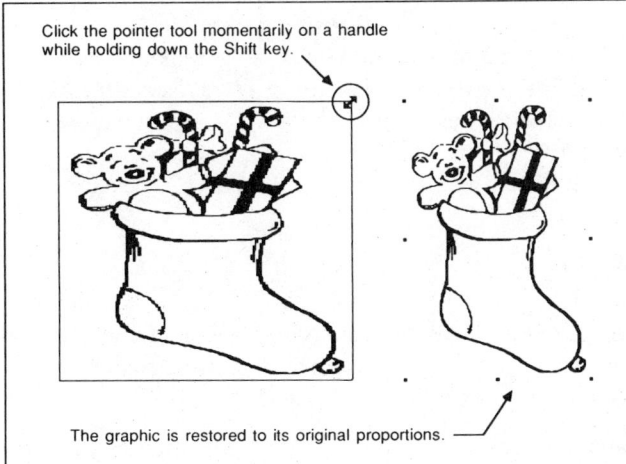

Fig. 7.11.

Restoring a distorted graphic to its original proportions.

Cropping Images

Any imported graphic (not images created in PageMaker) can be trimmed, as if using an X-ACTO knife, with PageMaker's cropping tool. The cropping tool changes the dimensions of the graphic on-screen without changing its size. You can crop an image horizontally, vertically, or in both directions at once. Select the image with the cropping tool and drag a side or corner handle. The part of the image you crop disappears from view, but, unlike trimming a picture with an X-ACTO knife, the missing part of the image is still there, hidden temporarily out of sight.

When you finish cropping, click the image with the cropping tool and hold down the mouse button. The cursor changes into a grabber hand that you can use to move the image under the newly sized window so that what was cropped off the image can be brought back into view. In this way, you can first crop an image to a specific size, then adjust the image for the best possible display.

Tip

To eliminate any possible image distortion when using Paint or black-and-white TIFF graphics, crop them to fit the page instead of scaling them. Unlike scaling, cropping affects neither print resolution nor image quality.

> **Warning**
> If you crop and scale a graphic up in size, PageMaker may not be able to pan the image in the cropped boundaries. If you see a message warning you of this problem, scale the graphic down in size to adjust it, and then scale it back up again after making your changes.

Moving Images

To move an image, click it with the pointer tool and hold down the mouse button as you drag. If you accidentally move something other than what you intended, immediately select Undo from the Edit menu.

If you click and start dragging immediately, a bounding box moves with your cursor. This box serves as an aid to placement. If you pause a moment after clicking, however, and continue to press the mouse button, the graphic changes into a transparent ghost image. The ghost image then moves with the cursor as you drag so that you can precisely position the graphic in its new location.

To move more than one image at a time, click-drag the pointer tool to form a selection rectangle around all the images you want to move. Then click on any image in the box and drag all the images as a group. You can add images to the group selectively by Shift-clicking each one. Use the Select All command on the Edit menu when you want to select all the elements on a page. To deselect any image, click it while holding down the Shift key.

These techniques can be used to select and move any combination of text and graphic elements on your pages. If using a selection rectangle to select text along with graphics, be sure to drag out a large enough area to include any outlying text block handles (see fig. 7.12).

If you want to select an image buried beneath other elements, hold down the Command key as you click over the image with the pointer tool. Repeated clicking cycles through the stack of elements, selecting each element in turn. When you reach the image you want, you can move or modify the image without changing its order in the stack, or you can use PageMaker's Bring To Front command on the Edit menu to place the image on top of the stack.

To move an image to another page in your publication, cut or copy the image to the Clipboard, change the page, and paste the image in its new location. You also can drag the image onto the pasteboard, turn to the new page, and drag the image back onto the new page.

To remove a graphic permanently from your publication, select the graphic and choose Clear from the Edit menu or press the backspace key.

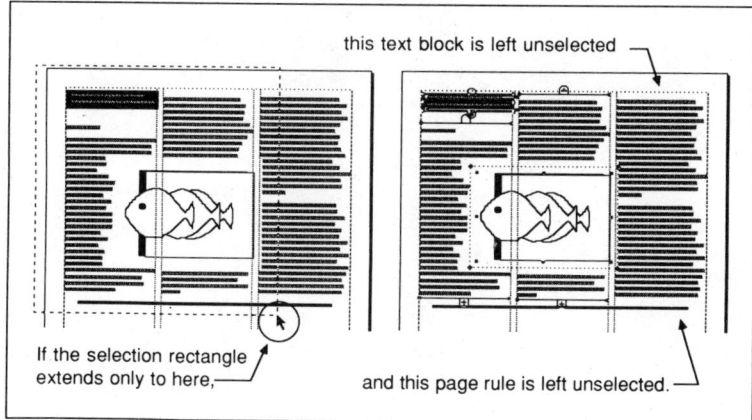

Fig. 7.12.

Dragging a selection rectangle around a group of elements selects just the elements that lie completely within the dotted boundary.

Exporting Graphics

To export graphics from PageMaker to another application, select and copy them to the Clipboard using the Edit menu's Cut or Copy commands. The Cut command completely removes a graphic from your publication, and the Copy command leaves the original image and places a copy on the Clipboard. Open the receiving application and paste the contents of the Clipboard into the new document. Original design elements created in PageMaker can be exported this way for use elsewhere.

Chapter Summary

In this chapter you learned how to work with several different kinds of graphic formats. You learned how to import and export images, and how to resize, reshape, and crop them to meet the requirements of your layouts. You found that although PageMaker isn't designed to create detailed original artwork, the program enables you to use various kinds of artwork created elsewhere. Page-Maker also provides you with a complement of easy-to-use drawing tools for creating simple design elements to dress up your publications.

Chapter 8 introduces you to PageMaker's advanced graphics-handling capabilities.

Formatting and Enhancing Graphics

8

PageMaker's advanced graphics-handling capabilities are exceptional. In addition to importing and manipulating a variety of graphics formats, PageMaker enables you to modify the flow of text to wrap around illustrations. You also can customize a wrap boundary to conform to any shape you like. With PageMaker, you can vary the contrast and brightness of Paint and TIFF images and apply custom halftone screens for special visual effect. If you import scanned grayscale TIFF photos into your layouts, you can adjust their gray levels separately. You even can apply spot color to text and graphics to enhance the look of your publications.

In this chapter you explore PageMaker's advanced graphics-handling capabilities. You learn how to wrap text around irregularly shaped graphics, modify scanned images, and add color to your pages. You discover, as with so much else in PageMaker, that these tasks are easy and fun to do.

Flowing Text around Graphics

Illustrations and photographs are important visual elements that help explain the content of a publication and add interest to what you read. Text and graphics must work together to effectively communicate thoughts and ideas. Fitting both kinds of elements together on your pages the way you want, however, is sometimes difficult. Some layouts are dominated by text, others by graphics. If text and graphics don't complement one another, you can end up with large, unsightly patches of white space. PageMaker's capacity to flow text around graphics helps fill these holes and give your pages a more polished look.

> **Warning**
> Flowing text around graphics is a powerful design technique, but it can be overused. Like any other design technique, overuse reduces effectiveness.

Using Text Flow and Wrap Options

PageMaker provides several options for flowing text around and over selected graphics. To pick the kind of wrap you want, you click icons in PageMaker's Text Wrap dialog box (see fig. 8.1). You can choose from three wrap options and three text-flow options. You also can enter standoff-boundary values directly from the keyboard (standoff boundaries determine the amount of white space between a graphic and the text that flows around the graphic).

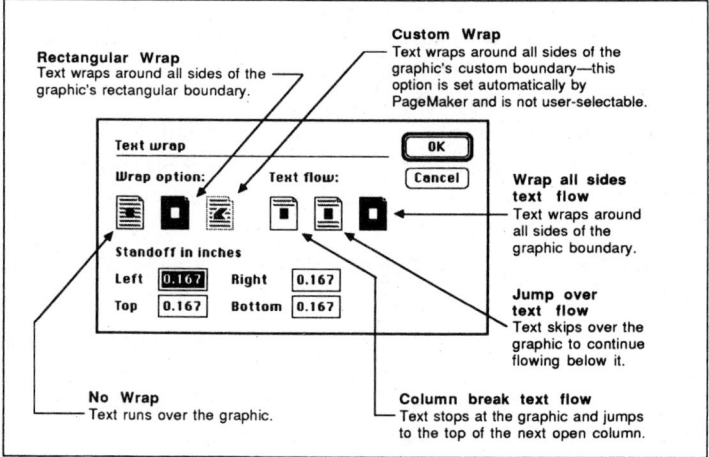

Fig. 8.1.

The Text Wrap dialog box.

PageMaker's wrap options work in combination with the text-flow options to determine the type of text wrap to occur. To assign text-wrap attributes to a graphic, first select the graphic with the pointer tool, then choose Text Wrap from the Options menu. In the Text Wrap dialog box that appears, click the appropriate Wrap option and Text flow icons for the kind of text wrap you want. Following is a list of the wrap options available.

- ❏ Clicking the *no wrap* icon tells PageMaker to ignore the graphic. Choosing this option disables (grays out) all the Text flow icons. As text flows down a column, it runs over the graphic as though the graphic wasn't there.

- ❑ Clicking the *rectangular wrap* icon tells PageMaker to wrap text around the graphic. Choosing this option enables all three `Text flow` icons. If you click the *column break text-flow* icon, PageMaker stops flowing text when the graphic is encountered and jumps to the top of the next open column to continue. If you click the *jump over text-flow* icon, PageMaker stops flowing text when the graphic is encountered, skips over the graphic, and resumes flowing text. If you click the *wrap all sides text-flow* icon, PageMaker wraps text around all sides of the graphic.

- ❑ The *custom wrap* icon cannot be selected by clicking. The icon is selected by PageMaker when you customize the wrap boundary.

If your text is already in place, selecting different text-wrap options for your graphics rearranges the text to conform to the new settings. Any existing text formats, such as indents and tabs, are retained. If you change the text-wrap attributes of a graphic in the Text Wrap dialog box from no wrap (the text runs over the graphic), to wrap all sides (the text runs around both sides of the graphic), for example, when you click OK, the text rearranges itself accordingly. Similarly, if you drag or paste a graphic with text-wrap attributes into an existing column of text, the text in the column instantly reflows to wrap itself around the graphic (see fig. 8.2).

Note

If you assign text-wrap attributes to graphics on your master pages, those graphics interact only with text on your master pages and not with text on your regular pages. The master-page graphics appear on regular pages, but the text-wrap attributes are ignored.

PageMaker's original default setting is no wrap that runs text over any graphics encountered. You probably want to change this setting. Make your preferred text-wrap settings into program or file defaults by choosing the Text Wrap command from PageMaker's desktop before opening a new publication or from within the open publication with no graphics selected.

Tip

PageMaker's no wrap option can be used to advantage by placing a large, lightly-shaded graphic behind your text to create a subliminal effect for sales fliers, announcements, and other forms of ad copy. Use PageMaker's image controls to make the shading of a Paint or TIFF graphic light enough so that the foreground text remains legible. (You learn how to use PageMaker's image controls later in this chapter.)

180 Part III: Graphics and Printing Techniques

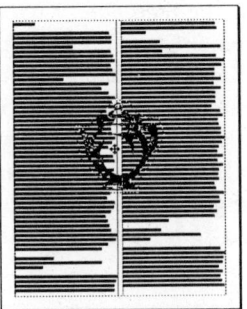

The selected graphic showing its custom text-wrap boundary.

Dragging the graphic into place on the page.

Fig. 8.2.

Text flows around a graphic after text-wrap attributes are assigned.

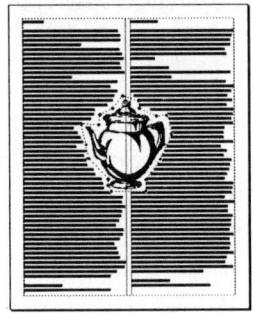

Surrounding text automatically reflows itself around the graphic.

The final page after enlarging and repositioning the graphic.

Specifying a Text-Wrap Standoff

PageMaker wraps text around a graphic outside a *standoff boundary*. This boundary surrounds the graphic and determines the width of the white space, or standoff, between the graphic and text. You can adjust the standoff by moving the standoff boundary with the pointer tool or by typing replacement values into the Standoff fields in the Text Wrap dialog box.

A nonprinting standoff boundary is created around a selected graphic when you first tell PageMaker to wrap text around the graphic (by clicking the rectangular wrap icon in the Text Wrap dialog box). The boundary is displayed on-screen as a dotted line with diamond-shaped handles. PageMaker assigns default standoff values of 0.167 inches, or 1 pica, on each side of the graphic. You can change these values individually, and even assign negative values to force text to fill space normally occupied by the graphic. To do the latter, type a minus sign before the number.

To change standoff-boundary dimensions using the pointer tool, click anywhere along the standoff boundary and hold down the mouse button. The pointer tool changes into a double-headed arrow. Drag to adjust the boundary as desired (see fig. 8.3). PageMaker updates the `Standoff` fields in the Text Wrap dialog box to reflect the new standoff dimensions.

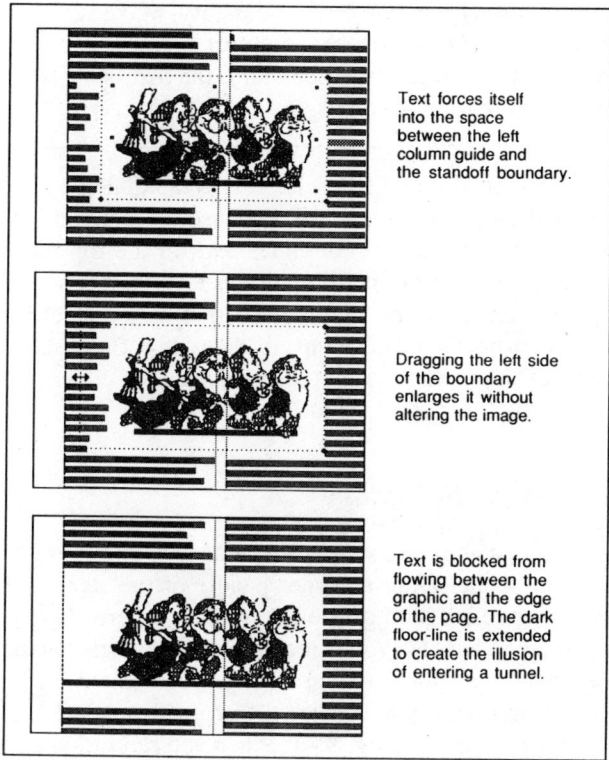

Fig. 8.3.

Dragging one side of a standoff boundary to block the flow of text on that side.

Note that if you drag a graphic-boundary handle (not a standoff-boundary handle) to resize or reshape the graphic, the standoff boundary moves with the graphic, and the standoff dimensions surrounding the graphic remain constant.

Tip

To keep text from wrapping around only one side of a graphic, increase the standoff on that side so that the standoff boundary touches a column guide.

> **Tip**
> If you place a caption next to a graphic to which you assign text-wrap attributes, the caption wraps like any other text. To avoid this problem, increase the standoff value on the side of the graphic where the caption is placed. Move the standoff boundary far enough away from the graphic so that the caption fits entirely within the boundary. Make sure that the text-block handles don't extend past the standoff boundary. As long as the caption lies completely within the boundary, the text is unaffected by the assigned text-wrap attributes.

Each `Text flow` option selected from the Text Wrap dialog box is affected by different parts of the standoff boundary. Because the column break text-flow option forms a column break and continues text on the top of the next open column, only the `Top` standoff dimension affects text wrap. The jump over text-flow option jumps text over the graphic, so that `Top` and `Bottom` standoff dimensions affect text wrap. The wrap all sides text-flow option flows text completely around the graphic, so that all four standoff dimensions determine the way text looks when wrapped around the graphic.

Creating a Custom Boundary

You easily can modify a graphic's standoff boundary to make text flow smoothly around an irregular shape. Drag a corner handle of the standoff boundary to adjust the boundary or click with the pointer tool anywhere along the boundary to create a new shaping handle. You can create as many new handles as needed to make the boundary conform to the edge of the graphic, no matter how complex the shape. In effect, you convert the original standoff rectangle into a multisided standoff polygon (see fig. 8.4). When you reposition a corner handle or create a new shaping handle, the custom wrap icon in the Text Wrap dialog box is highlighted.

> **Tip**
> Use ruler guides to effect precise placement of shaping handles when adjusting a custom standoff boundary. If the Snap To Guides command is checked in the Options menu, dragging the shaping handles to their new locations causes them to "snap" to the guides in perfect alignment. Use the Shift key at the same time to constrain handle movement to horizontal and vertical directions.

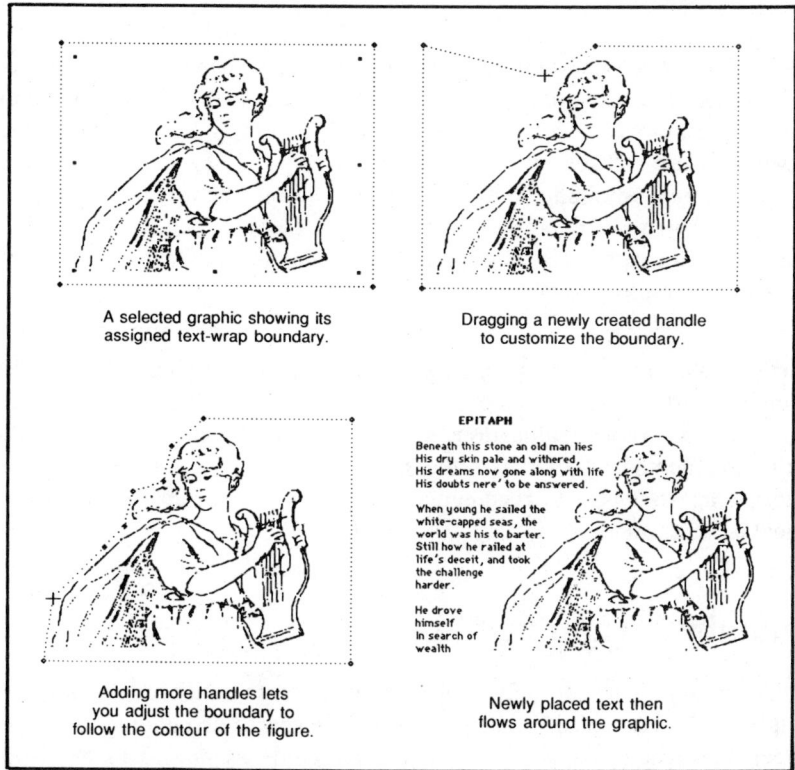

Fig. 8.4.

Creating a custom text-wrap boundary.

Custom-wrap standoff boundaries require a minimum of three handles. You can add as many new handles as you like, but try to limit the number. Each new handle requires additional calculations that slow screen redraws. If you want to make several quick adjustments to a custom-standoff boundary without redrawing the text each time you move a shaping handle, hold down the space bar as you make modifications. Release the space bar when you're done, and the text reflows. Remove excess handles by dragging them on top of adjoining handles.

> *Tip*
> When creating custom standoff boundaries around irregularly shaped graphics, drag the graphics off the page onto the pasteboard. You don't have to worry about holding down the space bar to stop repeated screen redraws when the image is on the pasteboard, and you can work on several graphics at the same time. When you're done creating customized boundaries, drag the graphics back onto your pages. Your text immediately rewraps around the graphics according to the adjustments made. Drag multiple graphics as a group to preserve their overall positioning.

> ***Tip***
> Wrapping text around both sides of an irregularly shaped graphic generally makes the text difficult to read because the eye is forced to jump across the graphic to complete each line. The best way to structure your layouts to use full text wrap and keep the text readable is to center the graphic across adjoining columns. In this position, the text in the column on the left wraps around the left side of the graphic, and the text in the column on the right wraps around the right side. The reader's eye then can travel down the page uninterrupted.

After a graphic's text-wrap boundary is defined, the boundary stays with the graphic no matter where you move it in your publication, and even if you copy the graphic to another publication. To eliminate a custom-standoff boundary, click the rectangular wrap icon in the Text Wrap dialog box. PageMaker resets the text-wrap attributes to rectangular wrap and the standoff values to their original default values.

Manually Wrapping Text

Manually wrapping text around graphics requires that you separate your text into multiple text blocks and size each block to fit the space surrounding the graphic. To keep line leading consistent, use a ruler guide as an aid to overlapping windowshade handles. Manually wrapping text is a tedious process and is generally not worth the effort.

You have little reason to wrap text manually. Manual wrapping is a hold-over from earlier versions of PageMaker when automatic text wrap did not exist, and is effective only with rectangular run-arounds. Minor adjustments to the standoff boundary can be made much more easily using automatic text wrap than with manual text wrap. If you make dimensional changes to graphics, manual text wrap must be done over again—manually. With automatic text wrap, updates occur automatically. In general, stay away from manual text wrap unless you have a rare instance where you cannot achieve desired results using automatic text wrap.

> **Tip**
> To wrap regular text around display text for special effect, draw a shape around the display text using one of PageMaker's tools. Customize the shape's text-wrap boundary, and use PageMaker's Send To Back command to place the graphic boundary behind the display text. Then assign the graphic a shade pattern of None and a line width of None. Regular text then wraps around the invisible graphic and the display text in front of the graphic. Use this technique to wrap regular text around a drop cap, headline, callout, or pull quote. By arranging two or more invisible graphics in a pattern on your page, you can flow regular text between and around them for interesting effect.

Working with Scanned Images

Scanned images include line art and photographs. These images can be edited using any of several popular drawing and image-enhancement programs before you import them into PageMaker. Scanned files are generally saved in Paint or TIFF format. After you bring the files into PageMaker, you can resize, reshape, and crop them like any other graphic. Additionally, PageMaker enables you to adjust their contrast, brightness, and gray levels and apply a variety of line screens for special effect.

Detailed line art is best scanned at the resolution of your printer. If you use a 300-dpi laser printer, for example, scan the image at 300 dpi. If your line art is composed mostly of straight lines and simple curves, however, try a lower resolution. The results are usually as good, but the files are smaller in size and easier to edit.

Scanning images at the size you want to print them is best. Resizing Paint and TIFF files often produces image distortion. Selectively combining different scanning resolutions with known scaling percentages, however, can result in graphics of the desired size that also reproduce well.

The trick is to plan ahead. If you know that you will shrink a scanned image by 50 percent after placing the image in PageMaker, for example, scan the image at half the required resolution. Halving the size later effectively doubles the resolution of the image when printed. Similarly, if you plan to enlarge a scanned image by 50 percent, scan it at twice the acceptable resolution.

Some scanners produce digital halftones when scanning photographs. Digital halftones are nothing more than sophisticated Paint files with resolutions typically varying from 75 dpi to 300 dpi, depending on the scanner, software, and settings used. The higher the resolution of your scanned image, the larger the TIFF file. Large TIFF files can take a long time to print, especially on a Linotronic; longer printing times increase production time and printing costs. Because many photos look good when scanned at 150 dpi or less, you don't always have to use the highest settings. Instead, assign the minimum resolution that produces acceptable results.

Gray-scale scans, even when scanned at low resolutions, also produce large files. Unlike digital halftones, however, gray-scale scans reproduce well when scaled. If you do a gray-scale scan of a photograph at 75 dpi, you usually get acceptable results when printing the photo on a 300-dpi laser printer. If you plan to enlarge the image before printing, increase the scanning resolution to 100 dpi, or even 150 dpi, to retain image quality. Otherwise, scan at higher resolutions only if you plan to print your publications using a Linotronic or other high-resolution output device.

Image Control

Scanned images, particularly photographs, frequently require slight modifications to produce acceptable output. PageMaker enables you to make small adjustments to contrast, brightness, and gray levels, and apply these changes to your screen image as you work so that you can gauge their approximate effect.

You also can change the number of lines per inch (lpi), or screen frequency, to produce a higher halftone screen resolution, and you can vary screen angle to change the orientation of the line screen. Lines-per-inch frequency and screen angle affect the number of grays that your printer can produce. As an example, a 53-lpi halftone screen set at 45 degrees—the default for the Apple LaserWriter—can produce 32 shades of gray. If you want a finer halftone resolution, you have to sacrifice some gray shades. In contrast, a 71-lpi halftone screen set at 45 degrees on the Apple LaserWriter can produce only 18 shades of gray. Only a few combinations of screen frequency and angle are mathematically possible. Generally, a screen angle of 45 degrees produces acceptable results on a 300-dpi laser printer.

Note
Lines per inch (lpi) and dots per inch (dpi) are two different things. Lines per inch describes halftone resolution; that is, the number of halftone cells per inch. Dots per inch, on the other hand, represents the resolution of your printer. If you remember that halftone dots are cells composed of printer dots, you should not be confused.

If you plan to print most of your publications on a 300-dpi laser printer, you should get by with an inexpensive four-bit gray-scale scanner that scans photos at 16 shades of gray. Six-bit gray-scale scanners that scan at 64 levels of gray and eight-bit gray-scale scanners that scan at 256 levels of gray represent overkill, unless you plan to print your publications on a Linotronic or other high-resolution output device. On a Linotronic L300 at 2540 dpi, you can print up to 256 shades of gray using a 150-lpi halftone screen (133 lpi at 256 shades of gray is considered magazine-quality printing—85 lpi at 64 shades of gray is considered newspaper-quality printing). The trade-off for such quality, however, is greatly extended print times: the more gray shades and the higher the image resolution, the longer printing takes.

With PageMaker, you can choose between a dot-pattern or line-pattern halftone screen. For normal photo reproduction, you usually use a dot-pattern screen, but you may want to employ the line-pattern screen for special effect. These settings, together with screen frequency and orientation, can be varied to create some striking visual effects, especially when screen frequency is set to a low number to produce large halftone dots or widely spaced lines, and screen angle is adjusted to an odd orientation (screen angle varies between 0 and 360 degrees, measured clockwise from the horizontal axis).

Modifying TIFF Files

PageMaker's Image Control dialog box (choose Image Control from the Options menu) may look intimidating, but the options are quite easy to use (see fig. 8.5). You can choose from three modes: `Black and white`, `Screened`, and `Gray`. All three modes can be applied to TIFF files. The following list presents descriptions of each mode.

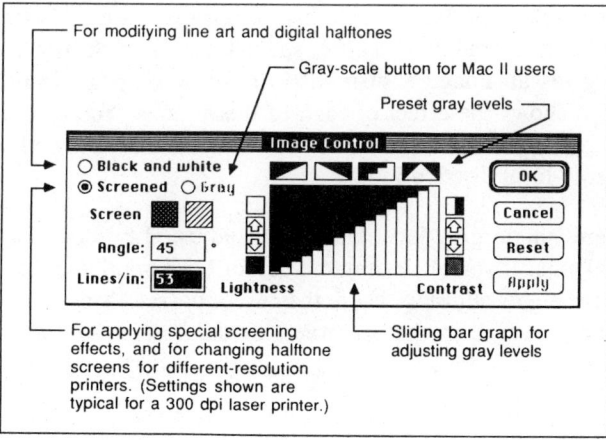

Fig. 8.5.

PageMaker's Image Control dialog box.

❑ `Black and white` mode generally applies to simple line art. This mode also can be used with gray-scale images, however, to convert them into high-contrast black-and-white renderings for special effect.

❑ `Screened` mode lets you set the lines-per-inch and angle settings for a halftone screen. This mode also lets you choose between dot-screen or line-screen patterns.

❑ `Gray` mode (for Mac II users) lets you adjust gray-scale images and view the effects of your work on-screen.

In the center of the Image Control dialog box is a dynamic vertical bar graph. This graph displays two wide bars (one black and one white) when the `Black and white` mode is selected, or 16 narrow bars when the `Gray` option is selected. The bars can be adjusted separately to vary the gray levels of gray-scale images.

When you first open the Image Control dialog box with a gray-scale TIFF graphic selected, the gray-level bars are arranged in an ascending pattern from left to right. This pattern is PageMaker's normal default gray-level distribution. Each bar represents one of 16 gray levels in a four-bit gray scan, with the lightest grays to the left, and the darkest to the right. If you use a six-bit or eight-bit scanner to create your images, each bar represents multiple levels of gray (4 for a 64-level gray scan, and 16 for a 256-level gray scan). Multiple gray levels are weighted proportionally in each bar to preserve the integrity of the image as adjustments are made.

Four icons at the top of the graph represent PageMaker's four preset gray levels. From left to right, the first is the *normal* preset that represents a normal gray-level distribution. The second is the *negative* preset that gives you a negative, or inverse, of your original image (like the negative film from which a photograph is produced). The third and fourth icons are *posterize* and *solarize*. Posterizing an image reduces the smoothness of its gray-scale graduations to dramatically heighten tonal contrast and is used for special effect. Solarization, another special effect, gives an image a surrealistic look by emphasizing the middle grays. Figure 8.6 shows the effect of each of these icons. You can click any of these icons to apply its effect to your selected image. The bar graph updates to show the new gray-level distribution.

The height of any single gray-level bar can be adjusted by clicking anywhere along its vertical axis. If you click-drag the cursor horizontally across the entire graph, all the bar heights adjust to where the cursor passed through their axes. If you want to change overall image brightness or contrast, click the appropriate scroll-bar arrows or the icons at each end of the scroll-bars.

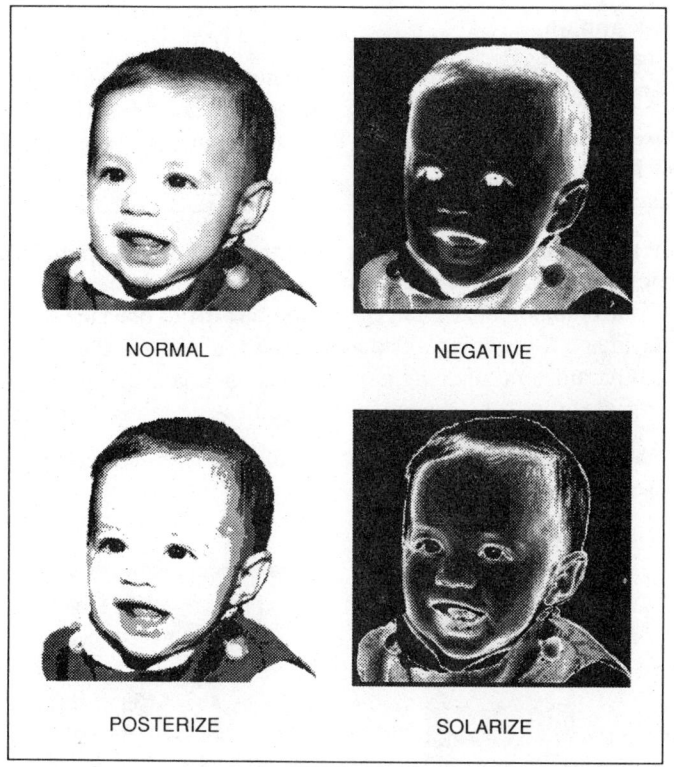

Fig. 8.6.

PageMaker's preset gray levels.

Adjusting image brightness moves all the bars up or down as a group and maintains their individual variances. At the extremes, you get an image brightness of all white or all black. Adjusting image contrast, on the other hand, changes gray-level distribution differently, depending on the preset gray-level icon selected at the time.

Note
All settings in the Image Control dialog box affect the entire image. You cannot selectively adjust part of an image.

If your TIFF scan is simple line art, the Image Control dialog box opens in the `Black and white` mode. To assign an image shade other than black, or a background shade other than white, click the `Gray` mode button. Then click the bar graph to vary the gray levels. In this way, for example, you can shade an image light gray before placing it behind text. Click the negative gray-level preset icon in `Black and white` mode to create a reverse image.

> *Tip*
> If you have a strong photographic background and spend much production time in a darkroom, examine your scanned photos as negative images in PageMaker. You may be able to pick up shading subtleties not immediately apparent in the normal view.

Clicking the `Apply` button in the Image Control dialog box applies changes to your graphic so that you can view them immediately on-screen without leaving the Image Control dialog box. Drag the dialog box off to one side to get a better view of your image if necessary. The `Reset` button restores the selected image to its original parameters, undoing any changes you made and giving you a way to start over gracefully if the special effects you assign fail to turn out well.

Figure 8.7 shows several different variations of an image and the Image Control dialog boxes used to create each.

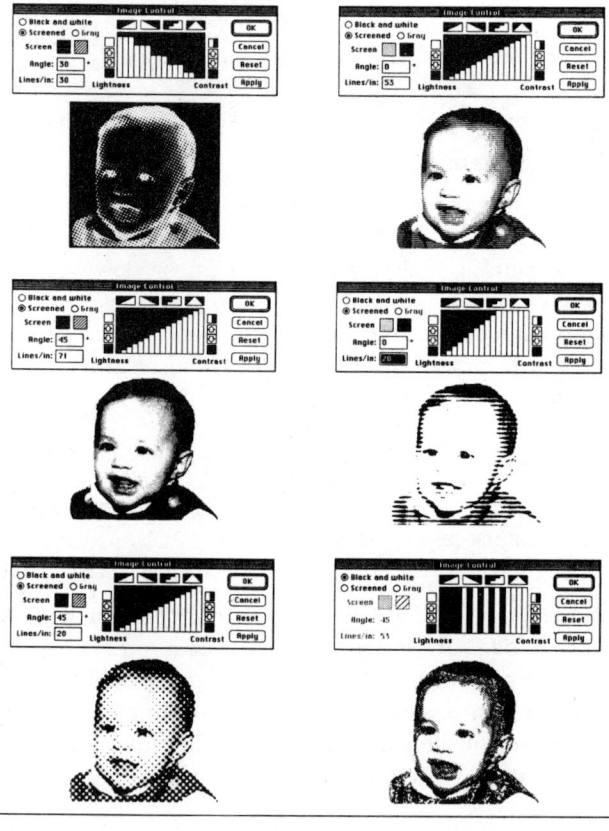

Fig. 8.7.

Different halftone frequency and angle settings produce different visual effects.

Modifying Paint Files

You also can use the Image Control command to apply special effects to your Paint graphics. You can convert black-and-white images to a lighter shade of gray, for example. You also can create many combinations of dot and line-pattern screens, screen frequencies, and screen orientations, to produce unusually vivid and striking illustrations. Anything you can do to a black-and-white TIFF image using PageMaker's Image Control command can be done to a Paint image (see fig. 8.8). Both types of files are bit-mapped graphics—only their dot sizes differ.

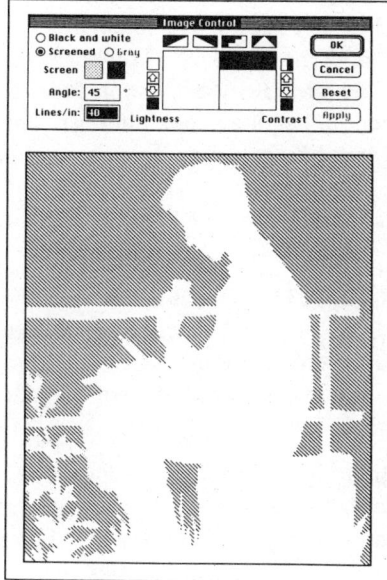

Fig. 8.8.

A bit-mapped Paint silhouette rescreened using PageMaker's Image Control dialog box.

Working with Color

With PageMaker, you can apply spot color to text and graphics to accent your publications. Note that spot color is not the same as full color. Full color is what you see in a color photograph: a wide variety of different colors are combined to make up a single image. Spot color, on the other hand, is more like a bunch of brightly colored balloons, with each balloon assigned a separate, solid color.

PageMaker can apply spot color to graphics selected with the pointer tool and to text selected with the text tool. Only one color can be assigned per item, although you can use any color you like. Colors can be defined using any of the following three color models:

- HLS—Hue, Lightness, Saturation. This model is similar to the HSB (Hue, Saturation, Brightness) model used by your Macintosh II system software. *Hue* represents a particular color and is defined by its angular position around the color wheel. *Lightness* (or brightness) defines a tonal value between totally bright (white) and totally dark (black). *Saturation* defines color intensity, or purity, which can be seen easily on the color wheel where saturation values increase as you move from the center toward the outer rim. HLS is generally your best choice for spot-color separations.

- CMYK—Cyan, Magenta, Yellow, and Black. This model separates colors into their primary subtractive components: cyan (blue), magenta (red), and yellow. Primary subtractive colors are overlaid and so subtract from one another to produce a composite color when light reflects off them. The CMYK model also includes black as an additional component to heighten color contrast. This model is frequently used by graphics programs to create separation overlays for full, or four-color, process printing. The CMYK model describes colors in terms of reflected light and is the kind of color you see on printed paper.

- RGB—Red, Green, Blue. This model is based on the primary additive colors (red, green, and blue) and describes color in terms of transmitted light. Primary additive colors are mixed, or added together, to produce a composite color. You see this kind of color on your color video monitor.

If you use a black-and-white video monitor, you cannot see the colors assigned to the elements, but PageMaker still generates the spot-color separations correctly (you learn more about color separations in Chapter 9, under "Color Printing").

Note

Although you can import full-color illustrations into your publications and display them in color on a color monitor, PageMaker cannot print the four-color separations needed to reproduce them properly. If you print a full-color illustration in PageMaker on a black-and-white laser printer, the colors are converted to black and white, instead of the subtle grays needed to faithfully duplicate the original tones of the image.

Four-color process printing requires four separate, precisely aligned color overlays per page to accurately reproduce an exhaustive range of graduated colors. With PageMaker, a separate spot-color overlay must be produced for every color you use on a page. If you use six colors (including black) on a page, for example, you need six spot-color overlays to reproduce all those colors. You cannot produce graduated color shadings in PageMaker.

Defining Colors

PageMaker's Define Colors command in the Options menu enables you to define and edit colors in the same way you define and edit styles, with many of the same benefits and advantages. A collection of colors is called a *color sheet*, just as a collection of styles is called a *style sheet*. The Define Colors dialog box lists currently defined colors in a scrollable window. New, Edit, Remove, and Copy buttons to the right of the list work much like the Define Style dialog-box counterparts.

To define a new color, open the Define Colors dialog box and click the New button. An Edit Color dialog box appears. In this box, you can assign a name to your color, choose one of the three color models (RGB, HLS, or CMYK), and adjust color percentages using sliding scroll bars to create the color of your choice. If a graphic is selected, click the Close button to save the color without applying it, or click OK to save and apply the color at the same time.

> *Tip*
> After you define a color using one of the color models, clicking the other Model buttons in PageMaker's Define Colors dialog box gives you an instant readout of the corresponding values for the other color models.

To edit a color, select it from the color palette (Choose Color Palette from the Options menu) or from the Define Colors dialog box list, then click the Edit button. If you select a color from the color palette, which displays a scrollable list of names of defined colors, hold down the Command key at the same time to bring up the Edit Color dialog box (see fig. 8.9). Type the values for the new color if you know them, or adjust the component scroll bars until you see the color you want. The original color is displayed in the color guide at the right of the dialog box; just above the original color, the revised color on which you are working appears. You can click the original color at any time to cancel any changes you made.

Fig. 8.9.

The Edit Color dialog box.

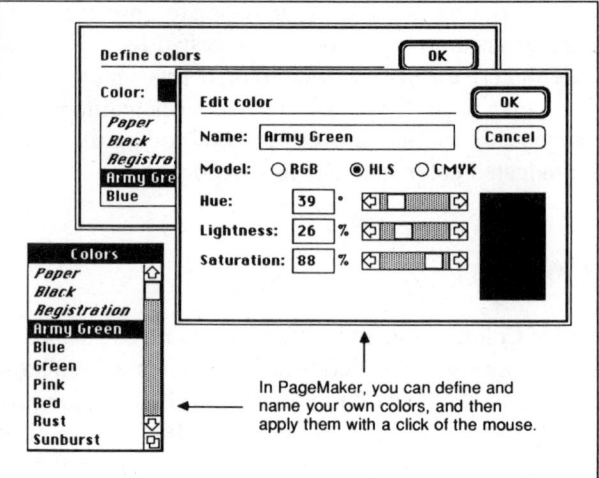

If you have a Macintosh II and prefer to use a color wheel to adjust HLS colors, hold down the Shift key as you click the Define Colors dialog box `Edit` button. This action displays the Apple color picker. You can type HSB or RGB values using Apple's numerical notation or use the color wheel exclusively by clicking the color of your choice. Drag the right scroll bar up or down to change color brightness (lightness). You can drag the pointer tool around the wheel to scroll your color choices in the color guide at the left. To learn more about the Apple color picker, consult the manual that came with your Macintosh II.

If you change the composition of a color, all items in your publication assigned that color are updated to the new shade. The same thing happens if you change the name of one color to the name of another color (you are given the chance to cancel this change if you assigned the matching name in error). These two features enable you to make global color changes in your publications without separately editing each color element.

To remove a color, click its name in the Define Color dialog box and click `Remove`. Elements in your publication assigned that color are reassigned the color black.

To copy colors from another publication, click the `Copy` button in the Define Colors dialog box. The Copy Colors dialog box appears, from which you can select another PageMaker publication and copy its color sheet. Click OK to copy the new color sheet into your current publication. New colors are added to the current color sheet, but colors having the same name replace existing colors (again, PageMaker gives you an opportunity to change your mind). This technique can be used to quickly update current color assignments.

Three colors are always present in the color list: `Paper`, `Black`, and `Registration`. `Paper` is the color of your page—usually white, but you can change the color using the Edit Color dialog box. Changing the color is useful if you plan to print your publication on color stock because you can visualize the color combinations that can be used successfully with that color paper. `Registration`, which applies to printing aids, is always black.

Applying Colors

Colors are applied only to areas of an image that are normally black. For example, text is normally black and can be assigned different colors. Similarly, object outlines, fill shades, and patterns are normally black and can be assigned colors. Surrounding areas that are normally white cannot be assigned any color other than `Paper`.

Colored text often is used to highlight critical paragraphs in a document. You may want to make certain text red in color, for example, to make important information stand out. Another popular use for color text is on letterhead stationary to highlight a company return address. The uses for colored text are limited only by your imagination.

To apply color to text, select a range of text using the text tool, then click the desired color in the color palette. The text takes on the assigned color and is displayed on-screen if you have a color monitor. Alternatively, you can pick a color in the Define Colors dialog box and click OK to make the assignment. You can assign a color text attribute to a style by clicking the `Color` button in the Edit Style dialog box to bring up the Define Colors dialog box. The color choice you make is saved as part of the style and applied each time that style is used.

> *Tip*
> Displaying your pages in color slows screen redraws and increases the time you spend putting together a publication. To speed things up, work with your color monitor set to black and white. (To learn how to set your color monitor to black and white, consult the manuals that came with Macintosh II and color monitor.) Apply color to your elements only as you near layout completion.

To apply color to a graphic, select the graphic using the pointer tool and click a color in the color palette; alternatively, choose a color from the Define Colors dialog box. If the graphic is a Paint or TIFF file imported with the Place command, the assigned color is displayed on-screen. If the graphic is a PICT or

EPS file, the image remains black, but prints as a spot-color overlay. Note that when Paint and TIFF images are saved in the Scrapbook, the images are converted into PICT format, and cannot display assigned colors in PageMaker.

Objects created in PageMaker using PageMaker's drawing tools also can be assigned only one color. The assigned color applies to the object outline and its shade pattern. If a shade pattern of None is assigned, only the outline is colored. If a line width of None is assigned, only the shade pattern is colored. Reverse lines and reverse text always take on the defined Paper color.

Tip

If you lose colored text in your publication, use the Select All command in the Edit menu to locate the missing text block. Check to see that you haven't accidentally assigned the color Paper to the block of text. If that's the case, drag the text tool through the invisible text to select it and reassign a visible color.

Tip

You can lose reversed text easily, especially if you set the text aside momentarily while creating the contrasting background. The text "disappears" because reversing text makes the text the same color as the page, and therefore invisible on-screen. To avoid this possibility, type an extra character, such as a •, —, or > in front of the text, and reverse everything but that character. You always can find the reversed text.

Chapter Summary

In this chapter you learned how to work with PageMaker's advanced graphics-handling capabilities, including the Text Wrap, Image Control, and Define Colors dialog boxes. You found that you can polish your layouts by wrapping text around irregularly shaped graphics and that PageMaker does most of the work for you. You also saw how PageMaker's image-control features let you apply special visual effects to your Paint and TIFF graphics. You learned how to adjust the brightness, contrast, and halftone screens of your scanned photographs to enhance printing. You also discovered new ways to add interest to your publications by including spot color on your pages.

Now that you know how to create your layouts using text and graphics in PageMaker, Chapter 9 explains how to successfully print your publications.

Printing Techniques   9

You have learned how to work with text and graphics to prepare your layouts in PageMaker, and now you're ready to print your publications. Printing is the one area where users most often encounter difficulty.

This chapter teaches you what you need to know to print your publications successfully every time. You learn how to adjust print options to set up, proof, and print your pages using different output devices. You also discover the secrets to using downloadable fonts. You learn when to favor traditional printing methods over laser-generated output, and when and how to use professional-caliber laser equipment such as a Linotronic ImageSetter (found in many print shops) to supplement those methods for better-looking results. You also explore the basics of color printing, and you discover how correct paper selection can make a difference in the finished product.

As you work through the material in this chapter, keep in mind that, without printing, you don't have a publication, no matter how good your documents look on-screen.

Getting Ready To Print

The obvious place to begin is with PageMaker's Page Setup dialog box because this box is displayed when you open a new publication. Verify the existing settings; don't just click OK immediately. In Chapter 2 you learned what each Page Setup option does, and in Chapter 3 you learned how to make those options into program defaults. If you always use the same parameters for all your publications, you can make those parameters into program defaults to save time. But you always should verify the settings before you begin working so that you can avoid making changes later that could disrupt your layouts.

Before verifying your page setup, go to the Apple menu and select the Chooser desk accessory. In the dialog box that appears, select the output device you are going to use to print your publication to help PageMaker match your publication's requirements to the characteristics of that printer. Selecting the output device also serves as a reminder to set your publication's page size and margins so that the text and graphics lie within the imaging area of the output device.

In Chooser, the icons represent printer drivers installed in your System folder. The names listed to the right of the icons represent the printers connected to your system (see fig. 9.1). (If you have more questions about using Chooser, consult your Macintosh manual.)

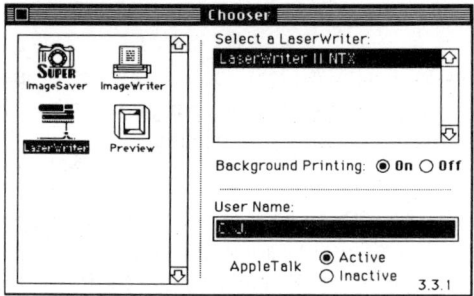

Fig. 9.1.

The Apple Chooser desk accessory dialog box.

As you set up your publications for printing, you may discover that different output devices produce different-size imaging (printing) areas for identically assigned page dimensions. At any Linotronic print resolution, for example, you can cover a full 8 1/2-by-11-inch area, but printing the same letter-size document on a 300-dots-per-inch (dpi) laser printer constrains the page image to lie within a smaller area; on all sides of the paper, an approximately 1/4-inch margin exists where nothing is printed. Any text or graphics that fall outside that margin are chopped off. The size of the printing area depends primarily on the printer's physical construction, but also can vary with output resolution because of the computational demands made upon printer memory.

Take into consideration printer imaging when you proof your publications, especially if you use a device different from the one on which you plan to generate your final output. Consult your printer's manual to determine the maximum printing area under different output conditions. The Apple Laser-Writer, for example, enables you to use two different-size printing areas for a given page size. The larger image area allocates less printer memory for downloading fonts, but enables you to include more text and graphics on a page.

> ***Tip***
> If your pages are too large to print properly, reduce them with the `Scaling` option from PageMaker's Print dialog box. PageMaker shrinks all page dimensions proportionally and centers the final output. Scaling is an easy way to reduce a legal-size layout to letter-size.

> ***Note***
> Because you can change printers and printing specifications at any time, you can print a copy of a publication on one printer, then immediately print a second copy on another printer. This feature comes in handy when you want to proof your work on a laser printer before downloading to a Linotronic.

Using the Print Options

Choose Print from the File menu to use the Print dialog box (see fig. 9.2). At the top of the dialog box, you see the name of the currently selected printer. If you want to change the printer assignment before printing, click Cancel and reopen Chooser to make a new printer selection.

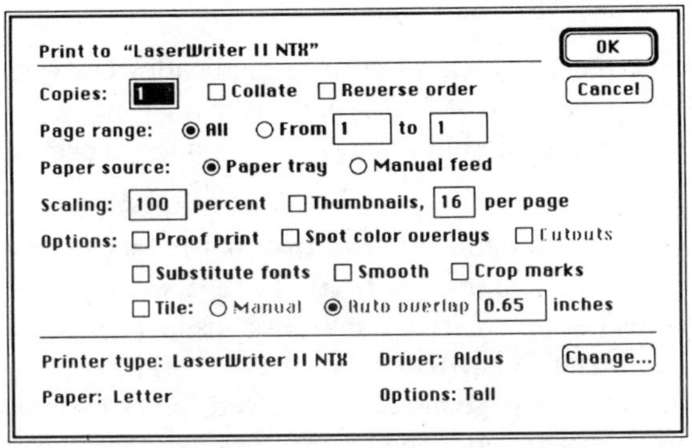

Fig. 9.2.

The PageMaker Print dialog box.

The PageMaker Print dialog box contains many options not normally available in the standard Apple Page Setup and Print dialog boxes. However, if you ever want to use Apple's page-setup features when printing a PageMaker document, hold down the Option key as you select Print from the File menu. You see a modified PageMaker Print dialog box containing only those options specific to PageMaker. Next you see Apple's Page Setup dialog box in which you can choose the particular options you want. Finally, you see the standard Apple Print dialog box in which you specify the number of copies to be printed (see fig. 9.3).

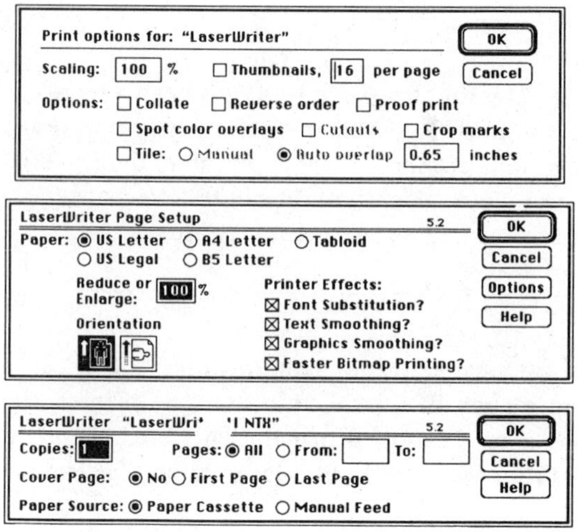

Fig. 9.3.

Using Apple's page-setup features when printing from within PageMaker.

Creating Multiple Copies

Using PageMaker's Print dialog box, you can print up to 100 copies of your publication at one time and even collate pages during printing. Normally, PageMaker prints all copies of one page before starting the next. If, however, you choose to collate pages, PageMaker prints the entire publication once through so that every page is in proper sequence, then repeats the cycle as many times as necessary to produce all the remaining copies (this method takes longer to print).

Collating pages saves time and means that your publications take longer to print because PageMaker has to download each page as many times as the number of copies to be printed. Several dissimilar pages take longer to print than multiple copies of the same page.

PageMaker normally prints a publication so that its first page lies on top of the stack of output pages (last page printed first). To reverse the output so that the first page lies on the bottom of the stack (first page printed first), choose `Reverse Order` from the Print dialog box before printing. Specify a page range by entering the desired page numbers. To feed sheets by hand (most laser printers require that you manually feed paper heavier than 24-pound), click `Manual Feed` in the Print dialog box.

Making Reductions, Enlargements, and Thumbnails

The Print dialog box enables you to reduce pages to as little as 25 percent or enlarge them to as much as 1,000 percent of the original size (the Apple Print dialog box enables you to enlarge only to 400 percent). If you enlarge your pages, you also should *tile* them (print them as overlapping images) to avoid alignment problems later when trimming pages for paste-up (you learn more about tiling later in this chapter).

You can assess your publication's overall layout by using thumbnail printouts (see fig. 9.4). Thumbnails are miniature publication pages. These printouts are complete pages and contain the same fonts and graphics as full-size pages. Displaying them side-by-side on a single page enables you to see how different parts of your publication tie together.

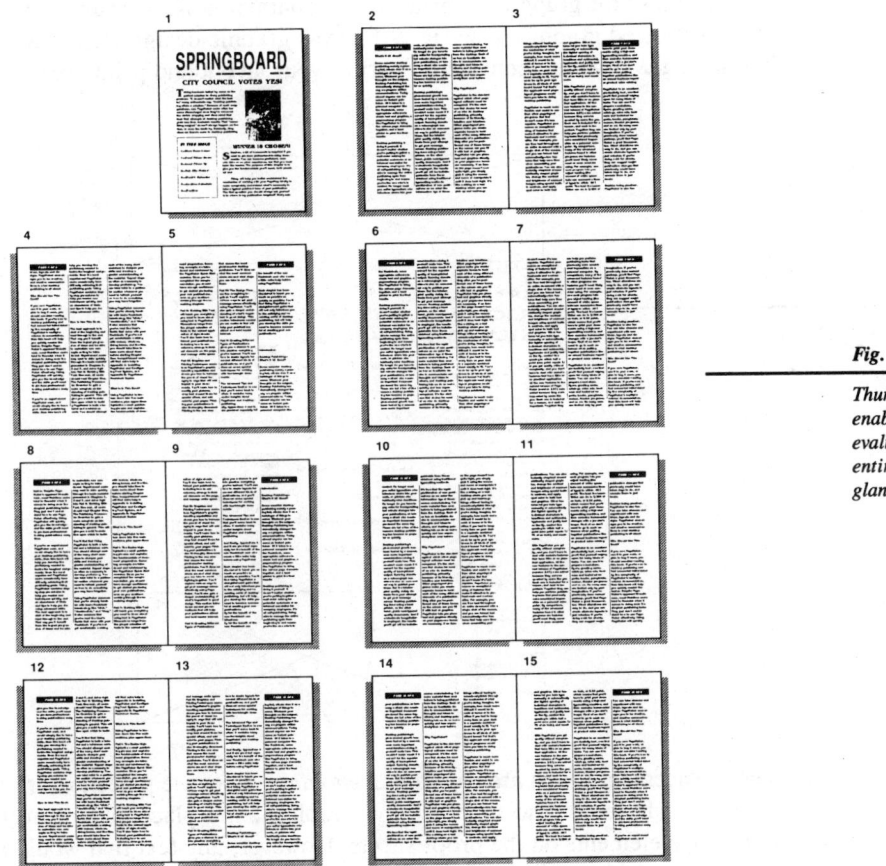

Fig. 9.4.

Thumbnails enable you to evaluate an entire layout at a glance.

Click `Thumbnails` in the Print dialog box to print up to 64 thumbnails on one sheet of paper. The size of each thumbnail depends on how many you assign per page and on the size of the paper. Facing pages are displayed as pairs. Because thumbnails are complete pages, they take at least as long to print as normal-size pages and usually longer because of the scaling involved.

> *Tip*
> Limit the number of thumbnails to 16 per page if you want to see layout details clearly.

Creating Proof Prints

You also can generate proof prints, complete pages without any imported graphics. Proof prints enable you to verify your text and layouts quickly without having to wait for graphics to print. Boxes containing Xs are substituted in place of the imported graphics (see fig. 9.5). Any graphic design elements you create within PageMaker are considered part of your layout and print normally.

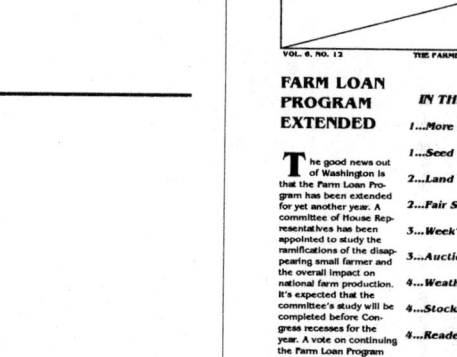

Fig. 9.5.

A proof print of the front page of the Barnyard Gossip *newsletter.*

The replacement boxes are called *placeholders*. Because placeholders mark the outer boundaries of the graphics they replace, the placeholders may overlap other page elements on the proof sheets. However, any text that would normally wrap around an imported graphic still wraps on the page exactly as if the graphic were there. To generate a set of proof prints, click `Proof Print` in the Print dialog box.

> *Note*
> Any headline text that you imported into PageMaker as a PICT file and sized to fit within your layout does not show when you generate proof prints. PageMaker considers text converted to PICT format to be a graphic, even though the text prints as text.

Changing Printer Specifications

You can change printer specifications any time by clicking `Change` in the Print dialog box. In the Printer-Specific Options dialog box, you can assign different APD files and switch between the Apple and Aldus printer drivers (see fig. 9.6). For each printer, you also can pick a different paper size, choose between `Tall` and `Wide` page orientations, and designate an alternate paper tray (if your printer has multiple paper trays). Two other options enable you to choose `Mirror` or `Invert` images for special printing requirements, such as outputting pages directly to film on a Linotronic.

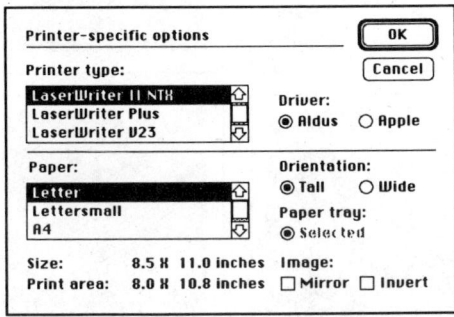

Fig. 9.6.

PageMaker's Printer-Specific Options dialog box.

As each page of your document is printed, PageMaker highlights the corresponding page icon at the bottom of the publication window. PageMaker remembers the print settings you choose and saves them with your publication so that the settings are available the next time you print.

> *Note*
> If you want PageMaker to remember revised print settings, save your publication before closing the file.

Tiling Large Documents

Enlarged pages must often be broken into sections and printed on separate sheets. You must then trim these sheets and paste them together to create composite pages. This process is called *tiling*. PageMaker enables you to create tiles automatically or manually.

To tile a document automatically, click `Tile: Auto overlap` in the Print dialog box and enter a value for the amount of overlap you want. Because most laser printers don't print fully to the edges of a page, some image overlap is necessary to ensure proper matching when pages are later assembled (see fig. 9.7). Make sure that the overlap is larger than the gap your printer leaves between the image area and the edge of the paper.

Fig. 9.7.

A tiled document ready for paste-up. Note how each segment overlaps the others.

Photo courtesy of Jeff Evans and *The Norwich Bulletin.*

> *Warning*
> The actual overlap may be several times the amount you specified in the Print dialog box, and many more tile sheets may be needed to print an enlarged page. Whenever possible, therefore, you should tile manually.

Manual tiling is useful when you want to avoid tiled pages splitting across text or graphics. (Joining tile pages so that split text or graphics line up perfectly is difficult.) To tile a document manually, click `Tile: Manual` in the Print dialog box. This option enables you to control precisely what is included in a tile block. Each tile block is printed with the upper left corner starting at the spot where you position the zero point of your rulers.

Only one manually tiled block is printed at a time. Before printing, check the ruler zero point to make sure that it is positioned properly. After each tile is printed, reposition the zero point for the next tile. Print as many tiles as necessary to reproduce the entire page.

> *Tip*
> Manually tiling a document is an effective way to create page bleeds (text or graphics that run off the page) when your output device cannot print to the edge of the paper. Tile your pages to include fully any bleed areas. After you cut and assemble the tile blocks, trim the composite pages to normal page size. Leave `Scaling` set to 100 percent in the Print dialog box and include crop marks to help determine where to trim each sheet.

Understanding Downloadable Fonts

Most laser printers contain several built-in PostScript fonts for printing text in high resolution. To use these built-in fonts, you should create your documents using the corresponding bit-mapped screen fonts. When PageMaker downloads your publication for printing, the built-in printer fonts are substituted for the screen fonts.

If you want to use PostScript fonts not built into your laser printer, the fonts must be downloaded separately to your printer's memory. You can download them permanently before printing by using any of several commercial or public-domain PostScript downloading utilities (a downloading utility is usually supplied with laser fonts you buy), or you can let PageMaker download them temporarily as you print each page.

Permanently downloaded fonts remain in your printer's memory, available for use until your printer is reset. Temporarily downloaded fonts are stored in your printer's memory only when being used. Then the fonts are purged to make room for new fonts and to free printer memory for other tasks. The only advantage to downloading fonts permanently is that you can save time if you print many different documents containing the same fonts, or if you collate pages. Otherwise, let PageMaker download fonts as the fonts are needed.

For each laser font you use, you must install a corresponding bit-mapped screen font in your System folder using Apple's Font/DA Mover utility (to learn more about the Font/DA Mover, consult your Macintosh manual). You need to install only one size of a particular screen font. If you choose other sizes from the Type Size menu, your fonts may look jagged on-screen, but they print smoothly. Installing separate screen fonts for each size you plan to use is helpful to improve on-screen accuracy for such tasks as manually kerning type.

For a downloadable laser font to print properly, you must store its PostScript file in your System folder. If your printer cannot locate the PostScript file for a particular screen font, the bit-mapped version is printed instead. Bit-mapped fonts not only take longer to print than laser fonts, but bit-mapped fonts lack the high resolution you expect from a laser printer.

If you click Substitute Fonts in the Print dialog box, a few commonly used bit-mapped fonts supplied with your Macintosh System software (Geneva, New York, and Monaco) are replaced by built-in laser fonts (Helvetica, Times, and Courier). However, you should avoid such substitutions. The character spacing of these laser fonts differs significantly from the spacing of the bit-mapped fonts. During printing, your text is reformatted differently from the way you composed the text on-screen.

Always prepare your publications with screen fonts that match your laser fonts. Never use bit-mapped fonts like Geneva, New York, or Monaco unless you intend to print your publications using a dot-matrix printer.

Using Printer Drivers and APD Files

Your printer driver is the software that handles the two-way communications between your computer and your printer. To print your publications, you must have the correct printer driver installed in your System folder. For printing on PostScript devices, you also must have the appropriate laser prep file installed. The laser prep file contains a set of PostScript commands used by the printer driver. Your Macintosh System software comes with a LaserWriter printer driver and a laser prep file. Aldus supplies its own laser prep software, Aldus Prep, designed for use with PageMaker's built-in printer driver.

The built-in Aldus printer driver has several advantages over the Apple driver. The Aldus driver provides faster printing and improved output resolution for reduced bit-mapped graphics. This driver also handles fonts more efficiently, shuttling them in and out of your printer as needed so that you can use any number of fonts in a single publication.

The Aldus printer driver also uses separately stored APD (A Printer Description) files. These text files contain descriptive information about different printers and their features, including available paper sizes and imaging areas for various page options, a list of printer-error alerts and warnings, a list of resident fonts, and other pertinent data PageMaker needs to process your documents properly. For PageMaker to work with a new printer or a new version of an old printer, place a new or updated APD file into your System folder (APD files also can be stored in your PageMaker folder), and select the appropriate APD file for your printer from the `Printer type` list in the Printer-Specific Options dialog box.

> *Tip*
> You can examine an Aldus APD file's contents by opening the file from within any word processor (see fig. 9.8). Be careful, however, not to make or save any changes unless you know what you're doing.

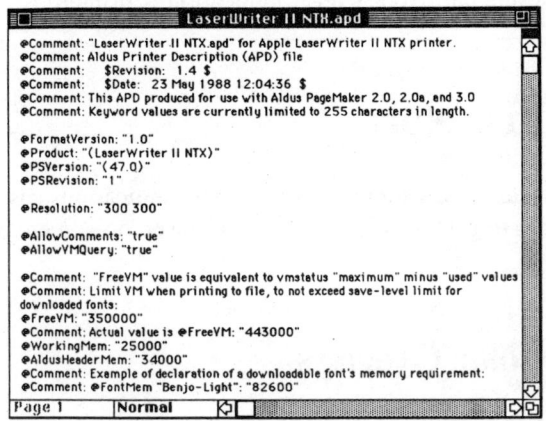

Fig. 9.8.

Examining the text of a PageMaker APD file in Microsoft Word.

Apple's printer driver has the advantage of enabling you to batch-print documents when operating under MultiFinder. The built-in Aldus printer driver does not support MultiFinder's background-printing capability. If you want to print PageMaker files as you continue working, you need to use third-party spooler software that intercepts printed files and processes them in the background or print your publications using Apple's printer driver. Apple's driver also provides better support for PICT graphics and should be used whenever imported PICT images don't print properly. To use the Apple printer driver, click `Driver: Apple` in the Printer-Specific Options dialog box.

Smoothing Graphics

If your laser printer supports smoothing, use PageMaker's Print dialog box to choose `Smooth` to help improve bit-mapped graphics processing. Smoothing can enhance the look of an image by eliminating some of the raggedness, but smoothing also can degrade some images by darkening and filling in details. However, you can partly offset unwanted darkening of a smoothed image by adjusting `Lightness` and `Contrast` using PageMaker's Image Control command from the Options menu. For the best reproduction of scanned images, always leave `Smooth` turned off.

Tip

Smoothed graphics take much longer to print than unsmoothed graphics. Also, smoothing is an option that normally applies to an entire print job. To assign smoothing to only a few pages, print those pages separately from the rest of your publication by assigning different page ranges successively for each print cycle until your whole publication is printed.

Printing in Color

Although PageMaker makes adding color to your publications easy, you need to know several things to get the colors you see displayed on-screen onto your final printed pages.

Preparing Color Overlays

When you click `Spot color overlays` in the Print dialog box, PageMaker produces separate overlays for each color (including black) you use on your pages. The one exception is the color `Paper` (accessed from the Define Colors dialog box) used only to visualize the color of your paper on-screen (see "Defining Colors" in Chapter 8 for more information about the color setting `Paper`). Each color element is printed on the overlay in the same position as it appears on the page. When you combine the separate overlays, you form a composite image of the entire page.

If your pages are smaller than the selected paper size, PageMaker adds registration marks, color labels, and corresponding page numbers to each color overlay you print; otherwise, you must add these items manually. To add registration marks to your overlays, draw the marks anywhere on your master pages using PageMaker's drawing tools, or import the EPS file labeled REGMARK.EPS from your PageMaker Templates disk. Use at least three registration marks per page to ensure proper alignment and assign each mark the color registration to have the marks appear on all overlays. You also can add registration marks individually to publication pages if you want them to print on the overlays for those pages alone.

> *Tip*
> If you assign colors to all your text and graphics so that no black remains, proof your text carefully before printing. If you miss assigning color to just one space or carriage return, PageMaker prints an extra overlay sheet for that page because the program thinks a black overlay is needed for any characters to which no color has been assigned. The overlay is blank, however, because the characters that PageMaker sees are invisible. Overlooking invisible text can increase printing costs greatly, especially when printing long publications on a Linotronic. To avoid this problem, create an insertion point in each story, and choose Select All from the Edit menu. Then reassign the desired colors to your text to color any overlooked invisible characters.

> *Tip*
> You can include registration marks, color labels, and corresponding page numbers on all your overlays in two ways. First, you can scale down your pages slightly so that enough extra room is on each page for PageMaker to include the information. Generally a 15 percent reduction (set Scaling to 85 percent in the Print dialog box) works well and may even improve the appearance of your pages. The second way is to print your pages on oversized paper, then trim them later. If you use this approach, include crop marks to help determine where to trim the pages.

Using Cutouts

PageMaker enables you to prepare cutout overlays for color images that overlap. Cutouts are blank areas within spot-color overlays; the missing shapes in one overlay exactly match the shapes of overlapping images in the next overlay (see fig. 9.9). With standard overlays, each colored image is printed in its entirety.

With cutout overlays, each colored image is printed in a way that, if all the overlays are stacked atop one another, the overlapping images fit together neatly like pieces of a jigsaw puzzle. To print cutout overlays, click `Spot color overlays` and `Cutouts` in the Print dialog box.

Fig. 9.9.

Spot color
overlay cutouts.

> *Note*
> Cutouts don't work with all colored elements. If you can see an element displayed in color on your color monitor, that element prints as a cutout. If an element does not display in color (some imported graphics don't), the element does not print as a cutout. If you have a monochrome display, you have to experiment to find out what works and what doesn't.

When you use cutout overlays, alignment problems can occur if your final registration isn't perfect. When different colors from adjoining areas abut one another, you may see thin white lines appear along area boundaries where no ink is placed during offset printing. These alignment problems usually occur because the feed transport system of a printing press isn't precise enough to ensure an exact paper feed every time or because the mounted offset plate isn't adjusted properly. Even the slightest shift can lead to improper registration.

To eliminate the gaps that result, commercial printers usually expand area boundaries by a fractional percentage so that adjoining colors overlap slightly (*trapping*). Because PageMaker doesn't give you a way to do trapping, check with your printer before using cutouts to determine if the printer can produce satisfactory color registration.

Using Commercial Printers

As easy as producing spot-color separations with PageMaker is, several variables still exist that, if left to chance, can ruin an otherwise perfect layout. The colors you see on-screen, for example, always differ greatly from the colors that get printed. The colors produced by transmitted light (as from a television screen or video monitor) look different to the eye than similar colors produced by reflected light (as from the pages of a printed publication). Much depends on the skill of the commercial printer in mixing and applying the required inks.

In most cases, you tell your print shop what colors to use and where the colors appear on the pages—specify Pantone Matching System (PMS) colors for best results. PageMaker doesn't support PMS colors, but your print shop can supply a PMS color guide from which you can pick them. Beyond that, you have little control over the color-printing process. If you use a direct-color printer of some kind, such as a dot-matrix, ink jet, or thermal-transfer printer, you can adjust your color choices to match the capabilities of that printer. But, even then, such printers are limited to producing only a narrow range of colors, and the color produced by one device may be matched only marginally by another device. Using such printers to produce multiple copies is very slow, and the printing cost per page is generally high. Using a direct-color printer may prove worthwhile only if you produce your publication in limited quantities.

The best way to produce color pages in quantity and ensure consistent results is to use a commercial printer. You and your printer should agree beforehand on the number and type of colors to be printed and the kind of paper you want to use. Find out whether you need to deliver camera-ready copy, or whether the print shop can produce the required separations directly from your disk files. Ask how scanned photographs and complex TIFF illustrations are handled. Some print shops may refuse to download slow-printing graphics to their Linotronics, and you may be asked instead to deliver photo originals from which quality halftones can be made and later stripped onto camera-ready paste-ups.

> **Tip**
> Instead of tying up a Linotronic to print complex TIFF graphics (and incurring large production costs at the same time), you can produce printouts of your graphics beforehand on a laser printer, then have the print shop reduce them for paste-up. Reducing them on-camera improves the resolution by the amount of the reduction. Reducing a 300 dpi TIFF graphic by 50 percent, for example, increases its resolution to 600 dpi.

Using the Linotronic

If your publications call for typeset-quality printing, you'll want to output your files to a Linotronic ImageSetter, found in many print shops and service bureaus across the country. The L300, for example, produces documents with resolutions up to 2,540 dpi, enough to satisfy the most demanding publishing requirements. Linotronic output, however, is much more expensive than normal laser-printer output. Because a Linotronic also occasionally refuses to process jobs that print readily on a regular laser printer, knowing how to prepare your documents properly pays off.

Proofing before Printing

Before printing on a Linotronic, always print a complete proof of your publication on a PostScript laser printer and check the text and graphics carefully. The Linotronic also uses PostScript as a page-description language, so that documents printed on both devices should be similar in appearance.

Check for typos, layout inconsistencies, and other errors. Then make sure that your publication is set up for Linotronic output. Choose the `Mirror` and `Invert` options from the Printer-Specific Options dialog box if you plan to print directly to film.

> **Tip**
> The Linotronic prints fully to the edge of a page, which makes the Linotronic ideal for doing bleeds. However, checking bleeds on laser-printed proofs is difficult because laser printers typically leave a small margin around the paper edges where nothing prints. To check pages with bleeds, run proof copies of them at reduced size. Scaling these pages to 90 percent and including crop marks enable you to verify that your bleeds are placed properly.

To avoid wasting time and money, use laser-printed thumbnails to assess your publication's complete layout before doing a final printout on a Linotronic. Thumbnails help you to spot any global errors or inconsistencies that might be overlooked during examination of the full-size page proofs.

You should be aware that what prints one way on a laser printer often prints entirely differently on a Linotronic. Hairline rules, for example, print thicker on a 300 dpi laser printer (where the dots are bigger) than on a Linotronic (where the dots are smaller).

On a laser printer, gray shades at the low end of the spectrum always turn out darker than when printed on a Linotronic. A 10 percent gray, for example, makes a good background shade when printed on a 300 dpi laser printer, but fades into nothingness when printed on a Linotronic. Similarly, gray shades at the high end of the spectrum always turn out lighter on a laser printer than on a Linotronic. When proofing work on a 300 dpi laser printer that is to be sent to a Linotronic, if the grays look just right, the tones probably will be off somewhat on your final prints. Make the necessary adjustments ahead of time by checking comparative gray-scale charts at your commercial printer.

Tip

When printing gray-scale images, such as scanned photos, on the Linotronic, use PageMaker's Image Control command to lighten the images about 10 percent before downloading. Scanned photos typically print darker on the Linotronic than on a 300 dpi laser printer, and this adjustment is necessary to accurately reproduce the originals. Also, increase the Lines/In setting to at least 90 lines per inch to take advantage of the Linotronic's finer output resolution.

Outputting Directly to Film

The main advantage of printing positives from a Linotronic is that the output can be treated as traditional high-quality camera-ready art. Preparing mechanicals (pasted up camera-ready copy) is therefore easier. The output also can be used on a high-speed copier.

Printing directly to film on a Linotronic, however, has the advantage of completely bypassing the camera when preparing your plates. Shooting mechanicals with a camera to produce plate negatives simply introduces one more step in the production process that increases the potential for unexpected problems. When you reproduce camera-ready copy using a camera, the image quality is degraded slightly. Going directly to film retains the clarity of the original, especially with ultrafine screens, to produce an output resolution that the camera cannot equal.

> **Tip**
> When you print directly to film using a Linotronic, you must select the `Invert` and `Mirror` options in the Printer-Specific Options dialog box. The `Invert` option produces the negative of the image on film; the `Mirror` option flips the image so that it comes out right after flipping the film. Flipping the film after it exits the Linotronic is important because the emulsion-side is placed against the printing plate during exposure. Placing the emulsion side down prevents light diffusion (caused by light passing through the celluloid thickness after striking the emulsion) from defocusing the image. Because the image is trapped in the emulsion and the emulsion is pressed tightly against the printing plate, the tiny dots produced by the Linotronic reproduce sharply.

Using the Linotronic

PICT files occasionally cause printing problems, especially if the files contain many smoothed polygons (multisided objects that have been converted mathematically into curves). Redrawing them requires many computations that can overtax printer memory.

When you create your files, even though you may conceal parts of some objects by overlapping them with others, all objects are seen in their entirety by the Linotronic and incrementally redrawn in layers. This process places additional burdens on printer memory.

Several other factors can significantly retard Linotronic print times and sometimes cause a print job to fail. These factors include using many detailed bit-maps (text or graphics) in your publications; excessively scaling or reshaping bit-mapped images; mixing large numbers of font types and styles on a page; and using many different shades, patterns, and line styles on a page. To compensate for printing slowdowns, the print shop may charge you for the actual time used to generate pages instead the usual flat-rate fee.

> **Tip**
> If you include Paint or TIFF bit-mapped graphics in your publications, set them up to print without Moiré patterns before you download them to the Linotronic. Select the `Linotronic APD` file in the Printer-Specific Options dialog box. Tune each graphic separately by clicking one of its reshaping handles while holding down the Command key. The image boundaries adjust to match the specific printing resolution of the Linotronic.

> **Tip**
> Unlike an ordinary laser printer, the Linotronic looks at all the text in a publication, including text residing on the pasteboard. Although text on the pasteboard isn't printed, it still is processed and can clog the Linotronic's limited memory. If your job fails to print, delete the text on the pasteboard before you try printing again.

Creating PostScript Files

When you send a publication to a commercial printer, you can avoid many problems by sending the publication as a pure PostScript file. That way, your print shop doesn't have to have a copy of PageMaker or the particular laser fonts you used to create your publication. All the data required is included in the PostScript file when you create the file.

To create a PostScript file from your publication, choose Print from the File menu and configure your desired print options. Select the APD file appropriate to the destination printer from the list in the Printer-Specific Options dialog box. Hold down the Option key as you click OK. The PostScript Print Options dialog box is displayed (see fig. 9.10). Click `Print PostScript to disk` and `Normal`, and set any other preferred options. Name your file and tell PageMaker where to store the file (click `Set file name`), and click OK. A PostScript file containing your publication is printed to disk.

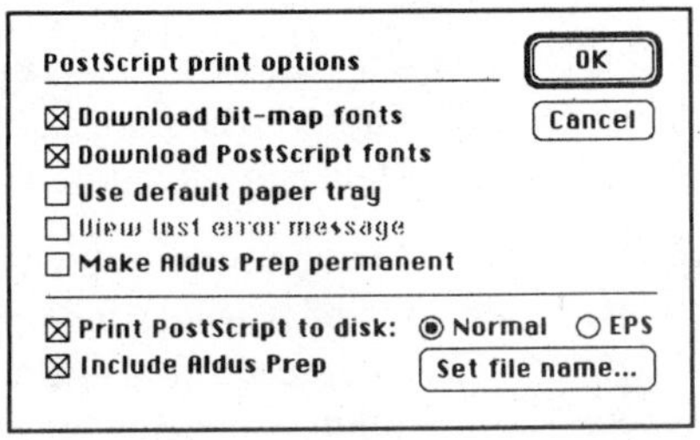

Fig. 9.10.

PageMaker's PostScript Print Options dialog box.

You should keep the following things in mind when creating PostScript files this way:

1. Aldus Prep is needed to process your publication properly. To make Aldus Prep a part of your PostScript file, click `Include Aldus Prep` if your commercial printer doesn't have PageMaker. If your print shop has PageMaker, tell your printer to download Aldus Prep to the printer and save file space by not selecting the `Include Aldus Prep` option when you create your PostScript file.

2. If you are going to print several publications in a row, create a separate PostScript file containing only Aldus Prep. Open a publication, leave it blank, and save the publication as a PostScript file. Click `Include Aldus Prep` and `Make Aldus Prep permanent`. This file can be used to download Aldus Prep to the printer, where Aldus Prep remains in memory while each publication is printed.

3. If the laser fonts used in your publication are not available on the destination printer, click `Download PostScript fonts`. The PostScript versions of each font used are added to your PostScript publication file. Click this option only if you are sure that the fonts are not available. If the fonts are already installed in the printer and you download them again, your publication may not print because the duplicate fonts choke the Linotronic's remaining memory.

> *Tip*
> If you are not sure what fonts are built into a particular printer, examine that printer's APD file using your word processor.

4. Click `Use default paper tray`.

5. If your PostScript file will be downloaded to a Linotronic for printing directly to film, set the `Mirror` and `Invert` options correctly in the Printer-Specific Options dialog box.

Each of the options in the upper half of the PostScript Print Options dialog box also can be used during ordinary printing.

- ❏ Select `Download bit-map fonts` if you want to use bit-mapped fonts in your publication (this option is PageMaker's normal default). Deselect the box if you want PageMaker to substitute Courier instead.

- ❏ Use the `Download PostScript fonts` option whenever you want to download third-party laser fonts to your printer (this option is PageMaker's normal default). If you deselect this option, Courier is substituted in their place. You should deselect this box only when creating a PostScript version of a publication that uses the same fonts resident in the destination printer.

- ❏ Select `Use default paper tray` if you are working on a network and sending files to a remote printer that has multiple trays. PageMaker uses whatever tray is available without displaying warning messages.

- Select `View last error message` if you want to see printer error messages when they occur. Selecting this option keeps you from regaining use of your Macintosh until after your document has been printed (normally your Macintosh becomes available immediately after a file has been fully downloaded).

- Use the `Make Aldus Prep permanent` option if you want Aldus Prep to remain in your printer's memory until you reset the printer (this option is PageMaker's normal default). Deselect this option only if you want Aldus Prep to be removed from your printer's memory as soon as your publication is printed. Deselecting this option keeps printer memory free for other uses.

Each time you print you must reselect these options from the PostScript Print Options dialog box if you don't use the default settings. PageMaker forgets your choices after each print job and reverts to its default settings.

Using Offset Printing

Small jobs cost less when run on high-speed copiers, but large jobs are cheaper when offset. Offset printing uses a printing press and plate to repeatedly transfer an image to paper. Choose offset whenever you must produce pages in large quantities or in color. You also should choose offset if you want to include photos, but don't have a scanner; if you want the superior resolution of half-toned photos instead of the marginal quality scanning sometimes produces; or if you want to print your publications using special paper sizes or weights that high-speed copiers cannot handle. Choose offset whenever you and your commercial printer conclude that offset is the best and most cost-effective way to produce your documents.

You generally save the most time and money by using PageMaker to do publication design and layout. However, after producing camera-ready copy, having the commercial printer finish the job is often more cost-effective.

Tip

Adjust the print-density control on your laser printer to a lighter setting if you plan to use your printouts as camera-ready copy. The camera gives lightly-printed text a crisp, clean look and makes dark type look even heavier. Use darker settings only for printouts intended as final copies.

Selecting the Proper Paper

Your choice of paper not only determines how good your final publication looks, but also how much the publication costs to produce. Keep in mind that paper usually makes up half or more of the expense of most print jobs.

Although you have many different weights, finishes, grades, and colors to choose from, in most instances, ordinary office or copier bond paper works well for laser-printed output. High-gloss and textured finishes, however, make poor reproductions. High-gloss paper doesn't hold toner well. The toner sometimes smears, occasionally chips and frequently heat-spatters during application. Textured paper doesn't accept toner evenly. The surface roughness causes uneven toner application and gives text and graphics a ragged look.

If you prepare camera-ready copy, a smooth, bright-white paper finish for heightened contrast is desirable. Several companies make such paper especially for use with laser printers. This paper costs two or three times as much as ordinary bond, but for important jobs, the added cost can be justified.

Tip

If you plan to print copies for later reproduction using a high-speed copier, print them on the heaviest paper you can put through your laser printer. Use a 70-pound paper, if available, to eliminate the severe curl you often get from feeding lighter-weight paper across your laser printer's internal rollers at high temperature and pressure. Paper curl is the biggest single cause of jams on high-speed copiers, and eliminating paper curl does much to ensure that your print job goes smoothly.

Chapter Summary

In this chapter you learned how to set up and print your publications using different kinds of output devices. You examined PageMaker's various print options in detail and discovered how to tailor them to meet your printing needs. In the process, you learned how to generate proof prints, do reductions and enlargements, print thumbnails, and tile oversized pages. You gained new insights into the role of printer drivers and APD files. You also learned how to produce color separations and how to download pages directly to film when preparing your publications for offset printing.

You discovered that you can convert PageMaker documents into pure PostScript files for direct processing by a commercial printer or print service bureau. Finally, you learned that, in the end, even the best print job can be undone by improper paper selection.

This chapter completes your introduction to the mechanics of using PageMaker. In the next chapter you begin your study of the design process, an essential step on your way to producing professional-looking publications.

IV
Creating Different Types of Publications

Includes

Planning Page Layouts

Designing a Newsletter

Designing Other Publications

Planning Page Layouts 10

This chapter focuses on designing and laying out your publications. Knowing how to use PageMaker does not automatically make you a successful designer; PageMaker is simply a tool for creating layout and design. If you want your publications to look good and appeal to your readers, you must study and practice sound design principles.

No one absolutely right way exists to design and lay out a document, but many wrong ways do exist. This chapter helps you avoid the more common pitfalls as you zero in on the right look for your publications. The ideas in this chapter will help you produce pages that sparkle with professionalism even if you are new to the magic of desktop publishing.

Communicating Ideas Effectively

To successfully convey thoughts, arguments, ideas, and feelings to your readers, your publication must be read. But before your publication can be read, it must be noticed, which is increasingly difficult in today's communications-intensive world. The rivalry for reader attention is intense. The following two things are necessary for any publication to be noticed:

1. To be successful, a publication must be tailored to meet the needs and expectations of its readership. For example, a journal containing nothing but page after page of text in small print could not hope to appeal to the graphic-design community. Similarly, a pamphlet with ornate graphics on every page would have little success among lawyers where concise, factual information is more highly valued.

2. A publication must stand out from the competition. Well-designed publications always have an edge. Few desktop publishers, however, have learned to apply design techniques that can give them that edge. Keep in mind that your publication's appearance helps set the tone of its message, even before the first words are read. Like a fishing lure, if your publication has the right look, you get many nibbles and eventually hook a good catch. Without the right look, you are reduced to reciting tales of the readers who got away.

Achieving the Right Look

To help you understand what is meant by the "right look," visualize a page containing nothing but text (see fig. 10.1A). You see a single text block that fills the entire area between the page margins and is fully justified. The unbroken lines of text are hard to read; your eyes must travel across the page without pause, and the layout has no counterbalancing white space. The result is an impenetrable wall of text tiring to look at and to read. This look is definitely wrong for almost everything but a deliberately intimidating legal contract.

In figure 10.1B, you see the same text with wider margins to allow plenty of surrounding white space. Because the left-right margin pair and top-bottom margin pair are equal and the text is fully justified, however, the page is monotonously uniform. This look may be right for formal announcements, but in larger doses will turn away readers.

In figure 10.1C the same layout has been improved. The text is set with unequal margins and ragged-right justification to heighten visual interest. Clockwise from the left, each margin is progressively wider than the last. The top margin is a little wider than the left margin (after binding); the right margin is a little wider than the top; and the bottom margin is widest of all.

The text block has been assigned *golden-rectangle* dimensions. A golden rectangle has a length approximately 1.62 times its width (1.61803398, to be exact). This ratio has been used for centuries to design everything from books to buildings (the most famous of which is the Parthenon in ancient Greece). The golden rectangle is attractive to the eye, and its use in page design makes reading a more pleasurable experience. Although this layout is less imposing than the last, the look still is somewhat formal. This layout is a good choice for books and other long manuscripts.

> **Tip**
>
> To make assigning golden-rectangle dimensions to text and graphics easy, create two golden-rectangle boxes (one vertical and one horizontal) using PageMaker's square-corner rectangle tool. Use your rulers as guides to size them accurately. Copy them individually to the Clipboard and paste them into your Scrapbook. After that, whenever you need a golden rectangle to use as a template for positioning ruler and column guides, use PageMaker's Place command to import a rectangle from your Scrapbook into PageMaker. (Be sure to use the Place command. If you simply copy from the Scrapbook and paste into PageMaker, the rectangles revert to squares when you hold down the Shift key and proportionally resize them.)

In figure 10.1D you see a typical three-column news format. The column rules, reversed running head, and increased white space help make the page more interesting, and, therefore, more likely to catch a reader's attention. The subheads help break up the flow of text into easily digestible chunks, and the narrower columns are easy to read. This format has a businesslike appearance without being imposing. The format is the right look for informational publications like journals and newsletters.

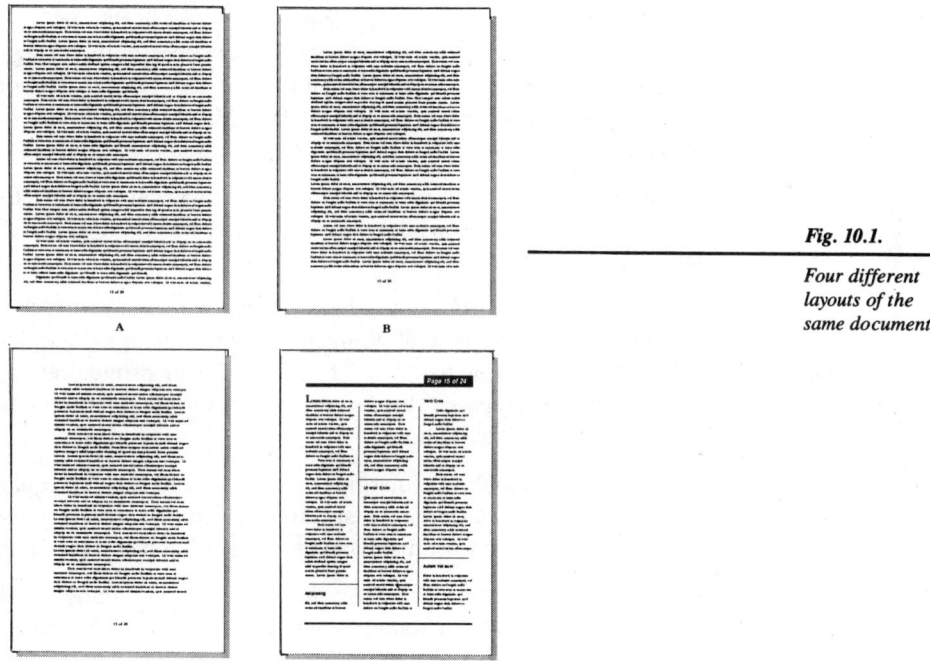

Fig. 10.1.

Four different layouts of the same document.

These examples show that even minor layout variations can produce dramatic differences in the appearance of a page. The right look for one publication, however, may be a totally wrong look for another. The trick to achieving the right look for a publication is to experiment with many different layouts until you find one that works best. But this doesn't necessarily mean endless trial and error. You can greatly improve your chances of success if you understand and apply a few universally accepted, fundamental design principles.

Understanding Structure

Every publication must have structure to accomplish its purpose. To make a particular point, a business report, for example, may include charts and tabular data alongside text. If, on successive pages, those graphics are arranged haphazardly, the lack of organization may subconsciously lower reader confidence in the data being presented.

Well-structured pages, on the other hand, inspire confidence, even before the data is examined. For example, many successful advertisements that, at first glance, seem unstructured, are actually placed according to an underlying grid that directs the structure of the elements on the page. Structure is the key to organizing and presenting your information.

The primary tool for laying out structured pages is the grid. Although PageMaker enables you to place elements on your pages without regard to a formal grid, good design practice entails using some sort of organizational framework to contain your text and graphics. In PageMaker, this framework consists of arrangements of nonprinting column, margin, and ruler guides.

You can lay out any kind of grid you want. PageMaker doesn't constrain your creativity. You should consider several things, however, as you formulate your publication's structure:

1. How large will your pages be, and how will they ultimately be folded, bound, and distributed? Remember that, although PageMaker lets you produce pages up to 17 by 22 inches, if your printer cannot accommodate paper that large, you have to tile your output to create camera-ready paste-ups.

2. How wide should the margins be, and should they be equal or unequal widths? If you decide on a specific-size image area, you will have to calculate margin widths manually from whatever paper remains.

3. Will your pages be laid out symmetrically or asymmetrically, and how will you allocate surrounding white space? If you intend to include bleeds, have you adjusted your page and paper sizes accordingly? (You

may have to use larger paper and trim later—check with your printer to see if you can change paper size without increasing production costs.) If you intend to print your publication double-sided, have you allowed enough gutter (inner margin) for proper binding?

> *Note*
> Most laser printers are not designed to handle large amounts of double-sided printing. Remelted toner can eventually accumulate on rollers and cause internal damage. Let your commercial printer produce any double-sided pages.

4. Does your publication call for multiple columns? If so, how many, and will they be all the same width or different widths? How much space will you need between them? Do you plan to vary the number of columns on different pages? If so, how will you balance facing pages to provide the most pleasing arrangement? Should you set your columns ragged right, or fully justify them? (If you don't need to justify, set the columns ragged right; they generally look better and are easier to read.) Remember that your columns are the pillars upon which your publication rests—they support your total layout design.

5. Will your headlines span multiple columns, or will they be confined to lie within column boundaries? How will you distinguish headlines and subheads from surrounding text? What's the most readable type size for your stories, and how much space should you insert between lines and paragraphs? Have you chosen workable type sizes for headlines, subheads, and captions?

> *Tip*
> If your headlines span two or more lines, selectively reduce the leading to tighten them up. If your headlines are set in large type, use negative values (values less than the existing type size). For example, a two-line, 60-point headline looks much better set with a negative leading of 52 points than at PageMaker's normal 72-points auto-leading setting (equal to 120 percent of type size). See figure 10.2 for an example of negative leading applied to a 24-point headline.

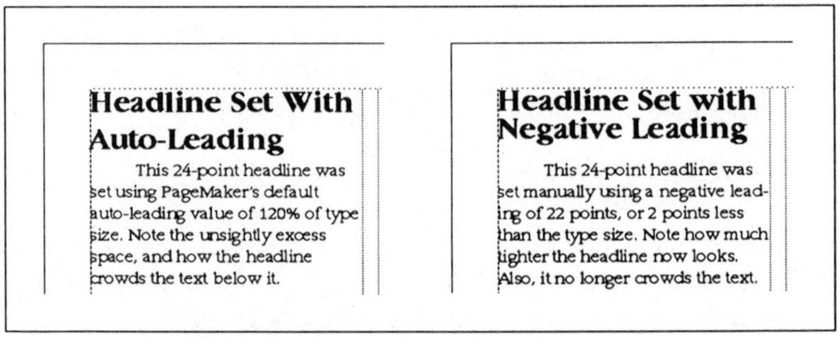

Fig. 10.2.

Assigning negative leading can improve the look of headline copy.

Headline Set With Auto-Leading

This 24-point headline was set using PageMaker's default auto-leading value of 120% of type size. Note the unsightly excess space, and how the headline crowds the text below it.

Headline Set with Negative Leading

This 24-point headline was set manually using a negative leading of 22 points, or 2 points less than the type size. Note how much tighter the headline now looks. Also, it no longer crowds the text.

6. How large should your photos and illustrations be? Will their boundaries coincide with column boundaries? Have you allowed enough extra space for frames? Where do you intend to place photo credits—below your photos or vertically alongside them? How will you handle illustrations that extend partway into a column? If you plan to use callouts (outlying captions that refer to different parts of illustrations), have you left room to include them?

7. What kinds of design elements are needed, and have you factored them into your layouts? For example, if you plan to use rules to separate adjoining columns, have you left enough space between columns to include them without crowding? How much extra space do you need for headers and footers? Where will you place page numbers?

8. Have you planned for consistency? If you use drop shadows, for example, will you use them with all your illustrations? Will boxes and rules always be the same thicknesses on facing pages? Will the same type sizes be used in the same way on all pages throughout your publication?

Answering these kinds of questions ahead of time helps you set up PageMaker's nonprinting guides to establish a consistent and uniform structure for placing text and graphics. A carefully implemented grid prepared in advance does much to give your publications a professional look that would otherwise be difficult to achieve.

Making the Story Fit

The best way to make your stories fit is to monitor character count as you go along. If you determine beforehand how many characters fit on a line, and how many lines fit on a page, you can calculate how many characters you should allocate for any story that has to fit in a particular layout. Remember, to be accurate, your character count must include punctuation marks and spaces as well as letters and numbers.

Be aware that story fit also can be affected by other variables, such as using different font types, sizes, and styles, and assigning different line leading and paragraph spacing. As you change these variables, you must adjust character count accordingly.

You sometimes may be tempted to alter a carefully planned layout to make room for a few extra sentences or paragraphs of a story. Don't; almost any story can be made to fit by careful and critical editing. If your story will suffer by editing, make slight adjustments in word spacing, leading, and hyphenation. If that fails, other things you can do to free up extra space include condensing headlines by rewriting them or reducing their size, cropping artwork and photos for a tighter fit, reducing the size and spacing of captions and credit lines, and reducing the spacing between paragraphs.

> *Tip*
> If a story that needs cutting contains a supplementary topic, extract the supplementary text and set the text apart from the story in a *sidebar*. A sidebar is a separate section of text, usually framed and shaded a light gray to distinguish it from the main story. You then can cut from the main story the transitional text that introduced that topic.

As you create your layouts, look for single or partial words left dangling at the bottoms of paragraphs or columns. Also watch out for single or partial words, or last lines of paragraphs, carried over into following columns (see fig. 10.3). These isolated bits of text cause a break in continuity that can interrupt a reader's concentration.

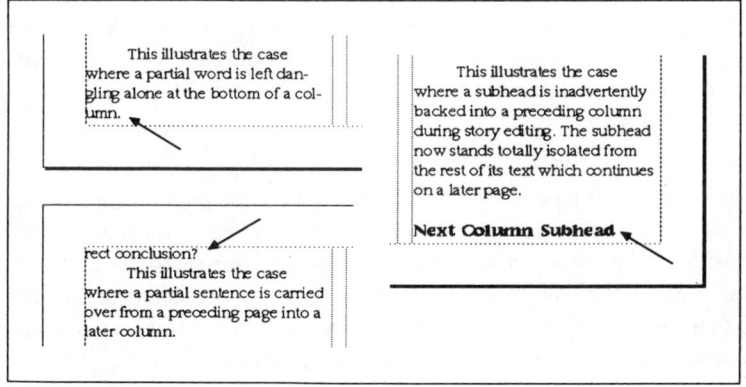

Fig. 10.3.

Examples of isolated text.

Using White Space

Think of white space as a design element in its own right, and use white space the same way you would a headline, rule, box, or illustration. Effective placement of white space is as important as the placement of any other element, and every page should be composed of at least 40 to 50 percent white space. Anything less generally gives a cluttered look that reduces visual appeal.

The biggest mistake you can make is to try to fit too much onto your pages. Including white space as a mandatory design element will help you avoid overcrowding. However, if you use large patches of white, confine them to only one or two areas on a page. Overuse of white space, like overuse of any other design element, can detract from the appearance of your publications.

When laying out your pages, consider the path the reader's eye normally follows as an aid to the placement of white space. The first place a reader usually looks is in the middle of the page, a little less than half way down from the top. The reader's eye typically travels from there upward, toward the right, then down across the page to the lower left corner, and finally back across the page to the lower right corner, carving out the letter Z in the process.

To use this information when preparing an advertisement or flier, you might place the dominant element, such as a graphic or headline, where the reader first looks in the upper center of the page and your closing statement, such as a sale price or discount coupon, prominently in the lower right corner. In this case, you should place white space in the upper left of the page and elsewhere to reinforce the anticipated path of eye travel (see fig. 10.4).

The liberal use of white space contributes to an elegant look for business publications, and an open look for advertising copy and other informal documents. White space also gives you more creative freedom when designing your page layouts. Because white space is light, not heavy, confine excess white space to the upper parts of your pages.

Tip

Whenever you lay out a publication with more than one page, always view your work in the facing-pages mode to see exactly what the reader will see. Look for areas where balance and symmetry are missing, and use white space as a compositional element to help correct deficiencies. Keep in mind that the reader never sees a single page by itself unless it's a front or back cover; facing pages always are viewed together.

Fig. 10.4.

The reader's eye normally follows a "Z" pattern when looking at a page for the first time.

Using Contrast, Balance, and Symmetry

The most eye-catching publications use contrast to enhance their pages. Contrast can be a matter of juxtaposing big illustrations alongside small ones, fancy lettering alongside plain, dark areas alongside light. It can be as straightforward as using graphics to enliven text (see fig. 10.5). Contrast can be used to draw attention to a particular spot on the page, or to highlight an important item. Contrast often results from your choice of a dominant page element (headline, text, or graphic), but sometimes contrast results from more subtle things, like setting a section of text in italics. Introducing contrast into your publications always makes them more interesting.

Contrast emphasizes disparity; balance does just the opposite. Balance represents the equal and harmonious distribution of weight within an environment. Because the weights on your pages are made up of visual elements, balance includes the attributes of shape, shade, and size. You can achieve balance in your layouts by offsetting asymmetrical elements with symmetrical ones, darker images with lighter ones, and a single large shape with several smaller ones.

Note that contrast and balance work hand-in-hand. The need for contrast, for example, may dictate a mixture of large and small graphics, and the requirement of balance demands a harmonious arrangement of those graphics on the page.

Fig. 10.5.

Strong graphics and bold type can add contrast to pages.

> **Tip**
> Always consider balance when laying out facing pages (see fig. 10.6). For example, placing running heads and page numbers near the outside margins on both facing pages not only balances those pages attractively, but also makes the running heads and page numbers easier to locate as your readers flip through your publication.

Symmetry refers to the individual and artful arrangement of elements on the page. Note that too much symmetry, where everything looks uniform and regimented, can make pages look dull and uninteresting. For example, having blurbs, quotations, or drop caps appear in exactly the same spot on every page will bore your readers quickly.

Balance brings harmony; symmetry affects mood. An asymmetrical arrangement, of course, can exhibit perfect balance, even while dramatically shifting emphasis among elements for heightened contrast (see fig. 10.7). Balancing a layout is like the fine art of Japanese bonsai, the pruning and shaping of dwarf trees. As you contemplate one of these miniature masterpieces, you see that the unstabilizing asymmetry of the individual branches is balanced by the wholeness of the tree.

Chapter 10: Planning Page Layouts   233

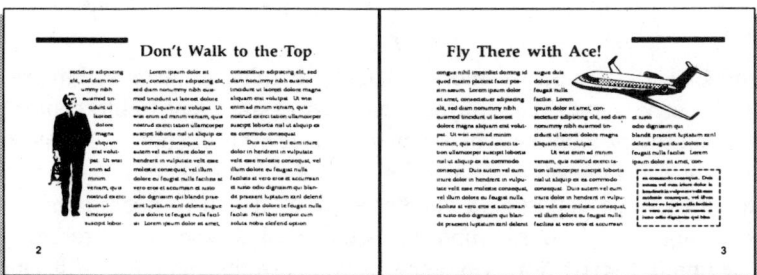

Balanced Facing Pages

Fig. 10.6.

Balanced pages are more appealing than unbalanced pages.

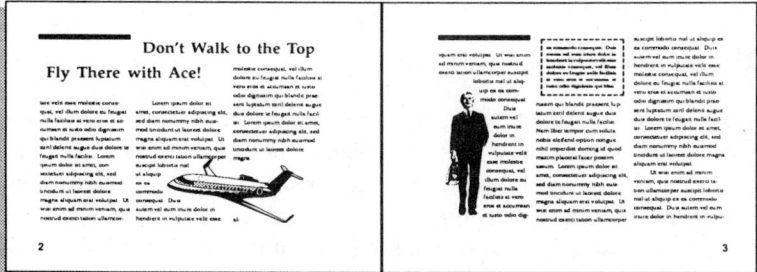

Unbalanced Facing Pages

Fig. 10.7.

An asymmetrical arrangement can sometimes be most effective.

> **Tip**
> Asymmetrical layouts are more difficult to manage than symmetrical ones, because symmetrical layouts have an easily identifiable center of gravity on the page about which you can place your elements. The center of gravity for an asymmetrical layout may lie somewhere off the page, with white space acting as a counterbalance. If you're not practiced at such arrangements, your compositions may look awkward and forced. In the beginning, strive for symmetry in your layouts, and you will enjoy more consistently rewarding results.

Creating Headlines

Without an effective headline, the reader might never consider your convincing argument, discover your well-written insights, or be persuaded to buy your superior product. A powerful headline is the irresistible bait you use to hook a reader's attention. Without headlines, one body of text would look the same as another, and there would be no compelling reason to favor one similar publication over another.

Your headlines should be larger than your body text and set in a contrasting typeface. Emphasizing headlines in bold also helps. Although they must necessarily be brief to fit within the allowable copy space, that doesn't mean that they should be dull. Your headlines should announce grandly, admonish severely, sparkle with wit, and call attention to themselves in every way possible. Headlines, like any other text, must be read to be effective. After all, what good is bait on a hook if the bait is ignored? Here are a few important rules to follow if you want your headlines to work:

1. Ideal type sizes for headlines range from 48 to 72 points. Headlines set in larger sizes become difficult to comprehend immediately at normal reading distances. Headlines set in smaller sizes lose their impact. Note that this constraint on larger type sizes doesn't apply to banners—banners are identifying logos and can be treated like graphics. This constraint on larger type sizes also doesn't apply in those cases where a headline normally is read at a distance of more than about two feet, as with newspapers displayed on a sidewalk newsstand.

2. Don't capitalize every word in a headline. Capitalize only the important words, leaving subordinate words in lowercase. Capitalizing every word slows reading comprehension. Never set headlines in all caps unless they're only one or two words long. Text set in all caps is difficult to read because the eye isn't accustomed to seeing words displayed that

way. Words are recognized by their shapes as much as by their letters (see fig. 10.8). When you set text in all caps, you eradicate recognizable shapes, leaving only constant-height letter groupings.

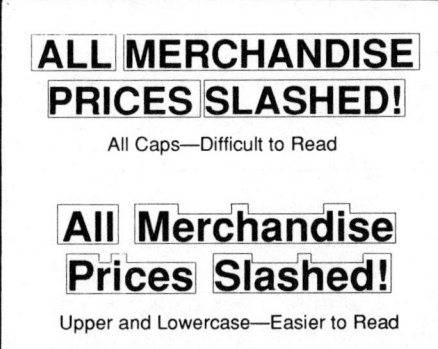

Fig. 10.8.

The eye uses word patterns as an aid to word recognition.

3. Don't use overly decorative type unless specifically called for by the theme of your publication. Headlines should contrast with body text, but not to the point where they become the entire center of focus. A headline's purpose is to stimulate interest in what follows.

4. Don't use several contrasting headlines on the same page. You don't want your headlines to compete among themselves for your readers' attention. Only one headline should dominate on any page.

5. Make your headlines as compact as possible. Kern individual letters as necessary to produce an even appearance, but not so much that serifs touch. Never justify a headline in an attempt to make it fit a particular space—justifying usually produces uneven and unsightly character spacing.

6. In earlier chapters, you learned that you could import text saved in PICT format and stretch it to fill a given space. Avoid doing this except for special effects. Stretching text can distort the regularity of the letterforms and reduce legibility.

7. Above all, make your headlines count by writing them with the reader in mind. For example, don't create headlines like the following:

    XYZ Company Announces New Product for Controlling Baldness

    Congress Cites Need for Additional Funding To Help Curb Hunger

Nobody really cares about XYZ Company or Congressional commentary. Such headlines succeed only in producing yawns. Instead, make your headlines interesting by stressing features and benefits, or by focusing on strong elements that provoke immediate reader reaction. You could rewrite the headlines as follows:

New Breakthrough Stops Hair Loss

Tax Increase Proposed in Fight against Hunger

Let each of your headlines clearly tell a story. Keep in mind that your headlines are likely to be remembered long after their accompanying articles are forgotten.

Tip

Most headlines are created as individual text blocks and later dragged into place above their articles. To ensure consistent spacing, use PageMaker's square-corner rectangle tool to draw a box the same height as the space you want between headlines and body copy. Store the box on the pasteboard, and drag the box onto your pages when you need to use it to help position a new headline. You also can use this trick for setting illustration captions.

Using Type Effectively

Mixing different but compatible type styles (for headlines, subheads, and body text) helps break up a page to make it more interesting. Mixing different type styles is especially important in newsletters and magazines, where dull pages often end up being dominated by nearby advertisements. You also can reduce the need for expensive color by careful use of bold type and other style variations to provide the necessary contrast.

Another type-related tool that can be used to good effect is the pull quote. Pull quotes are short segments of text extracted from stories and bracketed by horizontal rules. They're most often set in larger point sizes and in bold or bold-italic styles. Pull quotes highlight important topics of interest. They also help break up long blocks of text, and they add contrast to your pages (see fig. 10.9).

You can box your text with light background shading for increased emphasis. Sidebars in magazines and newsletters are good examples of boxed and shaded text. Often the type also is set in a different point size from the main story. For additional impact, use reversed type set against a dark gray or black background. This technique works best with short segments of text set in large point sizes.

> facilisi. Lorem ipsum dolor sit amet, consectetuer adipiscing elit, sed diam nonummy nibh euismod tincidunt ut laoreet dolore magna aliquam erat volutpat. Ut wisi enim ad minim veniam, quis nostrud exerci tation ullamcorper suscipit lobortis nisl ut aliquip ex ea commodo consequat. Duis autem vel eum iriure dolor in hendrerit in vulputate velit esse molestie consequat, vel illum dolore eu feugiat nulla facilisis at vero eros et accumsan et iusto odio dignissim qui blandit praesent luptatum zzril delenit augue duis dolore te feugait nulla facilisi.
> Lorem ipsum dolor sit amet, consectetuer adipiscing elit, sed diam nonummy nibh euismod tincidunt ut laoreet dolore magna aliquam erat volutpat. Ut wisi enim ad minim veniam, quis nostrud exerci tation ullamcorper suscipit lobortis nisl ut aliquip ex ea commodo consequat.
>   Duis autem vel eum iriure dolor in hendrerit in vulputate velit esse molestie consequat, vel illum dolore eu feugiat nulla facilisis at vero
>
> blandit praesent luptatum zzril delenit augue duis dolore te feugait nulla facilisi. Lorem ipsum dolor sit amet, consectetuer adipiscing elit, sed diam nonummy nibh euismod tincidunt ut laoreet dolore magna aliquam erat volutpat. Ut wisi enim ad minim veniam, quis nostrud exerci tation ullamcorper suscipit lobortis nisl ut
>
> ❝ *Concise but descriptive pull quotes stimulate reader interest.* ❞
>
> aliquip ex ea commodo consequat.
>   Duis autem vel eum iriure dolor in hendrerit in vulputate velit esse molestie consequat, vel illum dolore eu feugiat nulla facilisis at vero eros et accumsan et iusto odio dignissim qui blandit praesent luptatum zzril delenit augue duis dolore te feugait nulla facilisi. Nam liber tempor cum

Fig. 10.9.

Well-placed pull quotes can help draw readers' attention to a story.

Whether you're preparing headlines, subheads, captions, pull quotes, or body text, always pick fonts and type styles that suit your publication's theme. Documents identical in every way except the fonts used can look completely different from one another, and even convey completely different messages to your readers.

Every typeface has a unique personality (one reason they're called type "faces"). Figure 10.10 shows several type faces that project different personalities. Although this example is obvious, even subtle differences in type characteristics often dramatically affect the look of a page. Because font selection is critical to the acceptance of your work, you should take time to study how successful publications are typeset. Becoming type literate will help you to improve the effectiveness of your publications.

Tip

Whenever you use very small type sizes, avoid fonts that combine thick and thin strokes. Although they look elegant at larger sizes, these fonts tend to fall apart at tiny sizes. Unless the type is set on a Linotronic, the thin strokes often break up, making the type difficult to read.

Fig. 10.10.

Different typefaces convey different impressions.

Using Attention-Getting Graphics

Graphics can be an effective tool for sparking reader interest. You should select your graphics (illustrations, charts, graphs, and so on) to provide additional information to help your reader more fully understand the text. But be careful not to use meaningless illustrations; every graphic should have a specific purpose and should be related to your text.

You should place your graphics close to where they are referenced in your stories. Many readers skim through publications, stopping to read only those pages where an illustration appears. The longer a reader pauses to look at a picture, the better chance you have of getting him to read the accompanying text.

The size of a graphic often affects its placement on the page. Large graphics usually can be positioned at the top or bottom of the page with equally good results. If a graphic is less than a third of the height of the page, however, you should place it near the top of the page.

Graphics that span multiple columns can cause reader confusion when centered in the middle of the page. Such placement makes it difficult for the reader to find where a broken column of text continues. Narrow graphics, on the other hand, usually work well in any column, but are less effective if placed in the exact center of the page. Heavy or dark graphics do best when placed at the bottom of the page. Light, airy ones do better near the top of the page.

Tip

When you include several graphics on the same page, make the most important one the largest to help establish the correct hierarchy in your reader's mind.

Avoid framing graphics unless absolutely necessary. Most illustrations can stand alone without boxes around them—adding frames only dilutes their effectiveness. At times, however, you will want to frame illustrations for the sake of formality, especially photographs. In such cases, thin, simple frames usually suffice, but other designs also may be effective (see fig. 10.11). Be careful not to use overly heavy, ornate frames. They usually draw attention away from the illustrations they contain.

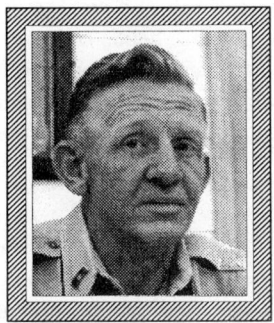

Fig. 10.11.

Different frames created within PageMaker produce strikingly different visual effects for the same image.

When a reader focuses on a graphic, you have another opportunity to set the hook. Use concise captions with your illustrations to encourage further reading. Captions should connect your illustrations to your stories in ways that stimulate reader interest. The more thought-provoking, the better.

> ***Note***
> Always center captions beneath your graphics. Otherwise they can become distracting.

Using Boxes, Rules, and Other Design Elements

Boxes, rules, drop caps, shadows, and other design elements are embellishments that dress up a publication and help give it a distinctive look. Using design elements is like wearing a colorful tie or a flashy pair of earrings. They help identify the uniqueness of your work.

However, design elements shouldn't be used just for the sake of distinctiveness. Each design element, to be effective, should grow out of a need to do a specific task. For example, if your publication uses running heads on each page, you might create a composite design element by overlaying reverse type on a heavy, black rule. However, the same need also could be addressed in dozens of other ways using many different design approaches.

Boxes and rules are eminently practical tools. They can be used to set off text and graphics and help bring organization to a page. Partitioning your pages with boxes and rules creates meaningful information groups (such as delineating ad copy from editorial copy), and helps focus reader attention on particular items (such as advertisements, pull quotes, illustrations, and announcements).

Shadows, shaded fills, and patterns enable you to emphasize the relative importance of elements on your pages by adding strong visual accents to blocks of text and graphics. Boxed sidebars, for example, are usually lightly shaded to stress the importance of the copy they contain. You can use drop shadows to make photos and text seem to leap off the page.

Ornaments are another wonderful design tool. They range from old-fashioned typographers' ornaments—intricate splashes of artwork—to the modern Zaph Dingbats font characters found in most PostScript laser printers. Ornaments can be used decoratively to heighten the visual appeal of a page, or more practically, as bullets, check boxes, and stylized pointers. The choice depends on the nature of your communication. However, even when used purely for decoration, ornaments always should be made to blend seamlessly with the rest of your publication.

Think of design elements as optional tools you can use to accomplish specific layout tasks. For example, if your columns crowd one another, you could simply widen the space between them, or you might place a vertical hairline rule between each pair of column guides. You also could box each column or apply light background shading to alternate columns. The task in this case is to distinguish more clearly one column from another to make reading the text easier. Design elements enable you to distinguish columns in a variety of interesting ways.

> *Tip*
> Boxed elements generally look best when the spacing between the box and the element contained is equal on all four sides.

Although you have a multitude of different design elements at your disposal, that doesn't mean that you have to use them all at once. In most cases, it pays to be conservative. Pick and choose carefully. Don't try to crowd too much onto your pages at once, or your publication may end up looking like a child's scrapbook.

Keep in mind that design elements have character, just as typefaces have personality. For example, thin, double rules used as square-cornered frames add a classical touch to any page. However, although they may be suitable for formal business documents, they may be totally inappropriate for more casual correspondence, such as wedding invitations, where the accompanying type and illustrations have gentle curves. Use design elements to complement your publications, not compete with them.

> *Tip*
> Select rule thicknesses to match the stroke weights of your fonts; avoid mixing light-weight rules with strong fonts, and heavy-weight rules with delicate fonts. For example, if you use a finely stroked serif font, a thin hairline rule might be the best choice. If you use a boldface sans serif font, a much thicker, heavier rule is called for. If the characters in your typeface combine thin and thick strokes, use a matching double rule having thin and thick lines.

Creating Drop Caps

Drop caps have been used for centuries to introduce chapters or new sections of manuscripts. The key word is introduce. Don't make the mistake of beginning every new paragraph with a large initial or drop cap. Drop caps, like any other design element, should be used sparingly. Use them to add flair to pages without overpowering the text.

Capitalizing the first few words in the first line after a drop cap is customary and provides a smooth transition into the text that follows. Modern usage frequently ignores this convention, but as a design technique, it lends subtle sophistication to your pages. If you choose to capitalize part of the first line, reduce the type size of the caps several points to make a more gradual transition into the following text.

Drop caps can be as ornate as the ones used in medieval manuscripts or as sleek as the ones in a modern news magazine (see fig. 10.12). You can place shadows behind them, or wrap text around them the same as graphics. They can be boxed, or they can stand alone. Most often they rise above the top of a paragraph, but they also can be completely embedded. In all cases, using a drop cap eliminates the need to indent the first line of a paragraph.

If you use heavy, black letters as drop caps, or if your drop caps have rounded bases, like O's, U's, and S's, let them sink slightly below the baseline of adjoining text. However, if your drop caps have square bottoms, like E's, H's, and L's, be careful to align them so that the baselines are even with the baselines of adjoining text. Avoid drop caps that hover above a common baseline. When in doubt, use a horizontal ruler guide to ensure accurate placement.

Fig. 10.12.

Drop caps can add interest to your pages.

Chapter 10: Planning Page Layouts **243**

To create a drop cap using existing text in PageMaker:

1. Select the first two lines of the paragraph in which you intend to create the drop cap and manually set the leading the same as PageMaker's auto-leading. This process keeps your lines from spreading when you enlarge the initial cap.

2. Select the first character of your paragraph and enlarge that character by choosing a new point size from the Type Size menu or Type Specifications dialog box. A point size three times the existing type size is usually a good starting point.

3. Add any styling, such as bold or italic and choose a different font type if appropriate.

Note

When you first enlarge an initial cap, the upper part of the letter may not show on-screen. The letter still prints properly, however. Switching to another view in PageMaker and back again causes the screen to refresh and properly display the full character.

---

4. Change the first few words of the first line (not the whole line) to all normal caps. Then manually kern the text immediately following the drop cap for a proper fit.

To create a drop cap using an imported PICT or bit-mapped letter graphic, do the following:

1. Import the letter graphic using the Place command from the File menu.

2. Using the Text Wrap command from the Options menu, assign a text-wrap boundary and specify a stand-off distance. If you prefer text to conform to the shape of the letter, customize the boundary accordingly.

3. Move the letter graphic into position at the beginning of the paragraph. Work in an enlarged 200 or 400 percent view for accurate placement. Use the leftmost column guide along with a horizontal ruler guide to align the letter with the left edge of the text and the adjoining text baseline. The text will reflow around the letter graphic. Make any minor adjustments to the custom boundary as needed.

4. Delete the first letter of the paragraph (the one you replaced with the letter graphic), and change the next few words to all normal caps.

Creating Drop Shadows

Drop shadows are offset shaded areas placed behind framed illustrations, text, or other design elements. They help create an illusion of depth.

Drop shadows can be any size and shape. You can offset them a little or a lot, and in any direction. Typically, they are black or gray, rectangular, and only slightly offset to focus attention on whatever elements lie in front of them. Because they create such a strong visual accent, they should be used judiciously, and only where additional emphasis is needed.

To create a drop shadow, do the following:

1. Select any of PageMaker's rectangular or oval drawing tools and draw a shape the same size or slightly larger than the element to which you want to add the shadow.

Note

If a graphic or block of text to which you want to add a drop shadow is transparent, you must first place a paper-colored shape of the same size behind it. Otherwise, when you add the drop shadow, the dark color will show through and obscure whatever lies in the foreground.

---

2. Assign the desired shade or color and a border line thickness (or None) to the shape, then drag the shape into position over the original element. Offset it slightly in the direction you want it to show.

3. With the shape still selected, choose Send To Back from the Edit menu. Your drop shadow is now in place. If minor adjustments in size or position are needed, scale or move the drop shadow like any other graphic.

Using Electronic Whiteout

Electronic whiteout is the equivalent of liquid correction fluid, that indispensable stuff used in offices around the world to make corrections. In PageMaker, whiteout is nothing more than lines and shapes that are the same color as your paper (usually white). You can use electronic whiteout to do many things, including touching up graphics and adding visual accents to text. One common use for electronic whiteout is to square off the ends of ragged rows of lines or leader dots.

To apply electronic whiteout, draw any shape using one of PageMaker's drawing tools. Assign your shape the color Paper from the Shades menu and a line width of None from the Lines menu. Drag the shape into position to "erase" what lies beneath. You also can use reverse lines as electronic whiteout.

Draw a line, assign any width, then choose Reverse Line from the Lines menu.

Electronic whiteout is a powerful design tool. You can use it to create new patterns and designs right in PageMaker. Experiment to discover the possibilities.

> *Tip*
> You can produce custom electronic whiteout using reversed text. For example, reversing typed symbols, such as the symbols contained in Zaph Dingbats (a font built into most laser printers), gives you an almost endless variety of shapes to work with for touching up your pages. Symbols and other special type characters also can be combined in many different ways to create innovative new designs. By using different type sizes for these characters, you can control precisely the effects produced.

Using Templates

With preformatted templates, you can produce publications more quickly and with less effort than you could if you had to build each new layout from scratch. Well-designed templates also give your publications more consistency. Another advantage is that they help employees who have little or no design experience become more productive within a shorter period of time.

Using Prepackaged Templates

Prepackaged templates let you create professional-looking documents without spending a long apprenticeship learning advanced design techniques. Because most of the preliminary layout work is already done, all you have to do is drop in text and graphics. With just a little additional customization, you can produce finished publications in a fraction of the time it otherwise might take. Among the best templates you can find anywhere are the ones from Aldus.

Aldus supplies 20 basic templates with PageMaker that cover a wide assortment of publishing needs. Included are templates for brochures, business reports, executive summary sheets, memos, newsletters, product specification sheets, some overhead transparencies, and other useful documents. Several of these templates include style sheets that you can import into your own publications. Consider these templates a starter kit and use them accordingly. Build on them and refine them until you have made them your own.

Aldus also markets several template packages, including Designs for Newsletters, Designs for Business Communications, and Designs for Manuals. These portfolios, contain a variety of templates, each saved with specific defaults intended to make them easier to use. Style sheets also are included.

The Designs for Newsletters portfolio, for example, contains 21 different newsletter templates. The manual guides you step-by-step through a detailed practice session to familiarize you with using templates. You then can choose the type of newsletter that most nearly matches your preferred publication style and follow the specific guidelines for placing your text and graphics. Character counts are provided for preformatted story lengths so that you can prepare your stories to fit.

Each of the other design portfolios is similar. The Designs for Business Communications portfolio contains several templates in traditional and contemporary formats for each of six different kinds of publications, including proposals, reports, handbooks, overhead transparencies, memos, and business plans. The Designs for Manuals portfolio contains 10 templates specifically designed for preparing books, manuals, and other long publications. Both accompanying manuals are filled with insights and advanced tips aimed at helping you produce quality publications with little or no prior experience. With all of Aldus's portfolios, however, you are expected to know how to use PageMaker and to have mastered the basics of working with text and graphics.

Creating Your Own Templates

Whenever you create a publication, you are creating a template. All it takes to convert your publication into a template is to save the publication as a template. To save your publication as a template, click `Save as template` in the Save As dialog box.

Before saving your publication as a template, replace existing graphics with shaded boxes and text with dummy text. (The Lorem Ipsum text file included with PageMaker is perfect for use as dummy text, and you see it used in many of the illustrations in this book.) What your placeholders look like doesn't matter, but you should strip them of any meaning so that you can concentrate on the form of your layout instead of on content. Publication content may change frequently, but your layout, as dictated by the template, should change very little. As you create your templates, be sure to make full use of your publication's master pages to handle repeating elements such as rules and nonprinting guides.

> ***Tip***
> A convenient template trick when using wraparound text in your publications is to customize the stand-off boundaries of your placeholders beforehand and make minor adjustments to the imported graphics later. If you click Replace Entire Graphic when you import your graphics, the graphics assume the same stand-off boundaries as the placeholders they replace.

Working with Templates

Templates are preformatted layouts that use placeholders to mark where imported text and graphics should go. You learned in earlier chapters how to import text and graphics to replace existing stories and illustrations. The principle is the same. Text placeholders, for example, are simply dummy stories. You replace them with your own stories by clicking `Replacing entire story` in the Place Document dialog box.

Text placeholders often have specific styles assigned. If you prefer to use an imported style, click the `Retain formatting` option in the Place Document dialog box. If styles imported from your word processor have names matching styles in the template style sheet, PageMaker uses the template styles. If the names don't match, PageMaker uses the imported styles. If you import your stories as text-only files, PageMaker applies the existing placeholder styles.

You generally don't want to import text to replace headlines, subheads, captions, and other short segments—that's inefficient. Simply select these elements with the Text Tool and type your replacement text. Whatever you type will take on the same styling as the original placeholders.

Graphic placeholders are shaded boxes that you replace with imported illustrations by clicking `Replacing entire graphic` in the Place Document dialog box. When you import graphics this way, they are scaled to fit within the existing placeholder boundaries. Adjust them as necessary to regain original proportions, crop unwanted areas, or configure for optimal printing.

Templates are easy to create and use. They greatly speed preparing your layouts and cut production time enormously.

> ***Note***
> Whenever you open a template, open a copy (PageMaker's default selection), not the original. That way the original remains intact for use another time. Click `Original` in the Open Publication dialog box only if you want to modify the template itself.

Avoiding Layout Mistakes

No rigid or unyielding rules govern layout design. The layout for one publication, for example, may vary enormously from the layout of another, depending on personal taste. New desktop publishers, however, often make several common mistakes. Avoiding these mistakes will help your publications look more professional.

1. Don't make your columns too wide or too narrow, or your text will be difficult to read. Keep line length to about 50 to 60 characters (10 to 12 words) for easiest reading.

2. Don't pick too large or too small a type size. Too large a type size can be overpowering and also may limit the amount of information you can include on your pages. Too small a type size makes reading your text difficult. Use 12-point type to start with and work from there.

3. Pick your fonts to match your message, and don't mix too many different typefaces or typestyles. Limit yourself to a maximum of three per publication. Avoid mixing sans serif faces. Don't use shadow, outline, and underline type styles. Strive for type consistency, or your publications may end up looking like ransom notes.

4. Don't use italic type for emphasis. Use bold instead. Italic doesn't stand out on a page unless the text also happens to be bold.

5. Don't crowd your margins. Give your pages breathing room. Without enough white space, you won't have a readable layout.

6. Don't use two spaces after periods and colons when using proportional type. Two spaces are required only when you are using a monospaced font like Courier. Also avoid straight apostrophes and quotation marks; use the curly kind instead. Never use double hyphens. Use the longer em-dashes (type a hyphen while holding down the Option key).

7. Don't juxtapose different kinds graphics on the same page (especially bit-mapped and EPS graphics) unless for special effect. Also be careful of mixing photographs of different composition. For example, don't place a close-up portrait photo right next to a full-length seated photo. Graphics should complement one another, not clash.

8. Don't design pages separately. Always work with facing pages to ensure proper balance. But don't be overly uniform or your publications will look sterile.

9. Avoid exact proportioning of elements on your pages. For example, if you place three illustrations on a page, don't size them all so that each occupies exactly a third of the page. Let one of the three illustrations dominate by being larger.

10. Don't print your publications without a final check. Proof your work accurately so that spelling, grammar, punctuation, and factual errors don't slip by. One oversight can spoil an otherwise perfect layout.

Chapter Summary

In this chapter you learned how to recognize and apply good layout and design techniques. You saw that achieving the right look is more than just a matter of style, and that it takes careful planning and coordination if you are to be successful.

You found that structure is crucial to the development of organized layouts, and that white space can be used effectively as a design tool. You learned that typefaces have personality and graphic elements have character, and you discovered that they can profoundly influence reader perception. You also learned that design elements can be used creatively to enhance your publications.

You saw how to use prepackaged templates to achieve design goals quickly. You also learned how to create your own templates so that you don't have to start over each time. Finally, you learned to avoid the mistakes beginning desktop publishers usually make when laying out publications. In the next chapter you learn how to apply these lessons to create winning newsletters.

Designing a Newsletter 11

Today more newsletters are desktop-published than any other kind of document. Their popularity as quickly digestible sources of specialized information cannot be contested.

Most newsletters are short, averaging no more than 4 to 16 pages long. Newsletters typically range from the traditional 8.5-by-11-inch all-text formats to 11-by-17-inch graphics-laden publications (like the bimonthly *Aldus Master Pages*—a newsletter sent free of charge to all registered PageMaker users).

Newsletters usually display a banner, masthead, and fixed column format. But that does not mean that newsletters all look the same. Even when two publishers use the same template as a starting point, the newsletters they produce usually look completely different from one another. Newsletter design is an intensely personal and creative undertaking.

In this chapter, you learn the basics of newsletter design. You learn how to assemble and lay out the key elements of a newsletter, including the banner, masthead, special editorial text, boilerplate, and graphic-design elements. You learn how to work with different column formats and achieve consistency in your newsletter layouts. You also discover how to use special visual effects to add interest to your newsletters and make them more appealing to readers.

Designing the Banner and Masthead

The words *banner* and *masthead* are frequently used interchangeably to mean the front-page title or nameplate of a newsletter. However, the masthead is actually the box that contains the name and address of the publisher, editors, writers, and other staff members. The masthead also may contain the issue or volume number, subscription rates, and other pertinent information. You can think of the masthead as the fine print of your publication.

Laying out a masthead is easy. You arrange one or more text blocks to present the required information in a hierarchical manner. You should box your masthead to set it apart from the main body of your newsletter. The masthead normally appears near the beginning of your newsletter, immediately following the cover page, but you can place the masthead near the end of your newsletter to de-emphasize it.

Banners are a different story. Whereas you should try to make your masthead invisible to the reader, you should make your banner highly visible, and preferably let the banner be the dominant element of your front page. The banner should be eye-catching to attract reader interest, yet succinct enough to tell the reader at a glance what your newsletter is all about. In that respect, you can think of your banner as a super headline.

You can include a logo as part of your banner, or you can make your banner highlight the theme of your newsletter. Because the banner introduces your newsletter, you should select an appropriate typeface when designing it. The type style you use should complement the publication style of your newsletter.

Tip

Design your banner in a graphics program like Adobe Illustrator or Aldus Freehand. These programs enable you to modify whatever type you use to achieve special design effects, and you can give your banner a distinctive flair. Save your banner as an EPS file and import the file into PageMaker. Importing the file in this way permits you to scale the banner to fit any page size without loss of resolution.

Choosing the Right Format

Formats range from single-column sheets to multiple-column pages. Most newsletters use between two and five columns. Again, the choice of format should be dictated in part by style and in part by content.

Using a Single-Column Format

Although a single-column format is rarely used, you might want to use this type of format to emulate typewritten copy for an informal look. When you use a single-column format this way, you should use Courier or some other monospaced font that accurately replicates typewritten characters. Be sure to increase your margins and leading. Increasing the margins makes the column lines a little shorter. That, along with increased leading, makes your copy easier to read. To achieve a true typewritten look, you also can break one of desktop publishing's cardinal rules and occasionally use underlined type for emphasis. Using underlined type makes your newsletter look like it was produced with a typewriter (see fig.11.1).

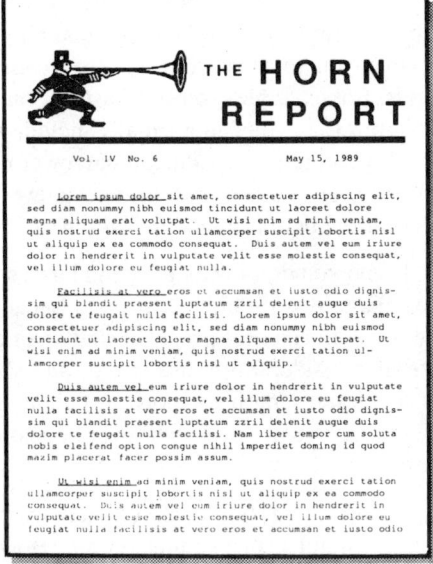

Fig. 11.1.

A single-column format designed to look like a typewritten page.

Using Multiple-Column Formats

Using multiple-column formats gives you greater flexibility when laying out your newsletters. Arranging text and graphics is much easier if you use three, four, or five columns per page instead of just one or two. You can introduce more story topics, and the shorter column line lengths make your copy easier to read. You also can more easily include different design elements to heighten visual contrast and stimulate reader interest.

The two-column format is the least cluttered and easiest to work with of the multiple-column formats. Although this format is not as flexible as three-, four-, and five-column formats, the two-column format yields a traditional look that is perfect for formal newsletters. The three-column format, on the other hand, is currently the most widely used format for newsletters. A three-column format is well suited for a formal or informal look, and three columns nicely accommodate almost any publication style.

A four-column format provides a more academic look than any of the other formats. This format is ideal for use where hard-hitting, specialized information must be conveyed in a concise manner.

The five-column format offers the most flexibility. This format combines many of the advantages of three- and four-column formats into one exceptionally versatile layout.

Three-, four-, and five-column formats take much planning to properly execute, but these formats enable you to vary your layouts readily to meet changing publishing requirements. For example, you successfully can include smaller-size graphics in narrow columns than you can normally include in the wider one- and two-column formats. (More columns also mean narrower columns.) Avoid fully justifying narrow columns, or you can end up with uneven and unsightly word spacing. Wider columns are a better choice for laying out fully justified text.

If your needs are simple and you don't want to spend large amounts of time doing complex layouts, use a simple two-column format. Because dual columns are fairly wide, you should use horizontal graphics that span a full column width. Vertical graphics take up considerably more space, and should be used only if they are at least half a column length or more in height. For three- and four-column layouts, vertical graphics are preferred over horizontal graphics because of the narrower columns.

If you use horizontal graphics, you should spread them over two or three column widths. Vertical graphics should span a single column. However, an exception to this rule applies when using portrait photographs, sometimes called mug shots. You may want to keep mug shots small so that the photos don't dominate your pages. Try fitting two mug shots in a single column width, or five mug shots in two column widths.

Headlines can be affected greatly by your choice of column formats. You can confine your headlines to lie within single-column boundaries, or you can have them span multiple columns (that encompass the same story). When placing headlines within multiple-column layouts, be sure to provide sufficient clearance between each headline and any accompanying graphics. Six to eight lines of text inserted between headlines and graphics should be enough. Place your headlines in the upper part of the page. Headlines near the bottom of the page lose their impact. Finally, avoid having all your headlines start at the same level on all your pages. Too much symmetry is boring.

> *Tip*
> When placing headlines on a multicolumn layout, keep the following guidelines in mind:
>
> 1. *Avoid tombstones*—two (or three) headlines placed side-by-side. For example, a two-column headline next to a three-column headline. Readers may mistakenly read the two different heads for one continuous and confusing headline.
>
> 2. *Extend a story's headline over the entire story.* If you have a three-column story, don't use a two-column headline.
>
> 3. *Make sure that any graphics or photos covered by the headline go with the story.* For example, if you have a three-column story about politics and a two-column photo of the recent snow storm, don't run a five-column headline above both. Readers expect the enclosed photograph to relate to the story.

When you use multiple columns, you don't have to flow stories down each and every column. A five-column format, for example, doesn't necessarily require five columns of text. Your choice of column layouts provides an underlying structure upon which you can later build. You can mix text and graphics on any column structure to achieve an interesting and informative layout for your newsletter. A three-column layout, for example, can be converted into an unequal two-column display, where one text block spans two underlying column widths, and another text block or graphic is confined to a single column width.

> *Tip*
> The most difficult task you face when preparing any newsletter is to make everything fit and still have your layouts look good. When planning story lengths and determining the numbers and sizes of headlines and graphics to include in your newsletters, allow for plenty of extra space. Leftover space can be manipulated easily to accommodate variable content from newsletter to newsletter, and plenty of space gives you room to make last-minute changes quickly or insert additional material.

Using Boilerplate

Boilerplate is text or graphics that remains unchanged from one issue of your newsletter to another. Boilerplate may be a declaration of editorial policy, an address line, an order form, your masthead, or a banner. Whatever your boilerplate is, you don't want to reproduce the material from scratch for each new issue. If you do, you are sure to introduce errors.

Using boilerplate adds consistency to your newsletter. If your boilerplate applies to only one publication, make it a part of that publication's template. If the boilerplate is to be used in several different publications, save it to your Scrapbook. After that, whenever you begin a new edition of your newsletter, use PageMaker's Place command to copy all your boilerplate from the Scrapbook onto the pasteboard. Then, drag individual items onto your pages as needed during layout.

> *Tip*
> Boilerplate text and graphics that you save as separate files for later placement into your newsletters can be difficult to find when you need them, especially if you have buried them deep within nested folders on your hard disk. A good way to identify them as boilerplate files is to prefix each file with BP (BP.EDITORIALPOLICY and BP.MASTHEAD, for example). The prefix groups all boilerplate files together in a folder when you sort that folder's contents by name. You also can more readily conduct searches using Apple's Find File desk accessory to search for files containing the BP letter designation.

Achieving a Consistent Look

The formality of your business newsletters is enhanced by the regular and consistent placement of text and graphics. Equal margins, centered headlines, justified text, and perfectly balanced layouts all contribute to a dignified look. To stress informality on your pages, do just the opposite—introduce variety into your layouts by using uneven margins, offset headlines, unjustified text, and asymmetrical arrangements. But, again, do so in a consistent fashion. Informality shouldn't breed disorder.

Your choice of typefaces, the placement of special editorial text, and the use of borders, rules, white space, and other design elements are all important factors to achieving consistency.

Using Type and Editorial Text

Limit type selection for your newsletters to traditional faces. Modern display faces that have an overly stylized or decorative look impede reading. Although these type faces may suit the theme of your newsletter because of their personality, they can put off your readers. Save ornate or unusual type for embellishment purposes only.

Never use more than three kinds of type, and preferably only two, in your newsletters, and choose contrasting faces for them. Avoid choosing similar type for headlines and body text, or your headlines do not stand out from the rest of the copy. Make sure that your headlines are large enough, and that your body text is a readable size. An 11- or 12-point type usually works well for body text.

For formality, fully justify your text; otherwise, keep your columns left justified (ragged right). Adjust word and letter spacing and modify hyphenation as necessary to achieve a uniform dispersion of type on the page. (Be careful not to let auto-hyphenation adversely affect headlines.) If you must use all caps, as for acronyms and abbreviations, set them in small caps so that they don't dominate surrounding text. Also make sure that your paragraph indents are all set the same.

You can add editorial refinements to your publication by including introductory text (sometimes called a *kicker*) above main headlines, or explanatory text (sometimes called *deck heads* or *subtitles*) just below main headlines (see fig. 11.2). These special headlines help draw the reader into a story by highlighting or summarizing what's to follow. When you use kickers or deck heads, set them in smaller italicized type to distinguish them from the accompanying headlines and stories and to emphasize their importance.

Fig. 11.2.

Kickers and deck heads can add interest to newsletter headlines.

Bylines are credit lines for stories. Usually, bylines immediately follow story headlines, but sometimes they close stories. For consistency, set bylines in the same type style as your headlines, but in a smaller point size.

Continuations, or *jump lines,* are short sentences at the bottom of columns that tell readers where to find the rest of a story elsewhere in your newsletter. Like kickers and deck heads, jump lines should normally be set in smaller, italicized type.

If your newsletters are long and include many stories, add a table of contents to the front page to help readers find the information of greatest interest to them. A table of contents also helps stimulate interest in your newsletter. Box or highlight the table of contents. Use a different type style to set the list apart from your stories. Double-spacing the entries in the table of contents also helps differentiate the table from the main text.

Using Borders and Rules

Use borders and rules sparingly to segregate or highlight important text and graphics. Use graphic elements to add emphasis where emphasis is needed, but avoid overuse. Otherwise, your newsletters may become cluttered. Most publications look better if you use only a few well-chosen design elements.

To help focus attention on your pages, add a hairline border around the entire margin. For improved readability, use vertical hairline rules to separate stories in adjoining columns. Use thicker rules to separate horizontal rows of text. To highlight graphics, set them apart with frames, but keep the line widths narrow. Hairline rules are often the best choice unless special emphasis is called for. For added consistency, if you use borders or rules on one page, use them the same way on all pages. Keep the spacing between them and any nearby text and graphics the same throughout your newsletter.

> *Tip*
> Boxing a graphic within a graphic to create an insert is an effective way to show how the bigger graphic (usually an enlarged section of the smaller graphic) relates to the smaller one (see fig. 11.3). Boxing also is a nice technique to use with photos. Use at least a one-point line width for the frame so that the smaller graphic is noticed.

Don't forget the importance of white space. Think of white space as the one element that can provide the most contrast for your pages. If you visit a museum, the most dominant element is the open space—on the floor and on the walls. All that open space emphasizes the importance of the few sculptures on the floor and the few paintings on the walls. If you completely filled the floor and the walls with works of art, how would you ever notice any one statue or painting?

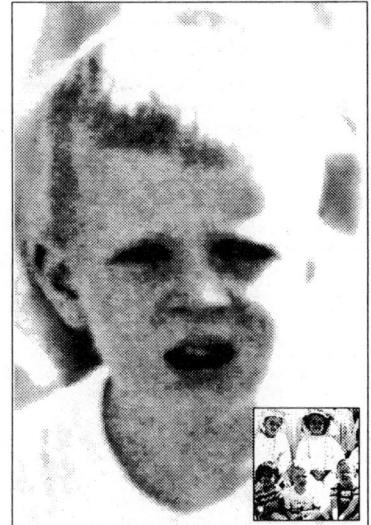

Fig. 11.3.
Graphic inserts help to raise the informational content of illustrations.

Using Special Visual Effects

Popular visual effects include screens, reverse type, and other custom elements. Like any other embellishment, special effects should be used cautiously. A little design emphasis goes a long way toward gathering and focusing reader attention—too much of a good thing can destroy the look of a publication.

Using Screens

Screens can be used effectively as backdrops to highlight text and graphics (see fig. 11.4). You can create a screen by drawing a shape with any of PageMaker's drawing tools, then filling the shape with a percentage shade from the Shades menu. In most instances, you should use the lightest shades. Darker shadings reproduce poorly on a 300 dpi laser printer and obscure whatever lies in front of them.

When you place a screen behind text or graphics, choose a line width of None from the Lines menu. Unless the screen also is to serve as a frame, rarely will you have to add a border to your screen by choosing a visible line width. Generally, framed screens have less appeal than unframed ones.

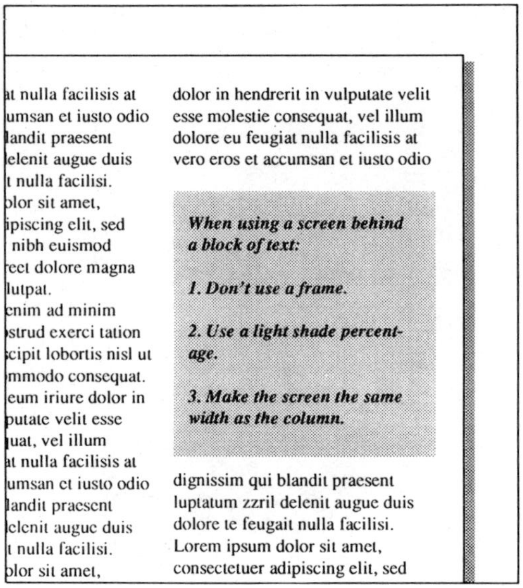

Fig. 11.4.

Placing a light screen behind a block of text helps emphasize its importance.

Using Reverse Type

In small doses, reverse type can be very effective. When employed as a design element, reverse type adds contrast to your pages and calls attention to items of significance. Reverse type also makes locating important information quick and easy. But in large doses, like the little shepherd boy who cried "wolf," reverse type can become ineffective quickly. If too many items compete for attention at the same time, none are noticed.

Because reverse type is difficult enough to read as is, take special care to ensure legibility. You should set all reverse type in bold using sans serif type in large point sizes. Making your text bold helps keep characters from closing in on one another, and setting text in large type helps the text stand out from the dark background. Keep reversed text short and to the point, and use upper- and lowercase lettering.

Using Photographs

Photographs have enormous reader appeal and are especially important for newsletters. Often a photograph can convey more information than many pages of text, and certainly more information than most hand-drawn graphics. You have already learned how to resize, reshape, crop, and enhance photographs in earlier chapters, but you should consider two additional things when you use them in newsletters.

Using Halftones

Most newsletters can benefit from the inclusion of scanned photographs. But sometimes scanned output is not good enough. To get crisp, unfuzzy photographs into your newsletters, your commercial printer must strip them in using traditional halftoning techniques.

TIFF files take such a long time to print on a Linotronic that having your commercial printer strip them in may be less costly, anyway. Even if you do go that route, scan your photographs first and place each photo in your newsletter to show where and how the photo should appear in the final printout. This placement serves as a guide to proper cropping and helps your printer match each photo with the correct caption.

Using Captions and Credits

Whenever you include photographs in your newsletters, you should provide descriptive captions. Captions help explain your photographs and also direct reader attention to the accompanying stories.

Make sure that you include a credit line in small type next to each photo. (Never use photographs without permission! To be safe, have a signed release from each recognizable person in a photograph, in addition to written authorization from the photographer.)

Chapter Summary

In this chapter, you gained useful insights into newsletter design. You learned how to combine the diverse elements of a newsletter into a unified whole and still keep your pages uncluttered and appealing to your readers. You discovered the important role that design consistency plays in preparing your layouts, and you learned how special visual effects can enhance the look of your pages.

In the next chapter you learn how to design a variety of other kinds of publications, ranging from brochures and fliers to catalogs and books.

Designing Other Publications

12

Now that you have mastered the basics of working with PageMaker and learned how to prepare quality layouts, you should consider the many ways you can put that knowledge to work. This chapter provides an introduction to the different publications you can produce using PageMaker. You learn approaches for designing and laying out short and long documents, and you are given some insights into preparing successful ads. When you complete this chapter, you will have a solid foundation on which you can build to produce your own publications.

Working with Short Documents

Short documents are often the most challenging to create and the most difficult to produce. Short documents are generally intended to induce prompt reader reaction. Whether you want the reader to reach an immediate management decision, respond appropriately to a sales pitch, or allocate time to attend an upcoming event, short documents must be tailored carefully if they are to get your message across.

Short documents come in many varieties, including documents that you come into contact with daily—overhead transparencies, brochures, fliers, mailers, greeting cards, certificates, and personal stationery.

Creating Overhead Transparencies

An entire industry has grown up around the concept of desktop presentations. You don't necessarily need specialized software, however, to prepare overhead transparencies. PageMaker does the job nicely.

Set up your page specifications for making overhead transparencies. Because most overhead projectors are configured to display a horizontal page, select Wide orientation in the Page Setup dialog box and choose a standard letter-size page.

Lay out any repeating elements, such as borders or company logos, on master pages.

Create each overhead transparency on a separate publication page in the same order as you plan to present them.

Print your publication normally, but, instead of paper, use clear acetate transparencies made especially for use in copiers or laser printers (to withstand the internal heat of your printer without melting).

Note
PageMaker's rounded-corner rectangles make excellent borders that match the shape of the cardboard holders many companies use to mount overhead transparencies. Figure 12.1 shows a sample overhead transparency.

Fig. 12.1.

A mounted overhead transparency created entirely in PageMaker.

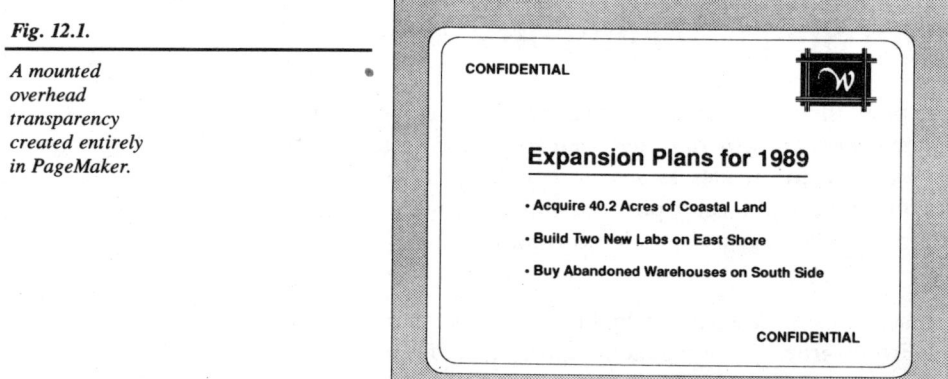

> ***Tip***
> You easily can shuffle the order of pages you have already created without having to do complex cutting and pasting.
>
> To swap the contents of two pages, for example, select everything on the first page and slide the elements onto the pasteboard (hold down the Shift key to keep them exactly on a horizontal axis). Do the same thing for the second page, but drag the elements off the page onto the opposite side of the pasteboard. Next, drag the first set of elements onto the second page and align them within the page margins (again, hold down the Shift key to keep them from shifting vertically). Finally, drag the second set of elements onto the first page.

Creating overhead transparencies in PageMaker enables you to import high-resolution EPS and TIFF files, apply various Image Control settings for added effect, do precision kerning for tighter headlines, and even generate accompanying handouts automatically (by printing pages of Thumbnails). If you do many presentations, convert your overhead transparencies into templates for later use.

> ***Tip***
> You can create multiple overlays for presentations by assigning colors to different elements on your pages. When you print your publication, choose `Spot Color Overlays` in the Print dialog box, and PageMaker prints a separate transparency for each assigned color. Stack the overlays in the correct order, making sure that they are properly aligned, then tape the edges of the sheets together. By flipping them over one at a time during your presentation, you can show a visual progression of information.

Creating Brochures and Price Lists

Brochures and price lists are short pamphlets, generally promotional in nature. These pamphlets usually are designed to sell or promote some item or service. They come in many different formats, but most often are seen as 8.5-by-11-inch or smaller booklets. To be effective, the layouts for these publications should be spacious and uncluttered.

When designing brochures and price lists, focus first on content; many a company has printed and distributed a sales brochure only to discover later that the company address and phone number were inadvertently omitted. Make up a detailed checklist of what should be in your brochure, then proof your publication carefully before printing. Double-check all numbers in all price lists. Transposing two numbers is easy to do and could prove costly.

Your brochure should stress your company's identity. Prominently display your company logo near the front of the brochure and follow the logo immediately by telling your readers what your company has to offer. Organize products or services into categories, but avoid a jumbled look of boxes and rules. Save boxes and rules for highlighting important information such as special discounts or free pickup and delivery announcements. For tabular material, such as price lists, use the same indents and spacing as much as possible throughout. Clear, logical, and consistent organization of material is crucial if you want to convey information successfully to your readers.

Your brochure should have an eye-catching front cover that captures reader interest. Don't list specific products, services, or prices on the front cover. Your goal should be to stimulate curiosity, not provide details. If you want to urge quick response to special offers, list them on the back cover as well as inside the brochure. But keep price lists entirely between the covers.

Be as creative as you like when designing brochures, but make every attempt to focus reader attention on your company. A memorable company identity helps to sell future goods and services. Use color where practical for additional emphasis and to help distinguish product categories. For best results, print brochures on a Linotronic, strip in photos where needed, and use high-quality paper for printing.

Creating Handbills, Fliers, and Mailers

Handbills and fliers are usually single-sheet documents printed on one or both sides. When used as mailers, these documents can be laid out and folded in various ways to help guide the reader through the information. Page formats for mailers can be flexible in design, and simple black-and-white or two-color reproduction at 300 dpi is usually adequate.

Handbills, fliers, and mailers are promotional vehicles that usually have a short life span; they often get thrown away as soon as they are looked at. To attract and hold the attention of readers, promotional documents should have a strong graphic element (see fig. 12.2). Headlines are important, but they, too, can be graphic; compose headlines in decorative or display type—the more decorative, the better. With short promotional pieces, glitz can be everything.

The first determination you have to make when composing handbills and fliers is whether the documents also will be used as mailers. Whenever you design a mailer, you must know ahead of time what kind of fold you plan to use and how

Fig. 12.2.

A handbill for a children's benefit performance.

heavy your paper is. The wrong choices can adversely affect your layouts and end up costing you extra postage. (Check with your post office to learn the current size and weight constraints for mailings.)

When creating a folded mailer of any kind, do a test fold and measure the results before creating your layout. Because folding documents subtracts usable space, generally about an 1/8th of an inch for every fold, you may have to offset your columns of text and artwork to compensate. A three-panel letter fold, for example, produces two equal panels and one unequal panel (to accommodate the inside fold).

The most popular mailer is a standard 8.5-by-11-inch, three-panel letter fold. One side of a three-fold mailer is divided into three separate vertical panels: the front cover, the back cover and the inside first fold. The second side typically presents a panoramic display when the mailer is fully opened. This side becomes your interior spread and is where your main message goes.

To create this type of mailer, perform the following steps:

1. Open a new PageMaker publication with two facing pages.
2. Set the side and top margins to 2.5 picas.

3. Set the bottom margin to three picas for a more balanced, eye-pleasing appearance.

4. Use a wide page orientation unless you plan to produce a mailer composed of all horizontal panels. In that case, set the page orientation to tall and work with rows instead of columns.

5. Assign three columns to your pages and adjust the spacing of the column guides to compensate for the folds so that you can properly center individual panel displays (a column spacing of 3 picas, or 0.5 inches works well in most cases).

6. Design the front cover. On the cover, you try to persuade the reader to open your mailer and discover what's inside. Keep the front cover simple. Try to elicit reader interest by using a strong visual element such as a headline or graphic.

7. Lay out the inside first fold. This panel serves as your introduction. Use this area to expand on the theme of the front cover. Because the reader sees the first third of your interior spread at the same time, try not to have the two clash.

8. Lay out your interior spread. Almost any arrangement of text and graphics is permissible, but try to keep your message concise and hard-hitting. Avoid including too much material, and make your text large enough to be easily read. For the best results, divide your message to fit within adjoining panels so that text flows across the page from left to right. Confine columns to individual panels, keep paragraphs short, and break up long text with subheads. Use illustrations and photos where appropriate to heighten reader interest and to provide contrast.

Tip

Center short hairline rules between columns in the top and bottom margins of your inside spread. Draw the rules just long enough so that the lines print on a laser printer without being clipped off. Use these rules as guides to ensure proper folding after your mailers are printed. Because the rules lie exactly on the folds, the rules are not noticed when the mailer is opened.

---

9. Finally, lay out your back panel. On the back, place your company name and address, and any pertinent ordering information. If your piece is a self-mailer, use this panel for the mailing and return addresses, and move company data and ordering information to your interior spread.

Creating Greeting Cards

Everyone enjoys getting greeting cards, and, with PageMaker, you easily can create your own. If you start with an 8.5-by-11-inch sheet, you can use several different folds to produce an attractive card. A standard "french" or double-fold format is a good choice because of its familiar look and because the format accommodates inserts nicely. This format also enables you to print all your panels on one side of the paper. To create a greeting card using a double-fold, perform the following steps:

1. Set up your page using two columns and split the page horizontally with a pair of ruler guides. Column spacing and the distance between horizontal ruler guides should be roughly 3 picas to accommodate folds.

2. Split each resulting quarter-panel horizontally and vertically with ruler guides to get four sets of cross hairs. Use these intersections to center text and illustrations. You also might consider initially setting page margins to zero; otherwise, they can prove unnecessarily distracting. If you later find that you are having difficulty centering objects, draw a frame in each panel as an additional guide. After you position your text and graphics, you can delete these extra boxes.

3. Center your text and graphics in each panel. Note that everything in the upper two panels should be placed upside down as displayed on-screen (these panels become right side up when you fold your card into fourths). Because PageMaker cannot rotate text or graphics, you must make the inversions within your graphics program before saving and importing the images. See figure 12.3 for a sample greeting card layout.

4. The right paper can make or break your card. Print greeting cards on 70-pound stock for best results. Paper heavier than 70-pound weight doesn't fold well, and paper lighter than that is too flimsy to stand upright after being folded.

Creating Certificates

Most people appreciate occasional well-deserved recognition. Easy-to-create certificates and awards are a popular way of giving recognition to others. To prepare a certificate in PageMaker, execute the following steps:

1. Choose a tall or wide page orientation for the kind of certificate to be produced, and set all page margins to 3 picas (0.5 inch).

2. Design a frame using PageMaker's drawing tools or import one from a separate drawing program. Size the frame so that the outer border lies just within the page margins.

Fig. 12.3.

A double-fold Christmas greeting card.

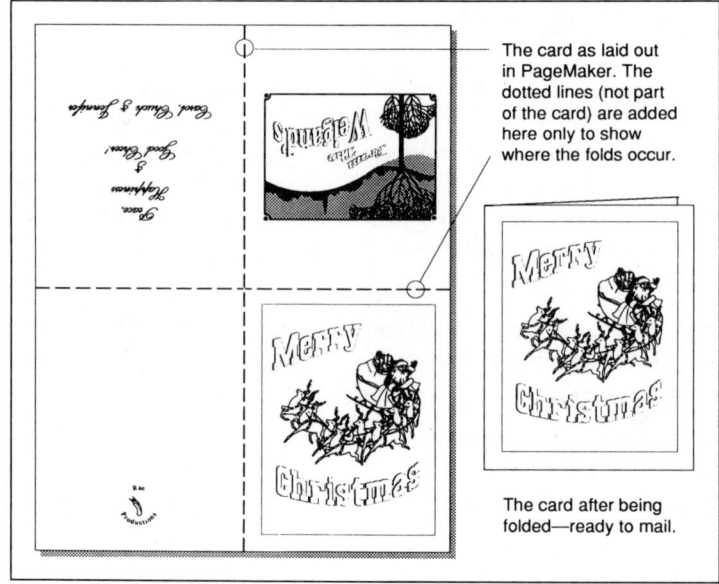

3. Type and center your text on the page. Use an appropriate mix of font types, sizes, and styles to suit the message. Be sure to include signature and date lines near the bottom of the certificate.

4. Import any graphics, including logos and seals, and place them in their proper locations on the page. To further dress up your certificate, enlarge a bit-mapped graphic, send it behind the text, and lighten the graphic to a faint shade of gray using PageMaker's image controls. This process creates an interesting visual backdrop that is appealing and professional-looking.

5. Print your certificates on a minimum 70-pound paper stock. If you routinely prepare many certificates or awards, seek out companies that supply special certificate paper. Certificate paper comes in a variety of styles preprinted with frames.

Creating Stationery and Business Cards

PageMaker is an excellent design tool for creating personalized stationery. For example, you easily can include your logo on letterhead stationery or on a business card, and you can preformat a set of templates to handle different kinds of correspondence. After you produce a design you like, you can have your stationery, including matching envelopes and business cards, printed in color on the paper of your choice by a commercial printer.

Your greatest challenge when designing letterheads, envelopes, and business cards is to produce a design that works equally well on all three document sizes. Start by identically arranging each element (return address, photo, logo, or other graphic embellishments) on all three pieces. Keep in mind that your design shouldn't intrude into the area of the envelope reserved for postage or the mailing address. You also need to allow at least a 0.25-inch margin on all sides of your design for text and graphics to remain within the imaging area of your laser printer. Vary the placement of elements until you arrive at a satisfactory arrangement that not only looks good, but also exhibits design consistency.

For stationery, stick with standard 8.5-by-11-inch paper and number 10 envelopes. Nonstandard sizes generally cost more and can be more difficult to produce. Business cards should always be 3.5-by-2 inches (21 by 12 picas). Lay the cards out five up and two across to a page to save printing costs; this arrangement yields 500 business cards for every 50 sheets you print. Print business cards on a minimum 100-pound paper stock.

To create a set of business cards in PageMaker:

1. Configure a single, tall-oriented, letter-size page with 0.75-inch side margins and 0.5-inch top and bottom margins.

2. Divide the page vertically into two halves using a ruler guide, then reset your ruler zero point to where the page margins intersect at the upper left corner.

3. Drag a horizontal ruler guide to each 2-inch ruler mark to divide the page horizontally into five sections. This process produces 10 boxes made up entirely of nonprinting guides into which you can place repeating text and graphics.

4. Draw short hairline rules at all margin and ruler-guide intersections and at the four page-margin corners to facilitate cutting your business cards after printing. Make these rules no longer than 1 pica long.

5. Drag additional ruler guides onto your page to create 1-pica margins inside each box. You can use slightly smaller margins if you like, but a minimum 1-pica margin looks best on a business card. With the Snap To Guides menu command turned on, use PageMaker's square-corner rectangle tool to draw a dashed rectangle along the inner margins of each card and a solid rectangle along the outer margins. These rectangles function as visual aids as you create your business card layout. The basic format is complete. Save the layout as a template for future use.

6. Next, produce your final design by typing the text, placing any logos or graphics, and adding any other design embellishments. Lay out only one business card in the box in the upper left corner of the page (see fig. 12.4).

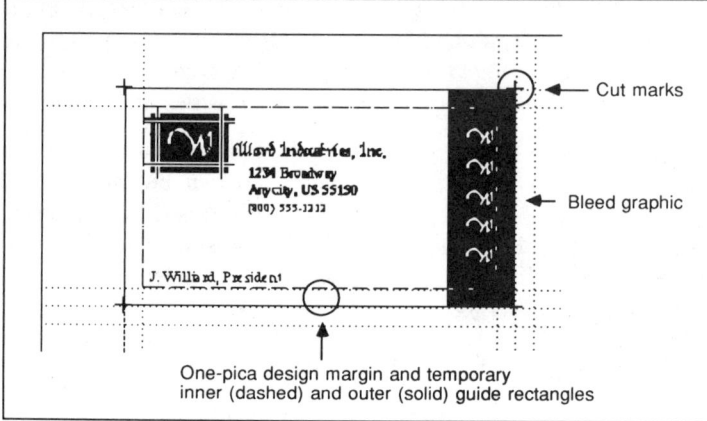

Fig. 12.4.

A business-card template showing the layout of the first card.

7. When you are satisfied with the layout, select all the elements of your card, including its margin rectangles, and copy them to the Clipboard. Repeatedly paste the contents of the Clipboard back onto your page, each time dragging them into a different box. The rectangles snap to the margin guides to center the elements within the box.

8. When your page is full, select and delete all the margin rectangles. Print your cards and cut them using the hairline rules as cutting guides. Your business cards will look as good as the finished sample in figure 12.5.

Fig. 12.5.

The final printed business card.

Managing Large Publications

Some large publications are easier to produce than others. For example, after an initial layout is completed for a long tract composed mainly of text, little effort is needed to produce the final document. Most large publications, however, require extensive planning and careful management to avoid production problems. Some types of large publications you may be called upon to produce include pamphlets, booklets, reports, proposals, catalogs, and directories.

Pamphlets and booklets are much like brochures, but usually lack the sales pitch and promotional graphics. The graphics included are used mainly to illustrate the text. Pamphlets can be thought of as short books and require much the same approach as books when preparing layouts.

Reports and proposals, on the other hand, can be short or long and can exhibit a variety of formats. Although some government reports consume thousands of pages, academic, business, and technical reports are usually more modest. These reports may range from a few dozen to several hundred pages. These publications frequently rely on diagrams and photos to supplement the text and often include detailed tables, charts, and graphs. Many include an executive summary or abstract to provide an overview of the contents. Proposals are similar in nature to reports, but their formats are more specifically aimed at winning support, usually financial, for some undertaking.

Catalogs require a thorough mix of text and graphics and are usually the most difficult of the large publications to produce, unless you standardize your layouts to provide regular placement of individual page elements. If you achieve an orderly and consistent arrangement of text and graphics, you can create new catalogs and update old ones easily from templates. Although catalogs are considered periodicals, they sometimes can be quite large and difficult to manage.

Directories range from everyday telephone books and registers to specialized listings of companies and products. The variety of subject matter is endless, but the format is often similar—two columns with stylized type to differentiate one entry or listing from another. After you establish a satisfactory layout for your directory, flowing the text is easy. Your main concern becomes ensuring consistent formatting for the proper display of information.

Layouts for large publications differ significantly depending on content. For example, technical books require a method of presentation quite different from that of novels. Self-help training manuals must be formatted differently than law books, and encyclopedias must be formatted differently from dictionaries (even though both may be organized alphabetically). Your first consideration whenever you take on a large publication should be to select a style of presentation appropriate to the subject matter.

Before you get started, identify the common elements in your layout for inclusion on your master pages. Then ask questions like the following to help decide on an appropriate format: If you have chapters, how will you define your chapter heads? Does your publication require multiple levels of headlines, and must the headlines be individually numbered, as in many textbooks and manuals? Do you want to use running heads throughout your publication? How are you going to handle the placement of any accompanying graphics?

Publications composed entirely of text, like novels, are easier to lay out than publications containing many illustrations. However, even when your page layout requirements appear simple and straightforward, be sure to pay close attention to the details of type selection, leading, paragraph spacing, and other typographical concerns. Only in that way can you obtain consistently good results.

Large publications often require forewords, introductions, acknowledgment pages, copyright pages, tables of contents, and indexes. You also may have to deal with footnotes, glossaries, and appendixes, all of which may require different formatting. In every case you need to estimate page counts accurately, determine page sizes, and select binding methods before beginning your layouts.

To achieve consistency, create and assign styles to different sections of your documents. When you pour the text, you find that you have fewer changes to make because of formatting errors.

After you pour your text, check to see that the tops and bottoms of columns on the same and adjoining pages are properly aligned. Make sure that you don't leave dangling pieces of text at the beginnings or ends of columns. Also make sure that spaces between paragraphs don't wind up sitting alone at the tops of columns.

If you properly set up your master pages to handle repeating elements, your final proofing goes more smoothly. Remember that you can always turn off master page elements on any one page to customize your layout individually.

Preparing large publications often presents special challenges simply because of complexity and sheer magnitude. Carefully plan your large-publication projects and break them into groups of tasks for easy management. Prepare comprehensive checklists to cover all possible contingencies and use them to ensure that nothing is overlooked.

Designing Successful Ads

PageMaker is an ideal tool for preparing ads because of its inherent flexibility. You can work like a graphic designer, moving items here and there on the page until you find a pleasing arrangement, or you can work like a copy editor, composing and editing text until the words fairly leap off the page.

Ads represent a special category of short documents. In advertising work, almost every kind of layout design has been tried, discarded, and tried again. Highly successful ads have ranged from tiny images centered in a sea of white space with nothing else on the page, to pages crammed full of text made to look like regular articles and news items. However, many ads using these same techniques have proven disastrous. In short, no one formula works every time. You can take certain steps, however, that improve your chances for success.

Your biggest constraint when designing ads is space. You generally are limited to a single page, or often to a small portion of a page.

Your graphics must be appropriate to your message, and your message must be concise. Tight copy is essential. You have to convey information compactly in a way the reader understands immediately, and you have to sell features and benefits while urging the reader to action. The whole purpose behind ads is getting readers to commit themselves—whether that commitment is to buy a product, join a cause, or vote a particular way. If your ad elicits the desired response, then, and only then, can you deem the ad successful.

In earlier chapters, you learned the basics of good layout design for newsletters and other publications. Those lessons apply equally to creating ads. The following are additional things to keep in mind when designing and laying out your ads:

1. Isolate the most important selling point and make it into a headline. Your headlines should offer something of value to your readers. Follow strongly worded headlines with supporting leads that help pull the reader further into the copy that follows.

2. Have each line of a multiple-line headline make sense. Be careful about the words you use and how you position them. Don't, for example, write a two-line headline with the phrase "Enjoy Retirement in" on the first line, leaving "Sunny Arizona" dangling on the second. Instead, let "Enjoy Retirement" stand alone on the first line as a complete thought that can be immediately assimilated by the reader, and then reinforce that upbeat introduction with "in Sunny Arizona" on the second line to complete your message. Appending the word "in" to the first line changes a positive phrase into a confusing question mark in the reader's mind.

3. If your copy calls for subheads, make them tell a complete story. Structure the subheads to get your message across, even if none of the accompanying text is read. Many readers scan headlines and subheads. Only if they are sufficiently intrigued do they read the ad copy.

4. In your ad copy, support any claims you make in your headlines. Don't disappoint your readers by using headlines in "bait-and-switch" fashion. Deliver on what you say by expanding on the headline. Prove your

claims before readers can mount any arguments. For example, don't write a headline that announces "End Baldness with Nobald," and go on to tell how shiny and thick-looking your hair is when you use Nobald without addressing the issue of baldness. Explain convincingly how and why Nobald ends baldness.

5. If you cannot squeeze everything of importance into your ad, include a coupon for a free brochure. Use the brochure to list additional details and close the sale. Focus your limited ad space to urge the reader to clip and mail in the coupon.

6. Don't forget to double-check your ads before printing. Many an ad has failed because the price of the product or the phone number wasn't included.

Chapter Summary

In this chapter, you discovered that you can produce a wide assortment of publications with PageMaker. You explored several different approaches for designing and laying out short and long documents. The types of short documents you examined include overhead transparencies, brochures, mailers, greeting cards, certificates, personal stationery, and business cards. Longer documents include pamphlets, books, reports, proposals, catalogs, and directories. You also learned how to compose winning ads. In the appendixes, you find some additional hints and tips that may prove useful to you in your work.

Your training in how to use PageMaker on the Macintosh is complete. You now possess all the basic skills necessary to start producing publications on your own. You should find desktop publishing a challenging and rewarding activity and PageMaker a most able assistant.

Dealing with a Commercial Printer

Use the following checklist as a guide when dealing with commercial printers, quick printers, and print-service bureaus.

1. Before deciding on a commercial printer, do some comparison shopping. Prices and quality vary enormously in the printing industry. Examine representative samples of each print shop's work before committing your project to a shop. Try to find a commercial printer knowledgeable about Macintosh desktop publishing and the PageMaker program.

2. Discuss your project in detail with each printer to find out the best and most cost-effective way to do the job. Ask specifically about different grades of paper. Paper is often your biggest expense, and the quality and cut of paper used can greatly influence the final cost of your job.

3. Ask for advice. Most commercial printers are happy to help, but reluctant to volunteer suggestions and information unless directly asked. Try getting input even before you begin your project—the ideas and tips you get may save you considerable time and money.

4. Specify the exact work to be done and obtain written, signed bids from each of the commercial printers whose services you're considering. You may find that costs at one location vary considerably from the costs at another location. If yours is a repeat-type job, such as a newsletter printed monthly, obtain new bids periodically to ensure that you still are getting a fair deal. Most printers gladly provide estimates with the understanding that the estimates may be exceeded by as much as 10 percent. If your job is a big one, or if you're on a stringent budget, try to arrange for a written contract instead. Don't forget to ask about discounts.

5. Agree beforehand on a firm schedule and identify drop-dead dates (absolute deadlines). Expect to pay premium surcharges for rush jobs, but realize that you also have to pay extra for any last-minute changes you make. Rush jobs and last-minute changes can double your estimated bill.

6. When you deliver your job to a commercial printer, include a cover sheet or on-disk Read Me file to eliminate guesswork and avoid potential problems. List the following information:

    - ❏ Your name, company name, address, phone number, purchase order or job number, and any other required billing information. Indicate when, where, and how the job is to be delivered.

    - ❏ The names of your publication files and of any accompanying documents (such as original TIFF scans). Indicate the disks on which the files are stored and specify which pages you want printed.

    - ❏ The names and type styles of all fonts used in your publications. If your commercial printer doesn't have the required fonts, you must supply the screen and printer versions of the fonts. Be careful not to violate licensing agreements when doing so. In such cases, convert your publications to pure PostScript files with the fonts embedded so that they are not accessible. If you convert your files to PostScript files, check beforehand to verify the resident fonts for the output device you are using to avoid potential printing conflicts.

    - ❏ The programs used to create the documents and the graphics contained by the documents. Be sure to include program version numbers. Also include the version numbers of the System and Finder used. To avoid printing anomalies, use the same version of the System and Finder used by your commercial printer, or be prepared to supply your System and Finder on-disk with your publication files.

    - ❏ How you want your documents printed. If in color, specify the pages and colors.

    - ❏ Any special instructions.

7. If your job is to be printed on a Linotronic ImageSetter, or if you include photos to be stripped in separately, supply a sample laser printout of the publication to serve as a guide to the operator (supply a rough mockup if you don't have a laser printer available).

8. Always keep a backup copy of all files and documentation in case the originals are lost or damaged.

9. Proof your work carefully before delivering it to the printer. Arrange to see photocopies of the mechanicals or the actual bluelines before printing takes place. Proof these copies just as carefully. Finally, check the completed job thoroughly before accepting it. After you sign for a job, it's yours. The printer is relieved of all responsibility, and if an error is discovered later, you have to pay extra to have the error corrected.

Installing PageMaker and Configuring Your System

PageMaker 3.01 requires a minimum 1M of memory to operate. Because the program is larger than 800K in size, PageMaker 3.01 doesn't fit on a single 800K floppy disk. The program comes in two parts with a built-in installer that joins the parts on your hard disk. The installation procedure is simple: all you do is double-click the PageMaker Install icon. PageMaker prompts you to insert additional disks as necessary until the installation is complete. Following are some key points to note:

1. You must run the installer from the floppy disks. You cannot copy the two parts of the PageMaker program to your hard disk and run the installation program there. To be safe, however, do not use the original disks. Make a backup copy of each disk and keep the originals in a safe place. Complete the installation using the backups. Make sure that your backups are exact copies of the originals. For the installation to work, even the names of the backup disks must be same as the original disks.

2. Before you begin, read the Read Me file included on your latest version disk. The Read Me file contains important information that may have been omitted from the manuals. Print a copy of the Read Me file for reference.

3. If you are updating PageMaker on your system, from Version 3.0 to Version 3.01, for example, even though you use a new installer disk, you may need the older version's program disk during the installation procedure (use your backup copy). Keep the disk handy.

4. If you receive error messages during the installation indicating that PageMaker is having problems with the installation and the cause of the problem is not immediately apparent, you may have a corrupted or outdated System file, or you may have conflicting INITs loaded into memory. Start over again after placing a fresh, current System onto your hard disk (follow the instructions in the manual that came with your Macintosh). Also drag all INITs out of your System folder, including any virus-protection INITs (be sure to check your floppies first using an anti-viral program). The installation should go smoothly. Drag the INITs back into your System folder when you're done.

Note

You must install PageMaker while operating in the Finder. The installer does not run under MultiFinder.

Warning

Make sure that you have only one System folder, System file, and Finder on your hard disk. Otherwise, you may encounter major problems, including system crashes, in the installation and during everyday operations.

---

5. Although you have some control over what is loaded onto your hard disk during installation, PageMaker normally loads all APD files, Apple's Teach Text application, and other utilities on the PageMaker disks. The total installation requires a little more than 3M of available hard disk space. After the installation is complete, remove any files you are sure that you don't need to free up extra room on your hard disk.

6. During the installation, a text file named PM CHRON.TXT is created and stored on your hard disk. This file can be read using any word processor, including PageMaker. The text file provides a history of the installation, documenting the files installed and what problems, if any, were encountered.

Installing Guidance

You can install the Guidance desk accessory directly into PageMaker so that Guidance is available whenever PageMaker is open. By installing Guidance into PageMaker, Guidance does not displace a slot under the Apple menu. To install Guidance into PageMaker, do the following:

1. Double-click the Guidance desk accessory, which opens Apple's Font/DA Mover and displays the Guidance's file name in the left window.

2. Hold down the Option key and click the `Open` button located under the right Font/DA Mover window. All kinds of files, including applications, are listed in the Open dialog box, not just desk accessories.

3. Locate `PageMaker` in the Open dialog box and double-click the file name. Font/DA Mover opens PageMaker in the right Font/DA Mover window, but the window remains empty, showing that no desk accessories are installed in the program.

4. Click `Guidance` in the left window of the Open dialog box, then click the `Copy` button. Font/DA Mover installs Guidance directly into PageMaker (see fig. B.1).

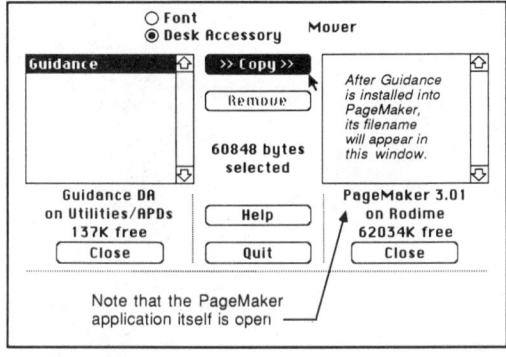

Fig. B.1.

Using Font/DA Mover to install the Guidance desk accessory directly into PageMaker.

5. Click `Quit` to exit Font/DA Mover. When you next open PageMaker, Guidance is available under the Apple menu for immediate use. Guidance does not appear under the Apple menu unless PageMaker is open.

Changing MultiFinder's Memory Allocation

As MultiFinder opens new programs, it partitions memory for the programs depending on what each program tells MultiFinder it needs. Occasionally, however, the allocations are not large enough to handle such memory-intensive tasks as working on long or complex documents. One indication of a PageMaker memory allocation that is not large enough is that PageMaker may suddenly and unexpectedly quit. If this happens more than once, try increasing the amount of memory that MultiFinder allocates for PageMaker.

To increase the amount of memory available to PageMaker, quit to the Finder desktop while still operating under MultiFinder. Click the PageMaker icon to select it, and choose Get Info from the File menu. In the Get Info window, change the number in the Application Memory Size box to reflect the desired memory increase (see fig. B.2). Assigning 1024K is large enough for almost any task. Be careful not to make the new number smaller than the value in the Suggested Memory Size box or your program cannot operate properly. Close the Get Info window to save your changes. When you reopen PageMaker, MultiFinder reserves the additional memory. To return to PageMaker's default memory setting, leave the Application Memory Size box empty.

Fig. B.2.

PageMaker's Get Info window.

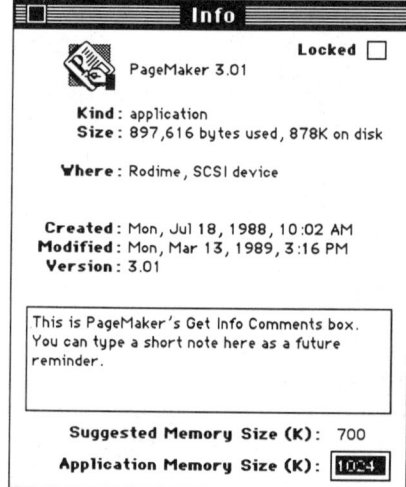

Additional Tips and Techniques

In this section, you find an assortment of important tips and techniques that didn't find a home in earlier chapters. Because these items are not arranged in any order, feel free to browse. You may find something that helps to increase your productivity when using PageMaker.

Recovering from a Crash

If you have an emergency and are unable to save current changes, you can use PageMaker's mini-save feature to recover your data. Use the following steps to effect a recovery:

1. Reboot your Macintosh and reopen PageMaker.

2. Choose Open from the File menu and look for the name of your file.

3. Select and open the file. PageMaker substitutes the last mini-saved version. When that document is open, you can revert to the last version you saved previously with the Save or Save As commands by choosing Revert from the File menu.

4. If you hadn't saved your document for the first time, look for a file named PMF000, and open that file as an original publication. This file, PageMaker's mini-saved version, most likely can be found in your System folder, but you may have to look in your PageMaker folder or the folder you were working in when the system crashed. If you have

accumulated several of these mini-saved files, the file you want to open is the one with the largest PMFXXX, where XXX represents a sequential three-digit number.

Converting PageMaker Pages into EPS Files

You can convert any PageMaker page into an EPS file for placement as an illustration in another publication, or even within the same publication. You also can open a PageMaker page saved as an EPS file into any program that accepts EPS documents for additional changes.

The trick is to set up PageMaker's Print dialog box to print just one page. Type the same page number in the `Page Range From` and `To` boxes. Then, hold down the Option key when you click the OK button to bring up PageMaker's PostScript Print Options dialog box. Click `Print PostScript to Disk` and the accompanying EPS button. Name your file, designate a storage location, and click OK. PageMaker prints your page to disk as an EPS file that can later be imported into PageMaker and manipulated like any other EPS graphic. This technique was used to prepare many of the illustrations in this book.

You also can create kerned headlines within PageMaker that you can save as EPS graphics for later resizing. When you reimport a headline saved as an EPS file, crop the page graphic to the edges of the headline and resize the image by dragging the reshaping handles with the pointer tool. Hold down the Shift key as you resize if you want to keep the same proportions.

Using Your Word Processor To Update Stories

If, after making extensive editing changes to a story in PageMaker, you decide you want to spell-check your work, or if you find that you need to execute one or more text searches to globally change or replace an item, export your story back into your word processor. Do your spell-checking and conduct your searches there. After making your revisions, reimport the story into PageMaker. Select `Replace Entire Story` in the Place Document dialog box to effect the update.

Improving Laser-Printed Output

You can get blacker blacks for crisper camera-ready copy by applying a non-glossy spray fixative to your pages. Use the same kind of spray artists use for fixing charcoal, pastel, and pencil artwork. You can find cans of fixative spray in any art supply store. Lightly spray your pages to bring out highlights, but don't overspray or your toner will spread.

Placing Stubborn TIFF Files

You may encounter a TIFF graphic that PageMaker does not accept (currently more than three dozen different TIFF formats exist, several of which are proprietary to specific scanners). To get around this problem, open the recalcitrant file into a compatible graphics program like Zedcor's DeskPaint, LetraSet's ImageStudio, or Silicon Beach Software's Digital Darkroom. Resave the file from there as a new TIFF file to regenerate the graphic in a revised TIFF format that PageMaker recognizes.

Drawing Quick White Lines

You can avoid the multistep process of drawing individual lines, selecting the lines, moving them into position over a black background, and choosing Reverse Line from the Lines menu. Draw lines in place to start with by using PageMaker's double- or triple-line styles. Because the spaces between the lines are opaque, they show up as solid white lines against the black background.

Adding Signatures to Documents

For that special personal touch, try including handwritten signatures in your documents. If you have a scanner, including signatures is easy. Sign your name on a sheet of paper as you normally would, but make your signature a little larger than usual for a cleaner scan. Then, scan your signature as line art at a medium resolution of 150 or 200 dpi. Save your scan as a TIFF file. When you place your signature into PageMaker, proportionally resize it down to increase the printing resolution. You can assign your signature any color, such as blue, if you print your documents as color separations.

Alternately, you can import your scan into a high-resolution drawing program like Adobe Illustrator or FreeHand. Trace the outline of your signature, fill the outline with black, and save the image as an EPS file. Your EPS signature retains its resolution when scaled to any size in PageMaker.

Reflowing Text Blocks from the Top

To reflow a text block that you have just placed, close up the windowshades, then click the top windowshade handle. You get the text placement icon again, ready to reflow the text. This trick can be used when you want to adjust a column's width and reflow the text from the original column to fit the new dimensions. The trick also works with the first text block in a story no matter when the block was placed—click the top, empty windowshade handle after closing up the text block to recover the text-placement icon.

Adding Color with Kroy

An easy way to add dazzling color to your PageMaker documents is to use a Kroy Kolor Processor. This remarkable machine applies a combination of heat and pressure to bond color ink from foil transfer sheets into the black toner on your laser-printed or photo-copied pages. The transfer sheets come in a wide variety of colors, including gold and silver metallics, that are perfect for dressing up invitations, certificates, awards, report covers, business cards, personal stationery, and other important documents.

Because you manually have to feed each sheet individually to add color, use of the Kroy Kolor Processor is limited to small production runs. The results you get, however, are so extraordinary that, if your printing requirements are modest, you should consider this alternative to using a commercial printer.

To obtain more information about the Kroy Kolor Processor, call Kroy Sign Systems at (800) 328-1306 or (602) 951-1593 and ask them to send you a free product brochure.

Easy Binding with Unibind

A quick, easy, and effective way to bind your publications and give them a uniformly elegant look is to use a Unibind Thermal Binding Machine. Several models are available, but all work on the same principle. Place your publication pages into a one-piece Unicover and insert the Unicover into the machine. The machine applies controlled heat to melt an inlaid thermoplastic adhesive that firmly binds the pages and cover together. It takes only seconds to produce a perfect, durable binding that enables even the thinnest documents to lay perfectly flat when open. You can even later reheat the binding to add or remove pages.

The Unibind system is far superior to most small-production binding tools. As with the Kroy Kolor Processor described above, if your printing needs are modest, consider this alternative to paying a commercial printer to prepare your bindings.

To obtain more information about Unibind Thermal Binding Machines, call Unibind at (415) 652-8345 and ask them to send you their free product brochure.

Keeping Updated with *ThePage*

An excellent continuing source of reliable information about PageMaker is *ThePage*, a monthly subscription journal that provides detailed coverage of PageMaker and other desktop publishing tools. Every issue of *ThePage* contains a wealth of valuable insights, including dozens of practical design and usage tips. The contents are well-illustrated (*ThePage* is subtitled "A visual guide to using the Macintosh in desktop publishing"), and the information is presented in a cleanly organized and concise manner. *ThePage* is published by PageWorks, a well-known graphic design and consulting firm. For a free sample issue of *ThePage* call (312) 549-4219 or write to: *ThePage*, P.O. Box 14493, Chicago, IL 60614.

Going Online for Information and Support

For additional help and information about PageMaker, go online with CompuServe and join the Aldus Forum. Just type *GO ALDUS* at the prompt. The forum is free, except for your connect time, and a wealth of valuable data can be discovered there. For example, you have access to a complete collection of PageMaker Technical Support Notes and an assortment of the most current APD files. The Forum also has a message board that enables you to exchange personal insights and information with other users, many who are qualified PageMaker experts. You can ask difficult technical questions and get prompt, in-depth answers, often directly from the folks at Aldus. To join CompuServe, call (800) 848-8199 or (614) 457-8650 and request an introductory kit.

Another excellent online data source is MacNet, a part of the expanding Connect Information Service. Aldus maintains a free forum on MacNet where up-to-date technical support notes, APDs, and other useful files and information are posted. Because of a prior agreement with CompuServe, Aldus representatives are unable to provide online conference support or take part in interactive technical discussions. The advantage of the MacNet interface is that it consists entirely of familiar windows and icons, exactly like your Mac's desktop. To join MacNet, call (800) 2-MACNET or (408) 973-0110 and order the MacNet software.

Another online service is the Macintosh Exchange on BIX. One conference of the MacExchange (mac.desktop) is devoted entirely to self-publishing. The flat fee subscription pricing contrasts favorably to the other services' hourly usage charge. For further information, call 1-800-227-2983.

Quick Reference

This section is for users who have forgotten a PageMaker procedure and need to access the information quickly. Step-by-step instructions take you through basic procedures—from opening publications to printing.

Some steps present more than one method for achieving the same result. These alternative procedures are introduced by "Or." Choose the method with which you are most comfortable.

Working with Files

Opening Publications

1. Choose New from the File menu to open a new publication.

2. Choose Open from the File menu to open an existing publication or template.

Reverting to the Last Saved Version of a Publication

1. Choose Revert from the File menu.

2. Click OK.

Saving Publications

1. Choose Save from the File menu to save an existing publication to the original file.

2. Choose Save As from the File menu to save a new publication, to save an existing publication under a new name or to a different disk location, or to save a publication as a template (or a template as a publication).

Viewing Your Publication

1. To view your publication's actual size, choose Actual Size from the Page menu.

2. To view your publication reduced to 75 percent of its original size, choose 75% Size from the Page menu.

3. To view your publication reduced to 50 percent of its original size, choose 50% Size from the Page menu.

4. To view your publication reduced in size to fit entirely within the publication window, choose Fit In Window from the Page menu.

5. To view your publication reduced in size with the entire pasteboard visible within the publication window, choose Fit In Window from the Page menu while holding down the Shift key.

6. To view your publication enlarged to 200 percent its original size, choose 200% Size from the Page menu.

7. To view your publication enlarged to 400 percent its original size, choose 200% Size from the Page menu while holding down the Shift key.

8. To toggle between Actual Size and Fit In Window, click on the part of the screen you want centered in the viewing window while holding down the Command and Option keys.

9. To toggle between Actual Size and 200% Size, click on the part of the screen you want centered in the viewing window while holding down the Command, Option, and Shift keys.

Hiding the Toolbox and Window Scroll Bars

1. To hide the toolbox, deselect the Toolbox command on the Options menu.

2. To hide the publication window's scroll bars, deselect the Scroll Bars command on the Options menu.

3. To redisplay the toolbox or scroll bars, choose the appropriate menu command from the Options menu.

Working with Graphics

Drawing Tools

1. Click on the square-corner rectangle, rounded-corner rectangle, circle, diagonal-line, or perpendicular-line tool icon in the toolbox.

2. Click on the page or pasteboard with the selected tool and drag to draw a square-corner rectangle, rounded-corner rectangle, oval, or line.

3. Hold down the shift key while dragging to make rectangles into squares, ovals into circles, and diagonal lines into exact multiples of 45 degrees.

Assigning Line Widths and Fill Patterns

1. Select graphic elements with the pointer tool (select only graphics drawn using PageMaker's drawing tools).

2. Choose a line width or line style (or None) from the Lines menu to assign that width or style to the borders of the selected elements.

3. Choose a shade or pattern (or None) from the Shades menu to assign that shade or pattern to the fill areas of the selected elements.

Reversing Lines and Border Shapes

1. Select a line or shape drawn with PageMaker's tools.

2. Choose a line thickness or line style from the Lines menu.

3. Choose Reverse Line from the Lines menu.

Resizing and Reshaping Graphics

1. Click on the graphic with the pointer tool to select it.

2. Click on a reshaping handle and drag. Release the mouse button when the graphic is the desired size and shape.

3. To resize a graphic proportionally, hold down the Shift key while dragging the reshaping handle.

4. To resize an imported bit-mapped graphic for the best printing resolution, hold down the Command key while dragging the reshaping handle. (The graphic must have been imported using the Place command in the File menu.)

Changing the Corner Radius of Rectangles

1. Select the rectangle.

2. Choose Rounded Corners from the Options menu.
3. Click on the desired corner-shape icon.
4. Click OK.

Importing New Graphics

1. Choose the Place command from the File menu to open the Place Document dialog box.
2. Select the file you want to import from the document selection window.
3. Click the `As new` graphic button.
4. Click OK.

Cropping an Imported Graphic

1. Click on the cropping tool icon in the toolbox.
2. Click on the imported graphic with the cropping tool to select the graphic.
3. Center the cropping tool over a boundary handle.
4. Click and drag in the direction you want to crop the graphic.

Centering a Cropped Graphic

1. To move or center a cropped graphic within its boundaries, click on the graphic with the cropping tool.
2. Continue holding down the mouse button. The cropping tool changes into a grabber hand.
3. Drag the grabber hand to adjust the display.

Modifying Scanned and Bit-mapped Images

1. Select the graphic to be modified.
2. Choose Image Control from the Options menu to open the Image Control dialog box.
3. Click the `Black and white` button to modify black-and-white images.
4. Click the `Screened` button to vary the contrast and brightness of black-and-white images, to adjust individual gray levels for gray-scale images, or to change screen assignments for both kinds of images.

5. Click the `Gray` button to individually adjust gray levels for gray-scale images (only if you are using a Macintosh II).

6. Adjust image contrast and brightness by scrolling the `Contrast` and `Lightness` scroll-bar arrows or by clicking in the bar-graph window to adjust the graph display (the `Screened` or `Gray` button should be selected). Note that each bar represents a different gray level and can be adjusted individually when modifying gray-scale or screened black-and-white images.

7. Click one of the four special-effect icons located above the bar graph if you want to apply the indicated effect (from left to right: `Normal`, `Negative`, `Posterize`, `Solarize`).

8. To change the screen assignment, click the `Screened` button.

9. To apply a dot-screen to your image, click on the dot-screen Screen icon. To apply a line-screen to your image, click on the line-screen Screen icon.

10. To change screen angle or lines-per-inch settings, type new values directly into the `Angle` and `Lines/In` fields.

11. Click the `Apply` button to view the effects of your modifications.

12. Click the `Reset` button if you want to undo modifications.

13. To better view your graphic, click in the title bar of the Image Control dialog box and drag the dialog box to another spot on-screen.

14. Click OK.

Substituting Graphics

1. Use the pointer tool to select the graphic to be replaced.

2. Choose the Place command from the File menu to open the Place Document dialog box.

3. Select the file you want to substitute from the document selection window.

4. Click the `Replacing entire graphic` button.

5. Click OK.

Working with Pages

Selecting Page Sizes

1. Choose Page Setup from the File menu to open the Page Setup dialog box.
2. Click the appropriate `Page size` button. The page dimensions are displayed in the `Custom Page size` fields.
3. To use a custom page size, type the desired page dimensions into the `Custom Page size` fields. The `Custom page size` button is selected automatically.
4. Click the `Tall` or `Wide` button to set the page orientation.
5. Click OK.

Setting Margins

1. Choose Page Setup from the File menu to open the Page Setup dialog box.
2. Type new margin settings into the margin fields.
3. Click OK.

Facing Pages

Turning Pages

1. To display a page or set of facing pages, click on the corresponding numbered page icons in the lower left corner of your publication window. Scroll the page icon display, if necessary, by clicking on the arrows at either end of the display.

   Or, choose Go To Page from the Page menu and type the desired page number into the `Page number` field.

2. To display your master pages, click on the left or right master page icons in the lower left corner of your publication window. Or, choose `Left master page` or `Right master page` from the Go To Page dialog box.

Viewing Facing Pages

1. Choose Page Setup from the File menu to open the Page Setup dialog box.

2. Click the `Double-sided` and `Facing pages` option checkboxes.

3. Click OK.

Numbering Pages

Assigning Automatic Page Numbers

1. To have PageMaker number all your pages automatically, type the Command-Option-P key combination on both master pages for double-sided publications and the right master page for single-sided publications. (Make sure that the Caps Lock key is toggled off.)

2. To have PageMaker number individual publication pages automatically, type the Command-Option-P key combination on just those pages you want numbers to appear. (Make sure that the Caps Lock key is toggled off.)

Setting the Number of Pages in an Existing Publication

1. Choose Page Setup from the File menu to open the Page Setup dialog box.

2. To change the beginning page number, type a new beginning page number into the `Start page #` field.

3. Click OK.

4. To change the total number of pages, choose Insert Pages or Remove Pages from the Page menu.

5. Type new values into the `Insert pages` or `Remove pages` dialog box fields.

6. Click OK.

Setting the Number of Pages in a New Publication

1. Choose Page Setup from the File menu to open the Page Setup dialog box.

2. Type a beginning page number into the `Start page #` field.

3. Type the planned total number of pages for your publication into the `# of pages` field.

4. Click OK.

Page Elements

Selecting Elements

1. Click on the pointer tool icon in the toolbox.

2. Click on the element you want to select or drag a selection rectangle completely around the element.

3. To select more than one element, hold down the Shift key while clicking on successive elements, or drag a selection rectangle completely around the elements.

4. To select an element from within a stack of elements or one that lies behind an overlapping guide, click on the element's location while holding down the Command key. Each successive click selects a different item in the stack.

5. To select all items on a page, choose Select All from the Edit menu.

Deselecting Elements

1. To deselect all currently selected elements, click on a blank area of the page or pasteboard or click on the pointer tool icon in the toolbox.

2. To deselect one or more elements from a group of currently selected elements, click on each element in turn or draw a selection rectangle around them while holding down the Shift key.

Hiding Master Elements

1. To hide the master elements on a publication page, deselect the Display Master Items command on the Page menu.

2. To redisplay the master items, choose Display Master Items from the Page menu.

Changing the Stacking Order of Elements

1. Select one or more elements with the pointer tool. To select an element buried within a stack, hold down the Command key and click repeatedly until the desired element is selected.

2. To move selected elements to the bottom of the stack, choose Send To Back from the Edit menu.

3. To move selected elements to the top of the stack, choose Bring To Front from the Edit menu.

Moving Elements on the Same Page

1. Select the elements to move using the pointer tool.
2. Click on one of the selected elements, continue holding down the mouse button, and drag the elements as a group to their new location on the page.

Moving Elements to Another Page

1. Select the elements to move using the pointer tool.
2. Choose Cut from the Edit menu.
3. Turn to the new page and choose Paste from the Edit menu. The elements will reappear in the center of your viewing window.
4. While the elements are still selected, drag them to their new location on the page.

    Or, drag the elements onto the pasteboard, turn to the new page and drag the elements back onto the new page.

Working with Rulers and Guides

Displaying Rulers

1. To display the rulers, select the Rulers command from the Options menu.
2. To hide the rulers, deselect the Rulers command from the Options menu.

Using Ruler Guides

1. Click the pointer tool in the horizontal or vertical ruler and drag to get a horizontal or vertical ruler guide.
2. Continue holding down the mouse button and drag toward the center of the viewing window. The ruler guide will follow. Use the ruler tick marks to help accurately position the guide on the page.
3. To reposition a ruler guide, click on it with the pointer tool and drag while holding down the mouse button.
4. Choose Snap To Rulers from the Options menu to activate the "magnetic" properties of the guides.

Resetting the Ruler Zero Point

1. Display the rulers by selecting the Rulers command from the Options menu.

2. Unlock the zero point if locked by deselecting the Zero Lock command from the Options menu.

3. Click the pointer tool on the crossed-lines icon in the upper left corner of the window where the rulers intersect.

4. Hold down the mouse button and drag the zero point to a new location on the page.

5. Release the mouse button.

6. To relock the zero point, select the Zero Lock command from the Options menu.

Selecting Units of Measure

1. Choose Preferences from the Edit menu to open the Preferences dialog box.

2. Click the `Measurement system` button that matches your preference to set the same units of measure for both rulers.

3. To set a different unit of measure for the vertical ruler, click the `Vertical ruler` button or type a custom point size into the `Custom points field`.

4. Click OK.

Using Column Guides

1. Choose Column Guides from the Options menu to open the Column Guides dialog box.

2. To specify the number of columns you want, type a whole number between 1 and 20 into the `Number of columns` field.

3. To specify the spacing between columns, type a numerical value into the `Space between columns` field.

4. Click the `Set left and right pages separately` checkbox if you are laying out facing pages and want to use a different column arrangement on each page.

5. Click OK.

6. To reposition a column guide, click on it with the pointer tool and drag while holding down the mouse button.

Using Snap To Options

1. To precisely align text or graphics to ruler tick marks, choose Snap To Rulers from the Options menu.
2. To precisely align text or graphics to column or margin guides, choose Snap To Guides from the Options menu.
3. To turn off either of these options, deselect the appropriate menu command on the Options menu.

Moving Guides to the Front or Back

1. Choose Preferences from the Edit menu to open the Preferences dialog box.
2. Click the `Guides Front or Back` button.
3. Click OK.

Locking Guides

1. To prevent the inadvertent movement of column and ruler guides, choose Lock Guides from the Options menu.
2. To unlock the guides, deselect the Lock Guides command on the Options menu.

Copying Master Guides

1. Turn to the page or facing pages to which you want to copy the master guide arrangement.
2. Choose Copy Master Guides from the Page menu.

Working with Text

Creating a Text Block

1. Click on the text tool icon in the toolbox.
2. Click between a pair of column guides to create an insertion point.
3. Type your text. The text wraps between the column guides.

    Or, click and drag the text tool if you want to create a text block of a specific width. When you type your text, it wraps to that width.

Resizing and Reshaping Text Blocks

1. Click on the text block with the pointer tool to select it.
2. Click on a windowshade handle and drag to lengthen or shorten the text block without changing its width.
3. To reshape the text block, click on a corner handle and drag. Release the mouse button when the text block is the desired shape.

Selecting Text

1. To select a range of text, click the text tool to create an insertion point.
2. Drag through the text while holding down the mouse button.

    Or, click the text tool to create an insertion point, then hold down the Shift key and click the text tool at the end of the range.

3. To select a word, double-click on the word with the text tool.
4. To select a range of words, double-click on the first word, then drag through the remaining words while holding down the mouse button.

    Or, double-click on the first word in the range, hold down the Shift key, and click the text tool on the last word in the range.

5. To select an entire paragraph, triple-click the text tool anywhere within the paragraph.
6. To select an entire story, click the text tool anywhere within the story to create an insertion point and choose Select All from the Edit menu.

Replacing Text

1. Select the text to be replaced using the text tool.
2. Type the new text from the keyboard.

    Or, paste text from the Clipboard.

    Or, import text using the Place command from the File menu. Make sure that the `Replacing selected text` button in the Place Document dialog box is selected.

Deleting Text

1. Select the text to be deleted using the text tool.
2. Press the Delete (Back space) key or choose Clear from the Edit menu.

    Or, choose Cut from the Edit menu to remove the text from your document and leave a copy of what was removed on the Clipboard.

Greeking Text

1. Choose Preferences from the Edit menu to open the Preferences dialog box.
2. Into the `Greek text below` field, type a point size below which you want Greeking to occur.
3. Click OK.

Changing Type Specifications

Changing Font Sizes

1. Use the text tool to select the text to be changed.
2. Choose Size from the Type menu.
3. Select a new font size from the pop-up Size submenu.

   Or, choose Type Specs from the Type menu.
4. Select a new font size from the pop-up Size menu in the Type Specifications dialog box.
5. Click OK.

Changing Font Types

1. Use the text tool to select the text to be changed.
2. Choose Font from the Type menu and select a new font type from the pop-up Font submenu.

   Or, choose Type Specs from the Type menu.
3. Select a new font type from the pop-up Font menu in the Type Specifications dialog box.
4. Click OK.

Changing Type Styles

1. Use the text tool to select the text to be styled. Choose Type Style from the Type menu and select a style from the pop-up Type Style submenu.

   Or, choose Type Specs from the Type menu to open the Type Specifications dialog box.
2. Select a new type style by clicking the appropriate type style in the Type Specifications dialog box.

3. Click more than one option to assign multiple styles simultaneously.

4. Click OK.

All Caps and Small Caps

1. Use the text tool to select the text to be styled.

2. Choose Type Specs from the Type menu.

3. Select All Caps or Small Caps from the pop-up Case menu in the Type Specifications dialog box.

4. To revert to your original type styling, select Normal from the pop-up Case menu in the Type Specifications dialog box.

5. Click OK.

Reversing Type

1. Use the text tool to select the text to be reversed.

2. Choose Type Style from the Type menu and select Reverse from the Type Style submenu.

   Or, choose Type Specs from the Type menu to open the Type Specifications dialog box.

3. Click `Reverse`.

4. Click OK.

Using Superscripting and Subscripting

1. Use the text tool to select the text to be super- or subscripted.

2. Choose Type Specs from the Type menu.

3. Select Superscript or Subscript from the pop-up Position menu in the Type Specifications dialog box.

4. To revert to your original type styling, select Normal from the pop-up Position menu in the Type Specifications dialog box.

5. Click OK.

Formatting

First-Line Indents

1. Use the text tool to select the paragraphs to be indented.

2. Choose Paragraph from the Type menu to open the Paragraph Specifications dialog box.

   Or, choose Indents/Tabs from the Type menu to open the Indents/Tabs dialog box.

3. Type the desired first-line indent value into the `Indents first` field.

4. To set a normal indent from the Paragraph Specifications dialog box, type a positive value.

   To set a hanging indent from the Paragraph Specifications dialog box, type a negative value. (Note that you must first type a larger positive value in the `Indents left` field to create enough room for the hanging indent.)

5. To set a normal indent from the Indents/Tabs dialog box, drag the first line indent marker to any spot along the ruler to the right of the left indent marker. The first line indent marker is the small upper triangle at the left end of the ruler. The left indent marker is the small lower triangle at the left end of the ruler.

   To create a hanging indent from the Indents/Tabs dialog box, drag the first line indent marker to any spot along the ruler to the left of the left indent marker. (Note that you must first move the left indent marker to the right to create enough room for the hanging indent.)

6. Click OK.

Left and Right Indents

1. Use the text tool to select the paragraphs to be indented.

2. Choose Paragraph from the Type menu to open the Paragraph Specifications dialog box.

   Or, choose Indents/Tabs from the Type menu to open the Indents/Tabs dialog box.

3. To set left and right indents from the Paragraph Specifications dialog box, type the desired left and right indent values into the `Indents Left` and `Indents Right` fields.

4. To set the left indent from the Indents/Tabs dialog box, drag the left indent marker to any spot along the ruler. The left indent marker is the small lower triangle at the left end of the ruler.

   To set the right indent from the Indent/Tabs dialog box, drag the right indent marker to any spot along the ruler. The right indent marker is the left pointing arrowhead at the right end of the ruler.

5. Click OK.

Setting Tab Stops

1. Use the text tool to select the text to which you want to assign tab stops.
2. Choose Indents/Tabs from the Type menu to open the Indents/Tabs dialog box.
3. Click `Clear` to remove any existing tab stops from the ruler.

   Or, to use the existing tab stops, adjust them one at a time by dragging them to new positions along the ruler.
4. Remove any tab stops you don't want by dragging them off the ruler.
5. Click `Left`, `Right`, `Center`, or `Decimal` for the kind of tab stop you want to set.
6. Click the appropriate button for the kind of leader style you want—dots, dashes, a solid line, a character of your own choosing, or none.
7. To style a new tab leader, click the rightmost leader style button. Type a one- or two-repeating character string into the leader style field.
8. Click on the lower or upper half of the ruler (not the ruler window) to make the tab marker appear along the ruler.
9. Drag the tab marker to the desired position along the ruler. Use the digital read-out at the right to check placement accuracy.
10. Click OK.

Non-breaking Spaces

1. To type an Em space, simultaneously press Command-Shift-M.
2. To type an En space, simultaneously press Command-Shift-N.
3. To type a thin space, simultaneously press Command-Shift-T.
4. To type a fixed space, simultaneously press Option-space bar.
5. To type a non-breaking hyphen, simultaneously press Option--(hyphen key).

Hyphenating

Adjusting the Hyphenation Zone

1. To adjust the width of the hyphenation zone (the area at the end of an unjustified line of text where PageMaker hyphenates words), choose Spacing from the Type menu to open the Spacing Attributes dialog box.

2. Type a new value into the Hyphenation zone field.

3. Click OK.

Automatic Hyphenation

1. Use the text tool to select the paragraphs to be hyphenated.

2. Choose Paragraph from the Type menu to open the Paragraph Specifications dialog box.

3. Click Hyphenation Auto to have PageMaker hyphenate your paragraphs automatically.

4. To turn auto-hyphenation off for selected paragraphs, deselect Hyphenation Auto.

5. Click OK.

Discretionary Hyphenation

1. To add a discretionary hyphen to a word, click on the word with the text tool to create an insertion point where you want the hyphen to appear.

2. Type the hyphen while holding down the Command key. The hyphen remains invisible until PageMaker splits the word.

3. To delete a discretionary hyphen from a word PageMaker has split, click with the text tool just after the hyphen to create an insertion point, then press the Delete (Back Space) key.

4. To delete a discretionary hyphen from a word PageMaker has not split, use the text tool to select the letters on both sides of the hyphen, then retype the letters.

Prompted Hyphenation

1. Use the text tool to select the paragraphs to be hyphenated.

2. Choose Paragraph from the Type menu to open the Paragraph Specifications dialog box.

3. Click **Prompted Hyphenation** to have PageMaker prompt you with suggested hyphenation whenever it encounters a word that doesn't fit at the end of a line. (The words are displayed sequentially one at a time in a dialog box.)

4. Click on the displayed word to the left of the blinking bar to insert new hyphens. Backspace over existing hyphens if you want to delete them. Delete all the hyphens and then place a hyphen in front of the word if you don't want the word hyphenated.

5. Click **Add word to dictionary** checkbox to add the word to the supplementary hyphenation dictionary (auto-hyphenation must be turned on).

6. Click **Next** to see the next word or **Stop** to cancel prompted hyphenation.

7. Click OK.

Updating the Supplementary Hyphenation Dictionary

1. Open the PMUSDISK.DCT file with any text editor.

2. Type new words, delete old ones, or make corrections. Add hyphens normally wherever you want PageMaker to hyphenate the words. If you don't want a word to be hyphenated, include it without any hyphens.

3. Resave PMUSDISK.DCT as a text-only file.

Importing and Exporting

Importing a New Story

1. Choose the Place command from the File menu to open the Place Document dialog box.

2. Select the file you want to import from the document selection window.

3. Click the **As new story** button.

4. Click the appropriate options to retain the original story format, convert straight quotes and apostrophes to curly ones, or import style tags.

5. Click OK.

Autoflowing Text

1. Choose Autoflow from the Options menu.

2. Import your text. PageMaker will autoflow your story and create additional pages and columns as necessary to hold the text.

3. To stop autoflowing text, click the mouse. To resume autoflowing text, click on the + symbol in the column windowshade handle.

4. To semi-autoflow imported text, hold down the Shift key when clicking with the text-placement icon.

5. To change text-flow modes from automatic to manual, or manual to automatic, hold down the Command key when clicking with the text-placement icon.

Replacing a Story

1. Use the text tool to create an insertion point in the story to be replaced.

2. Choose the Place command from the File menu to open the Place Document dialog box.

3. Select the file you want to import from the document selection window.

4. Click `Replacing entire story`.

5. Click OK.

Replacing Selected Text

1. Use the text tool to select the range of text to be replaced in the story.

2. Type the new text.

   Or, paste the text from the Clipboard.

   Or, choose the Place command from the File menu to open the Place Document dialog box.

3. Select the file you want to import from the document selection window.

4. Click `Replacing selected text`.

5. Click OK.

Inserting Text into a Story

1. Use the text tool to create an insertion point in the story for the new text.

2. Type the new text.

   Or, paste the text from the Clipboard.

Or, choose the Place command from the File menu to open the Place Document dialog box.

3. Select the file you want to import from the document selection window.

4. Click `Inserting text`.

5. Click OK.

Exporting Text

1. Use the text tool to select the text or story to be exported.

2. Choose Export from the File menu to open the Export Document dialog box.

3. To export the entire story, click the `Entire story` button.

4. To export a selected range of text, click the `Selected text only` button.

5. Select an export file format from the File Format scroll box.

6. Assign a name to your exported file and a disk destination.

7. Click OK.

Spacing

Justifying Text

1. Use the text tool to select the paragraphs to be aligned.

2. Choose Alignment from the Type menu.

3. To left justify your text, choose Align Left from the pop-up Alignment submenu.

4. To right justify your text, choose Align Right from the pop-up Alignment submenu.

5. To center justify your text, choose Align Center from the pop-up Alignment submenu.

6. To fully justify your text, choose Justify from the pop-up Alignment submenu.

Or, choose Paragraph from the Type menu to open the Paragraph Specifications dialog box.

7. Click the appropriate `Alignment Left`, `Right`, `Center`, or `Justify` button for the desired alignment.
8. Click OK.

Adjusting Word and Letter Spacing

1. To adjust the word spacing of a story, use the text tool to create an insertion point in the story.
2. Choose Spacing from the Type menu to open the Spacing Attributes dialog box.
3. Type the desired word spacing values into the `Word Space Minimum`, `Desired`, and `Maximum` fields. All field values must fall within the range 0 to 500 percent.
4. Type the desired letter spacing values into the `Letter space Minimum`, `Desired`, and `Maximum` fields. Minimum field values must fall within the range −200 to 0 percent, and Maximum field values must fall within the range 0 to 200 percent.
5. For unjustified text, adjust as necessary the width of the hyphenation zone (the area at the end of an unjustified line of text where PageMaker hyphenates words) by typing a new value into the `Hyphenation zone` field.
6. Click OK.

Paragraph Spacing

1. Use the text tool to select the paragraphs for which you want to change the spacing.
2. Choose Paragraph from the Type menu to open the Paragraph Attributes dialog box.
3. Type the desired spacing values into the `Spacing Before` and `After` fields.
4. Click OK.

Automatic Kerning

1. Use the text tool to select the paragraphs to be kerned.
2. Choose Paragraph from the Type menu to open the Paragraph Specifications dialog box.

3. To have PageMaker automatically kern your text, click the `Auto Pair kerning` button.

4. In the `Auto above points` field, type the point size above which you want auto-kerning to be applied.

5. Click OK.

Manual Kerning

1. Use the text tool to create an insertion point between two characters you want to kern.

2. To remove space, press the Delete (Backspace) key while holding down the Command key. Repeat to remove additional increments of space.

3. To add space, press the Delete (Backspace) key while holding down the Command and Shift keys. Repeat to add additional increments of space.

Wrapping Text

Wrapping Text Around Graphics

1. Select the graphic around which you want to wrap text.

2. Choose Text Wrap from the Options menu to open the Text Wrap dialog box.

3. Click on the wrap option icon (the middle icon) to set a rectangular graphic boundary.

4. Type desired standoff values into the `Standoff Left`, `Right`, `Top`, and `Bottom` fields.

5. Click on a text flow icon to set the desired type of text flow.

6. Click OK.

Creating a Custom Text Wrap Boundary

1. Select the graphic that has a text wrap boundary you want to customize.

2. To change the shape of the boundary, click on any diamond-shaped handle with the pointer tool, hold down the mouse button, and drag the handle to a new position.

3. To create additional handles, click anywhere along the text-wrap boundary.

4. To move a whole text-wrap boundary line, click on the line with the pointer tool, hold down the mouse button, and drag the line to a new position.

5. To prevent the screen from being redrawn each time you adjust the boundary, hold down the space bar until all changes are complete.

Leading

Adjusting Line Leading

1. Use the text tool to select the text to be changed.
2. Choose Leading from the Type menu.
3. Select a new leading value from the pop-up Leading submenu.

   Or, choose Type Specs from the Type menu.
4. Select a new leading value from the pop-up Leading menu in the Type Specifications dialog box.
5. To specify a leading value other than those listed in the pop-up menu, type the new value directly into the Type Specifications dialog box `Leading` field. Half-point sizes are permissible.
6. Click OK.

Assigning Automatic Leading

1. Use the text tool to create an insertion point in your story.
2. Choose Leading from the Type menu.
3. Select Auto from the pop-up Leading submenu.

   Or, choose Type Specs from the Type menu.
4. Select Auto from the pop-up Leading menu in the Type Specifications dialog box.
5. To change the way PageMaker computes auto-leading, choose Spacing from the Type menu to open the Spacing Attributes dialog box.
6. Type a new value into the `Auto-leading % of point size` field.
7. Click the `Proportional` or `Top of caps` leading method button.
8. Click OK.

Using Styles

Applying Styles

1. Use the text tool to select the paragraphs to which you want to apply a style.

2. Choose Style Palette from the Options menu to display the Styles palette. Click on a style in the Styles palette list to apply it to the selected paragraphs. Hold down the Shift key when you click to preserve any existing overrides.

   Or, choose Style from the submenu. Select a style name from the pop-up Style submenu to apply that style to the selected paragraphs.

   Or, choose Define Styles from the Type menu to open the Define Styles dialog box. Select a style from the Define Styles dialog box style list.

3. Click OK.

Defining and Editing Styles

1. Choose Define Styles from the Type menu to open the Define Styles dialog box.

2. To define a new style, click `New` to open the Edit style dialog box. To edit an existing style, click the name of the style to be edited, then click `Edit` to open the Edit Style dialog box.

   Or, if the Styles palette is displayed, click the name of the style to be edited (click `No style` to create a new style) while holding down the Command key. This opens the Edit Style dialog box.

   Or, in the Type Style submenu, click the name of the style to be edited (click `No style` to create a new style) while holding down the Command key. This opens the Edit Style dialog box.

3. If defining a new style, assign a name to your style by typing it into the `Name` field. Type a style name into the `Based on` field if your new style is to be based on an existing style.

4. Click `Type` to open the Type Specifications dialog box. Set the desired type specifications and then click OK.

5. Click `Para` to open the Paragraph Specifications dialog box. Set the desired paragraph specifications and click OK.

6. Click `Tabs` to open the Indents/Tabs dialog box. Set the desired indents and tabs and click OK.

7. Click `Color` to open the Define Colors dialog box. Specify the desired color and click OK.

8. Click OK to return to the Define Styles dialog box.

9. Click OK to save the style and apply it to selected text.

    Or, click `Close` to save the style without applying it to selected text.

Copying Styles

1. Choose Define Styles from the Type menu to open the Define Styles dialog box.

2. Click `Copy` to open the Copy Styles dialog box.

3. Click on a publication or template name in the list.

4. Click OK to import that publication's or template's style sheet and return to the Define Styles dialog box.

5. Select a style from the style list and click OK to apply the style to selected text.

    Or, click `Close` to save style-sheet changes without applying a style to selected text.

Deleting Styles

1. Choose Define Styles from the Type menu to open the Define Styles dialog box.

2. Click on the name of the style in the style list.

3. Click `Remove` to delete that style.

4. Click `Close` to save changes to your style sheet.

Working with Color

Applying Colors

1. Use the pointer tool to select the graphics to which you want to apply a color. Use the text tool to select the text to which you want to apply a color.

2. Choose Color Palette from the Options menu to display the Colors palette.

3. Click on a color name to apply that color to your text or graphics.

   Or, choose Define Colors from the Options menu to open the Define Colors dialog box.

4. Select a color name.

5. Click OK.

Defining and Editing Colors

1. Choose Define Colors from the Options menu to open the Define Colors dialog box.

2. To define a new color, click New to open the Edit color dialog box. To edit an existing color, click the name of the color to be edited, then click Edit to open the Edit Color dialog box.

   Or, if the Colors palette is currently displayed, click the name of the color to be edited while holding down the Command key. This opens the Edit Color dialog box.

3. If defining a new color, assign a name to your color by typing it into the Name field.

4. Click the appropriate RGB, HLS, or CMYK color model button to select the color model with which you prefer to work.

5. Adjust the color scroll bars to achieve the desired color.

   Or, type the known color values directly into the color fields.

6. Observe the top half of the color display to view your new color changes. The bottom half of the color display shows the color with which you started.

7. Click on the bottom half of the color display when you want to restore your color settings to their original values.

8. Click OK to return to the Define Colors dialog box.

9. Click OK to save and apply the color to selected text or graphics.

   Or, click Close to save the color without applying it to selected text or graphics.

Editing Colors with the Apple Color Picker

1. Choose Define Colors from the Options menu to open the Define Colors dialog box.

2. Hold down the Shift key and click `Edit` in the Define Colors dialog box to open the Apple Color Picker dialog box.

3. Click and drag around the wheel to change the color hue.

4. Click and drag inward toward the center or outward toward the rim of the wheel to change the color saturation.

5. Click and drag the scroll bar up or down to change color brightness.

   Or, type the known values for your new color directly into the `Hue`, `Saturation`, and `Brightness` (or `Red`, `Green`, and `Blue`) fields.

6. Observe the top half of the color display to view your new color changes. The bottom half of the color display shows the color with which you started.

7. Click on the bottom half of the color display anytime you want to restore your color settings to their original values.

8. Click OK to return to the Define Colors dialog box.

9. Click OK to save and apply the color to selected text or graphics.

   Or, click `Close` to save the color without applying it to selected text or graphics.

Copying Colors

1. Choose Define Colors from the Options menu to open the Define Colors dialog box.

2. Click `Copy` to open the Copy Colors dialog box.

3. Click on a publication or template name in the list and click OK to import that publication's or template's color sheet and return to the Define Colors dialog box.

4. Select a color.

5. Click OK to apply the color to selected text or graphics.

   Or, click `Close` to save color sheet changes without applying a color to selected text or graphics.

Deleting Colors

1. Choose Define Colors from the Options menu to open the Define Colors dialog box.

2. Click on the name of the color.

3. Click Remove to delete the color.
4. Click Close to save changes to your color sheet.

Printing

Changing Printers

1. Select Chooser from the Apple menu.
2. Click the printer icon to select a printer.
3. Close the Chooser window.
4. Choose Print from the File menu to open the Print dialog box.
5. Click the Change button to open the Printer-Specific Options dialog box.
6. Select the matching Printer APD from the Printer type scroll box.
7. Click OK.

Changing Printer Drivers

1. Choose Print from the File menu to open the Print dialog box.
2. Click the Change button to open the Printer-Specific Options dialog box.
3. Click the Aldus or Apple Driver button.
4. Click OK.

Printing Multiple Copies of a Publication

1. Choose Print from the File menu to open the Print dialog box.
2. Type the desired number of copies into the Copies field.
3. Click Collate to automatically collate your output.
4. Click Reverse order to have the first page of your publication printed first (so it ends up on the bottom of the output stack).
5. To print copies of only a specific page range, type the beginning and ending page numbers into the From and To Page range fields.
6. Click OK.

Setting PostScript Print Options

1. Choose Print from the File menu to open the Print dialog box.
2. Hold down the Option key and click OK to open the PostScript Print Options dialog box.
3. Select desired options by clicking the appropriate checkboxes and buttons.
4. Click OK.

Generating Proof Prints

1. Choose Print from the File menu to open the Print dialog box.
2. Set the desired page range.
3. Click `Proof print`.
4. Click OK.

Scaling Page Output

1. Choose Print from the File menu to open the Print dialog box.
2. Type a value between 25 and 1000 percent into the `Scaling` field. Pages printed at less than 100 percent size are reduced and centered on the paper. Pages printed at greater than 100 percent size require tiling.
3. Click OK.

Smoothing Bit-mapped Graphics

1. Choose Print from the File menu to open the Print dialog box.
2. Click `Smooth` to automatically smooth bit-mapped graphics during printing.
3. Click OK.

Generating Spot Color Overlays

1. Choose Print from the File menu to open the Print dialog box.
2. Set the desired page range.
3. Click `Spot color overlays`.
4. Click `Cutouts` if cutouts are desired.
5. Click `Crop marks` if crop marks are desired.
6. Click OK.

Substituting Fonts

1. Choose Print from the File menu to open the Print dialog box.

2. Click Substitute fonts to automatically replace New York, Geneva, and Monaco bit-mapped fonts with Times, Helvetica, and Courier laser fonts during printing.

3. Click OK.

Printing Thumbnails

1. Choose Print from the File menu to open the Print dialog box.

2. Click Thumbnails.

3. Type the desired number of thumbnails (up to 64 per page) into the Thumbnails per page field.

4. Click OK.

Tiling Page Output

1. Choose Print from the File menu to open the Print dialog box.

2. Click Tile and Manual or Auto overlap for manual or automatic tiling.

3. To control what part of the page is tiled during manual tiling, reset the ruler zero point on your page to where you want the upper-left corner of the tile to start (repeat for each tile on the page).

4. To control automatic tiling, specify the amount of image overlap by typing a numerical value into the Auto overlap field.

5. Click Crop marks.

6. Click OK.

Index

10% fill command, 88
200% Size command, 50, 292
400% Size command, 50
50% Size command, 292
75% Size command, 292

A

About PageMaker command, 36
Actual Size command, 50, 292
ads, 274-276
Aldus Prep, 206, 215-217
Alignment command, 143, 310
APD (A Printer Description) files, 31, 206-208, 215, 282
Apple Color Picker dialog box, 316-317
Apple LaserWriter, 20
Apple menu, 36, 53, 198, 283, 318
ASCII text files, 17
Auto command, 134
Autoflow command, 106, 109, 309
autoflow text-placement icon, 106
autoflowing text, 309
automatic
    hyphenation, 141, 307
    kerning, 119, 311-312
    leading, 313
    text flow, 106-108

B

Backspace key, 307
banner for newsletter, 251-252
batch-printing documents, 207
bit-mapped
    fonts, 206
    graphics, 155-156, 243, 294-295
    smoothing, 319
bleeding pages, 68
boilerplates in newsletters, 256
borders, 258
boxes, 169, 240-241
Bring To Front command, 174, 298
brochures, 265-266
business cards, 270-272

C

Canvas, 18-19
captions, 182, 261
Case menu, 114, 116-117
certificates, 269-270
characters, kerning, 311-312
Choose Color Palette command, 193
Chooser command, 318
Chooser desk accessory, 198
circle tool, 44
circles, drawing, 169
Clear command, 112, 165, 174, 302
clip art, 22-23
Clipboard, 130, 161, 165, 174-175, 225
    copying graphics to, 165
    text on, 109-110
Close command, 40
CMYK (Cyan, Magenta, Yellow, Black) color model, 192
color, 315-318
    adding with Kroy, 288
    applying to text, 195-196
    copying, 317
    defining, 316
    deleting, 317-318
    editing, 193, 316-317
    graphics, 191-196
    models
        CMYK (Cyan, Magenta, Yellow, Black), 192
        HLS (Hue, Lightness, Saturation), 192
        RGB (Red, Green, Blue), 192
    overlays, 208-209
    PMS (Pantone Matching System), 211
    printing, 208-212
Color Palette command, 315
color sheet, 193
column break text-flow icon, 179
Column Guides command, 69-72, 80, 123-124, 128, 300
Column Guides dialog box, 70-71, 123, 300
columns, 123-124
    aligning text, 143-144
    changing, 70-72
    guides, 127-128, 300
    master pages, 63
Command key, 48, 127

Command—[hyphen] (discretionary hyphen) keyboard shortcut, 118
Command-backspace (remove space between characters) keyboard shortcut, 120
Command-G (go to page) keyboard shortcut, 49
Command-Option-P (number pages automatically) keyboard shortcut, 63-64, 83, 117, 297
Command-Shift-+[plus] (superscript) keyboard shortcut, 117
Command-Shift—[minus] (subscript) keyboard shortcut, 117
Command-Shift-> (one incremental-size larger type) keyboard shortcut, 115
Command-Shift-backspace (add spaces between characters) keyboard shortcut, 120
Command-Shift-H (small caps) keyboard shortcut, 117
Command-Shift-K (all caps) keyboard shortcut, 117
Command-Shift-M (em space) keyboard shortcut, 117, 306
Command-Shift-N (en space) keyboard shortcut, 117, 306
Command-Shift-space bar (return to original format settings) keyboard shortcut, 117
Command-Shift-T (thin space) keyboard shortcut, 306
Command-Shift-Tab (one page backward) keyboard shortcut, 49
Command-Tab (one page forward) keyboard shortcut, 49
commands
    10% fill, 88
    50% Size, 292
    75% Size, 292
    200% Size, 50, 292
    400% Size, 50
    About PageMaker, 36
    Actual Size, 50, 292
    Alignment, 143, 310
    Auto, 134
    Autoflow, 106, 109, 309
    Bring To Front, 174, 298
    Choose Color Palette, 193
    Chooser, 318
    Clear, 112, 165, 174, 302
    Close, 40
    Color Palette, 315
    Column Guides, 69-72, 80, 123-124, 128, 300
    Copy, 112, 175
    Copy Master Guides, 65, 73, 301
    Cut, 112, 130, 175, 299, 302
    Define Colors, 193, 316-317
    Define Styles, 148, 314-315
    Display Master Items, 65-66, 91, 298
    Export, 122, 310
    Find, 54
    Fit In Window, 50, 131, 292
    Fit In World, 50
    Get Info, 55, 284
    Go To Page, 49, 296
    Guidance, 53
    Guides, 74, 128
    Image Control, 191, 208, 213, 294
    Indents/Tabs, 99, 101, 136, 138, 305-306
    Insert Pages, 63, 124, 297
    Leading, 313
    Lock Column Guides, 70
    Lock Guides, 63, 73, 87, 127, 301
    New, 37, 79, 291
    None, 88, 168, 259
    Open, 36, 40, 53, 285, 291
    Page Setup, 37-38, 60-61, 296-297
    Paper, 245
    Paragraph, 119, 135-136, 141, 305, 307, 310-311
    Paste, 112, 161, 299
    Place, 84-86, 98, 101, 103-106, 142, 161-166, 225, 243, 293- 295, 302, 308-310
    Preferences, 38, 46, 60, 300-301, 303
    Print, 56, 92, 199, 215, 318-320
    Remove Pages, 63, 124-125, 297
    Reverse, 83
    Reverse Lines, 168, 245, 287, 293
    Revert, 55, 151, 285, 291
    Rounded Corners, 294
    Rulers, 46, 74, 299-300
    Save, 54-56, 92, 285, 291
    Save As, 54-56, 92, 285, 291
    Scroll Bars, 52, 292
    Select All, 102, 174, 196, 209, 298, 302
    Send To Back, 87, 185, 244, 298
    Size, 303
    Snap To Guides, 70, 73, 111, 126, 130, 166, 182, 271, 301
    Snap To Rulers, 67, 70, 73, 76, 91, 126, 135, 144, 166, 299, 301
    Solid, 82
    Spacing, 134, 144-146, 307, 311, 313
    Style Palette, 148, 314
    Text Wrap, 86, 107, 178, 243, 312
    Toolbox, 45, 292
    Type Specs, 90, 114, 134, 303-304, 313
    Type Style, 83, 303-304
    Undo, 73, 125-126, 151
    Undo Page Setup, 71
    Zero Lock, 47, 75, 300
configuring system, 281-282
Control-Shift-F1 (Pointer tool) keyboard shortcut, 167
Control-Shift-F2 (Diagonal-line tool) keyboard shortcut, 167
Control-Shift-F3 (Perpendicular-line tool) keyboard shortcut, 167
Control-Shift-F4 (Text tool) keyboard shortcut, 167
Control-Shift-F5 (Square-corner rectangle tool) keyboard shortcut, 167
Control-Shift-F6 (Rounded-corner rectangle tool) keyboard shortcut, 167
Control-Shift-F7 (Circle tool) keyboard shortcut, 167
Control-Shift-F8 (Cropping tool) keyboard shortcut, 167
Copy Colors dialog box, 194, 317
Copy command, 112, 175
Copy Master Guides command, 65, 73, 301
Copy Styles dialog box, 315
copying
    colors, 317

Index **323**

master guides, 301
styles, 149, 315
text into PageMaker, 97-98
crash, recovering from, 285-286
Cricket Draw, 19
Cricket Paint, 18-19
cropping graphics, 173-174
cropping tool, 44-45
custom wrap icon, 179
Cut command, 112, 130, 175, 299, 302

D

deck heads, 257
defaults, 59-62
Define Colors command, 193, 316-317
Define Colors dialog box, 193-195, 208, 315-317
Define Colors menu, 168
Define Styles command, 148, 314-315
Define Styles dialog box, 148-150, 152, 314-315
deleting
    colors, 317-318
    styles, 149, 315
    text, 302
    text blocks, 131
designing
    newsletters, 251-261
    publications, 223-249
        ads, 274-276
        attention-getting graphics, 238-240
        boxes, rules, and design elements, 240-241
        contrast, balance, symmetry, 231-234
        drop shadows, 244
        electronic whiteout, 244-245
        headlines, 234-236
        large publications, 272-274
        short documents, 263-272
        templates, 245-247
        type styles, 236-237
desk accessories
    Chooser, 198
    Find File, 256
    Guidance, 53-54, 283
    Key Caps, 117
DeskDraw, 19
DeskPaint, 18-19, 287
desktop publishing, 1-2, 9-33
diagonal-line tool, 43
dialog boxes
    Apple Color Picker, 317
    Column Guides, 70-71, 123, 300
    Copy Colors, 194, 317
    Copy Styles, 315
    Define Colors, 193-195, 208, 315-317
    Define Styles, 148-150, 152, 314-315
    Edit Color, 193, 195, 316
    Edit Styles, 148-149, 314

Export Document, 122, 310
Get Info, 55
Go To Page, 49, 296
Image Control, 187-190, 294-295
Indents/Tabs, 305-306, 314
Insert Pages, 125
Open, 283
Open Publication, 40, 247
Page Setup, 37-40, 48, 60-61, 63, 65-66, 69, 71, 73, 76, 79, 92, 124-125, 127, 197, 199, 264, 296-297Paragraph Attributes, 311
Paragraph Specifications, 119, 135-136, 141, 305, 307, 310-311, 314
Place Document, 84, 100-104, 109, 150, 162, 165, 247, 286, 294-295, 302, 308-310PostScript Print Options, 215, 217, 286
Preferences, 46-47, 51, 60, 67, 69, 74-75, 87, 127, 135, 140, 300-301, 303
Print, 56, 92, 199-206, 208, 210, 265, 286, 318-320
Printer-Specific Options, 203, 207-208, 212, 214-216, 318
Save As, 54-55, 246
Spacing Attributes, 134, 144-146, 307, 311, 313
Text Wrap, 178-182, 184, 312
Type Specifications, 90, 99, 113-115, 134, 147, 243, 303-304, 313-314
dictionaries, 141-142
    editing, 142
    updating, 308
Digital Darkroom, 19, 287
discretionary hyphenation, 118, 142-143, 307
Display Master Items command, 65-66, 91, 298
documents, 37-40, 59-77
    adding handwritten signatures, 287-288
    batch-printing, 207
    closing, 40
    defaults, 59-62
    editing, 40
    jump to any page, 49
    layout, 67-70
    linking graphics, 163
    printing, 56, 318
    rulers, 74-77
    saving, 54-56
    tiling, 204-205
    viewing, 49-53
dots per inch (dpi), 186
downloadable fonts, 205-206
drawing, 166-170, 287
drop caps, 88-89, 242-243
drop shadows, 244

E

Edit Color dialog box, 193, 195, 316
Edit menu, 38, 46, 60, 71, 73, 87, 102, 112, 125-126, 130, 151, 161, 165, 174-175, 196, 209, 244, 298-303
Edit Styles dialog box, 148-149, 314

editing
    colors, 193, 316-317
    dictionaries, 142
    documents, 40
    styles, 148-149, 314-315
    text, 91-92, 110-120
EPS files, 17-19, 115, 157-158, 165, 196, 265, 288
    converting pages to, 286
Export command, 122, 310
Export Document dialog box, 122, 310
exporting
    files, 308-310
    graphics, 175
    text, 121-122

F

facing pages, 39, 65-66, 79
    see also pages
    turning, 296
    viewing, 296-297
File menu, 36-38, 40, 54-56, 60-61, 79, 84, 92, 98, 100-104, 106, 122, 142, 151, 161-165, 199, 215, 243, 284-285, 291, 293-297, 302, 308-310, 318-320
files
    Aldus Prep, 206, 215-217
    APD (A Printer Description), 31, 206-208, 215, 282
    ASCII text, 17
    defaults, 60-62
    EPS, 17-19, 115, 157-158, 165, 196, 265, 288
    exporting, 308-310
    hiding toolbox and window scroll bars, 292
    importing, 308-310
    opening publications, 291
    Paint, 195-196, 214
    PICT, 18-19, 86, 115, 157, 165-166, 195-196, 203, 214
    PM CHRON.TXT, 282
    PMF000, 285
    PMUSDISK.DCT, 308
    PostScript, 215-217
    Read Me, 281
    REGMARK.EPS, 209
    reverting to last saved version, 291
    saving publications, 291
    TIFF, 17-19, 160, 163-165, 172, 185-187, 195-196, 212, 214, 261, 265, 287
    viewing publication, 292
fill patterns, 293
Filter Installer utility, 98
Find command, 54
Find File desk accessory, 256
Finder, 282
Fit In Window command, 50, 131, 292
Fit In World command, 50
fliers, 266-268
Font/DA Mover, 114, 206, 283
fonts, 112-117
    bit-mapped, 206
    downloadable, 205-206
    laser, 206
    PostScript, 205-206
    selecting, 89-90
    serif, 89
    sizes, 115-116, 303
    substituting, 320
formatting
    graphics, 177-196
    paragraphs, 132-143
    tables, 138
    text, 123-152, 305-306
        global, 147-152
Freehand, 19, 252, 288
FullPaint, 18

G

Get Info command, 55, 284
Get Info dialog box, 55
Get Info window, 284
global text formatting, 147-152
Go To Page command, 49, 296
Go To Page dialog box, 49, 296
graphic-placement icons, 162
graphics, 26, 155-175, 238-240, 293-294
    aligning, 301
    bit-mapped, 155-156, 243
    centering cropped, 294
    choosing, 21-23
    color, 191-196
    copying to Clipboard, 165
    cropping, 44-45, 173-174, 294
    drawing tools, 293
    Encapsulated PostScript (EPS), 157-158
    enhancing, 177-196
    exporting, 175
    flowing text around, 177-185
    formatting, 177-196
    importing, 85-86, 161-166, 294
    line widths and fill patterns, 293
    linking to document, 163
    modifying, 170-174
        scanned and bit-mapped, 294-295
    moving, 174
    object-oriented, 157
    opaque objects, 166
    Paint, 165
    PICT, 157, 243
    placing, 85-86
    resizing and reshaping, 171-172, 293
    reversing lines and border shapes, 293
    scanned images, 159-160, 185-186
    shades and patterns, 169-170
    smoothing, 208, 319
    software, 18-19

standoff boundary, 180-184
substituting, 295
supported by PageMaker, 155-160
transparent objects, 166
wrapping text around, 312-313
gray-scale scanned images, 160
greeking text, 51, 303
greeting cards, 269
Guidance desk accessory, 53-54
Guidance menu, 53-54
guides, 73-74, 299-301
    adjusting, 127-128
    column, 127-128, 300
    copying master, 301
    locking, 301
    margin, 127-128
    moving, 301
    ruler, 127-128
Guides command, 74, 128

H

halftones, 261
handbills, 266-268
headlines, 25, 234-236
help, 53
HLS (Hue, Lightness, Saturation) color models, 192
hyphenation, 141-143
    automatic, 141, 307
    discretionary, 118, 142-143, 307
    nonbreaking, 118
    prompted, 141-142, 307-308
    zone, 307

I

icons
    autoflow text-placement, 106
    column break text-flow, 179
    custom wrap, 179
    graphic-placement, 162
    jump over text-flow, 179
    manual text-placement, 105
    master page, 62
    negative, 188
    no wrap, 178
    normal, 188
    page, 48-49
    PageMaker, 284
    PageMaker Install, 281
    posterize, 188
    rectangular, 179
    solarize, 188
    text-placement, 103, 108-109
    wrap all sides text-flow, 179
Illustrator, 252, 288

Image Control command, 191, 208, 213, 294
Image Control dialog box, 187-190, 294-295
ImageStudio, 19, 287
importing
    files, 308-310
    graphics, 85, 161-166, 294
    stories, 308
    styles, 150
    text, 97-109
indents, 135-138, 305-306
Indents/Tabs command, 99, 101, 136, 138, 305-306
Indents/Tabs dialog box, 305-306, 314
Insert Pages command, 63, 124, 297
Insert Pages dialog box, 125
inserting pages, 124-125
installing
    Guidance desk accessory, 283
    PageMaker, 281-282

J-K

jump over text-flow icon, 179
justified text, 143-144, 310

kerning, 97, 119-120, 311-312
    automatic, 119, 311-312
    manual, 120, 312
Key Caps desk accessory, 117
keyboard shortcuts
    Command--[hyphen] (discretionary hyphen), 118
    Command-backspace (remove space between characters), 120
    Command-G (go to page), 49
    Command-Option-P (number pages automatically), 63-64, 83, 117, 297
    Command-Shift-+[plus] (superscript), 117
    Command-Shift—[minus] (subscript), 117
    Command-Shift-> (one incremental-size larger type), 115
    Command-Shift-backspace (add spaces between characters), 120
    Command-Shift-H (small caps), 117
    Command-Shift-K (all caps), 117
    Command-Shift-M (em space), 117, 306
    Command-Shift-N (en space), 117, 306
    Command-Shift-space bar (return to original format settings), 117
    Command-Shift-T (thin space), 306
    Command-Shift-Tab (one page backward), 49
    Command-Tab (one page forward), 49
    Control-Shift-F1 (Pointer tool), 167
    Control-Shift-F2 (Diagonal-line tool), 167
    Control-Shift-F3 (Perpendicular-line tool), 167
    Control-Shift-F4 (Text tool), 167
    Control-Shift-F5 (Square-corner rectangle tool), 167
    Control-Shift-F6 (Rounded-corner rectangle tool), 167
    Control-Shift-F7 (Circle tool), 167
    Control-Shift-F8 (Cropping tool), 167

Option--[hyphen] (nonbreaking hyphen), 118, 306
Option-Command-Click (toggle between Fit In Window and Actual Size view), 52
Option-Command-Shift-< (one incremental-size smaller type), 115
Option-Command-Shift-> (one point-size larger type), 115
Option-Command-Shift-Click (toggle between 200% Size and Actual Size view), 52
Option-space bar (fixed space), 117, 144, 306
keys
    Backspace, 307
    Command, 48, 127
    Option, 51
    Shift, 109
    Tab, 37, 140
kickers, 257
Kroy Kolor processing, 288

L

laser
    font, 206
    printers, 287
layouts, 24-28, 67-70
leading, 47, 133-135, 313
    automatic, 313
    negative, 227
Leading command, 313
Leading menu, 133-134
letter spacing, 311
lines
    drawing, 43, 167-168
    reversing, 293
    widths, 293
Lines menu, 43, 88, 168, 245, 259, 287, 293
lines per inch (lpi), 186
linked text blocks, 102
Linotronic ImageSetter, 212-215
Lock Column Guides command, 70
Lock Guides command, 63, 73, 87, 127, 301
locking
    guides, 301
    templates, 55

M

MacDraft program, 19
MacDraw, 19, 157
MacPaint, 18, 155-156
MacWrite, 17, 98
mailers, 266-268
manual
    kerning, 120, 312
    text flow, 105
    text-placement icon, 105
    wrapping text, 184-185

margins, 40, 79, 296
    guides, 127-128
markers
    master-page, 63
    tab, 138-140
master elements, hiding on pages, 298
master pages, 62-66, 80
Master Styles publication template, 148
masthead for newsletter, 251-252
menus
    Apple, 36, 53, 198, 283, 318
    Case, 114, 116-117
    Define Colors, 168
    Edit, 38, 46, 60, 71, 73, 87, 102, 112, 125-126, 130, 151, 161, 165, 174-175, 196, 209, 244, 298-303
    File, 36-38, 40, 54-56, 60-61, 79, 84, 92, 98, 100-101, 103-104, 106, 122, 142, 151, 161-165, 199, 215, 243, 284-285, 291, 293-297, 302, 308-310, 318-320
    Guidance, 53-54
    Leading, 133-134
    Lines, 43, 88, 168, 245, 259, 287, 293
    Options, 45-47, 52, 63, 67, 69-71, 74-75, 80, 86-87, 91, 106-107, 109, 111, 123, 126-128, 130, 135, 144, 148, 166, 178, 193, 208, 243, 292, 294, 299-301, 309, 312, 314-317
    Page, 49-50, 63, 65, 73, 91, 124, 131, 292, 296, 298, 301
    Position, 114, 116-117
    Shades, 82, 88, 169-170, 245, 259, 293
    Styles, 148, 150-152
    Type, 83, 90, 99, 101, 113-114, 119, 134-136, 138, 141, 143-145, 148, 151, 303-307, 310-311, 313-315
    Type Size, 90, 115, 206, 243
Microsoft Word, 17, 98, 100, 121-122
Microsoft Works, 17, 98
modifying
    graphics, 170-174
    Paint files, 191
    TIFF files, 187-190
moving
    elements on pages, 299
    graphics, 174
    guides, 301
    text blocks, 126-127
MultiFinder, 282, 284

N

negative icon, 188
negative leading, 227
New command, 37, 79, 291
newsletters, 79-93
    banners, 251-252
    boilerplates, 256
    borders and rules, 258
    captions and credits, 261
    designing, 251-261

Index

drop caps, 88-89
editing text, 91-92
halftones, 261
making text fit, 86-87
master pages, 80
masthead, 251-252
multiple-column format, 253-255
page formats, 252-255
photographs, 260-261
positioning
    logo, 81
    page numbers, 82-84
printing, 92
rules, 91
saving, 92
selecting fonts, 89-90
single-column format, 253
snap to guides, 91
special visual effects, 259-260
table of contents, 87-88
type selection, 257-258
no wrap icon, 178
nonbreaking hyphen, 118
None command, 88, 168, 259
normal icon, 188
numbering pages, 38-39, 297
    automatically, 63, 297

O

object-oriented graphics, 157
on-line support, 289-290
Open command, 36, 40, 53, 285, 291
Open dialog box, 283
Open Printer Interface (OPI), 160
Open Publication dialog box, 40, 247
Option key, 51
Option—[hyphen] (nonbreaking hyphen) keyboard shortcut, 118, 306
Option-Command-Click (toggle between Fit In Window and Actual Size view) keyboard shortcut, 52
Option-Command-Shift-< (one incremental-size smaller type) keyboard shortcut, 115
Option-Command-Shift-> (one point-size larger type) keyboard shortcut, 115
Option-Command-Shift-Click (toggle between 200% Size and Actual Size view) keyboard shortcut, 52
Option-space bar (fixed space) keyboard shortcut, 117, 144, 306
Options menu, 45-47, 52, 63, 67, 69-71, 74-75, 80, 86-87, 91, 106-107, 109, 111, 123, 126-128, 130, 135, 144, 148, 166, 178, 193, 208, 243, 292, 294, 299-301, 309, 312, 314-317
output device, selecting for printing, 198
overhead transparencies, 264-265

P

Page menu, 49-50, 63, 65, 73, 91, 124, 131, 292, 296, 298, 301
Page Setup command, 37-38, 60-61, 296-297
Page Setup dialog box, 37-40, 48, 60-61, 63, 65-66, 69, 71, 73, 76, 79, 92, 124-125, 127, 197, 199, 264, 296-297
PageMaker
    basics, 35-57
    graphics supported, 155-160
    help, 53-54
    installing, 281-282
    opening, 36-40, 79
PageMaker icon, 284
PageMaker Install icon, 281
pages
    bleeding, 68
    changing
        columns, 70-72
        stacking order, 298
    double-sided, 39
    elements
        deselecting, 298
        moving, 299
        selecting, 298
    facing, 39
        turning pages, 296
        viewing, 296-297
    formats for newsletters, 252-255
    gutter, 40
    hiding master elements, 298
    icons, 48-49
    inserting, 124-125
    jump to any in document, 49
    layouts, planning, 223-249
    margins, 40, 296
    master, 62-66
    numbering, 38-39, 63, 297
    order of printing, 200
    orientation, 38
    positioning page numbers for newsletter, 82-84
    removing, 124-125
    scaling output, 319
    size, 38, 296
    tiling, 320
Paint files, 155-156, 171-172, 185, 195-196, 214
    modifying, 191
PaintDesk, 86
Paper command, 245
Paragraph Attributes dialog box, 311
Paragraph command, 119, 135-136, 141, 305, 307, 310-311
Paragraph Specifications dialog box, 119, 135-136, 141, 305, 307, 310-311, 314
paragraphs
    formatting, 132-143
        importing text, 99-101
    indenting, 305-306

spacing, 135, 311
Paste command, 112, 161, 299
pasteboard, 41-42, 131-132
patterns in graphics, 169-170
perpendicular-line tool, 43
photographs, 260-261
PICT files, 18-19, 86, 115, 157, 165-166, 195-196, 203, 214, 243
Place command, 84-86, 98, 101, 103-106, 142, 161-166, 225, 243, 293-295, 302, 308-310
Place Document dialog box, 84, 100-104, 109, 150, 162, 165, 247, 286, 294-295, 302, 308-310
PM CHRON.TXT file, 282
PMF000 file, 285
PMS (Pantone Matching System) colors, 211
PMUSDISK.DCT file, 308
pointer tool, 42-43
Position menu, 114, 116-117
posterize icon, 188
PostScript
    files, 215-217
    fonts, 205-206
PostScript Print Options dialog box, 215, 217, 286
Preferences command, 38, 46, 60, 300-301, 303
Preferences dialog box, 46-47, 51, 60, 67, 69, 74-75, 87, 127, 135, 140, 300-301, 303
price lists, 265-266
Print command, 56, 92, 199, 215, 318-320
Print dialog box, 56, 92, 199-206, 208, 210, 265, 286, 318-320
printer drivers, 206-208, 318
Printer-Specific Options dialog box, 203, 207-208, 212, 214-216, 318
printers
    Apple LaserWriter, 20
    changing, 318
    changing specifications, 203
    Linotronic ImageSetter, 212-215
printing, 197-219, 318-320
    color, 208-212
        cutouts, 209-211
        registration marks, 209
    commercial printers, 211
    documents, 56
    multiple copies, 200, 318
    newsletters, 92
    offset, 217
    order of pages, 200
    outputting to film, 213-214
    proof prints, 202-203
    proofing on LaserWriter before printing on Linotronic, 212-213
    selecting
        output device, 198
        paper, 218
    thumbnails, 201-202, 320
    tiling, 201, 204-205

programs
    Canvas, 18-19
    Cricket Draw, 19
    Cricket Paint, 18-19
    defaults, 60
    DeskDraw, 19
    DeskPaint, 18-19, 287
    Digital Darkroom, 19, 287
    FreeHand, 19, 252, 288
    FullPaint, 18
    Illustrator, 19, 252, 288
    ImageStudio, 19, 287
    MacDraft, 19
    MacDraw, 19, 157
    MacPaint, 18, 155-156
    MacWrite, 17, 98
    Microsoft Word, 17, 98, 100, 121-122
    Microsoft Works, 17, 98
    PaintDesk, 86
    SuperPaint, 18-19
    WriteNow, 17, 98, 122
prompted hyphenation, 141-142, 307-308
proof prints, 202-203, 319
publications
    binding, 288-289
    designing, 223-249, 263-276
    fitting stories, 228-229
    laying out, 223-249
    opening, 291
    saving, 291
    viewing, 292
    white space, 230
    window, 41-46
pull quotes, 236

Q-R

quick reference, 291-320

Read Me file, 281
rectangles, changing corner radius, 293-294
rectangular icon, 179
registration marks for printing color, 209
REGMARK.EPS file, 209
Remove Pages command, 63, 124-125, 297
reshaping
    graphics, 171-172
    text blocks, 302
resizing
    graphics, 171-172
    text blocks, 128-131, 302
Reverse command, 83
Reverse Lines command, 168, 245, 287, 293
reverse type, 260, 304
Revert command, 55, 151, 285, 291
RGB (Red, Green, Blue) color model, 192
Rounded Corners command, 294
rounded-rectangle tool, 44

rulers, 46-47, 74-77, 136, 299-301
    changing unit of measure, 46-47
    displaying, 299
    guides, 63, 73-74, 127-128
    hiding, 74
    measurements, 74-75
    units of measure, 300
    zero point, 47, 75, 300
Rulers command, 46, 74, 299-300
rules, 240-241, 258
    drawing, 43
    newsletters, 91

S

Save As command, 54-56, 92, 285, 291
Save As dialog box, 54-55, 246
Save command, 54-56, 92, 285, 291
saving
    documents, 54-56
    newsletters, 92
scanned images, 22-23, 159-160, 185-186, 294-295
Scrapbook, 165, 225
screens, 259
scroll bars, 52
Scroll Bars command, 52, 292
Select All command, 102, 174, 196, 209, 298, 302
semiautomatic text flow, 108
Send To Back command, 87, 185, 244, 298
serif fonts, 89
Shades menu, 82, 88, 169-170, 245, 259, 293
Shift key, 109
sidebars, 229
Size command, 303
smoothing graphics, 208
Snap To Guides command, 70, 73, 111, 126, 130, 166, 182, 271, 301
Snap To Rulers command, 67, 70, 73, 76, 91, 126, 135, 144, 166, 299, 301
solarize icon, 188
Solid command, 82
Spacing Attributes dialog box, 134, 144-146, 307, 311, 313
spacing between paragraphs, 135
Spacing command, 134, 144-146, 307, 311, 313
special characters, 117-118
spot color overlays, 319
square-corner rectangle tool, 82
square-corner tool, 44
standoff graphic boundary, 180-184
stationery, 270-272
stories
    importing, 308
    inserting text, 309-310
    replacing, 309
Style menu, 150-152
Style Palette, 150-152
Style Palette command, 148, 314

style sheets, 147-152, 314-315
styles, 314-315
    assigning, 150-151
    copying, 149, 315
    defining, 148-149, 314-315
    deleting, 149, 315
    editing, 148-149, 314-315
    importing, 150
    overriding, 151-152
    text, 147-149
subscript, 99, 116, 304
subtitles, 257
SuperPaint, 18-19
superscript, 99, 116, 304
system, configuring, 281-282

T

Tab key, 140
    highlighting fields in dialog boxes, 37
tab marker, 138-140
tab stops, 306
table of contents, newsletters, 87-88
tables, formatting, 138
tabs, 135-140
templates, 59, 245-247
    locking, 55
    Master Styles publication, 148
text, 20-21, 25, 97-122, 301-302
    aligning, 143-146, 301
    all caps, 116
    attributes, 61, 113, 115
    autoflowing, 309
    case, 116
    color, 195-196
    columns, 123-124
    copying into PageMaker, 97-98
    deleting, 302
    drop caps, 88-89, 242-243
    editing, 91-92, 110-120
    exporting, 121-122
    fitting in newsletters, 86-87
    flow, 104-109
        around graphics, 177-185
        automatic, 106-108
        manual, 105
        semiautomatic, 108
    formatting, 123-152, 305-306
    greeking, 51, 303
    hyphenating, 141-143
    importing, 84, 97-109
    inserting into stories, 309-310
    justified, 143-144, 310-311
    kerning, 97
    leading, 133-135
    manually wrapping, 184-185
    newsletter, 84-85

normal, 116
placing, 102-104
position of, 116
rearranging elements, 126-132
replacing, 302, 309
searching for, 54
selecting, 302
sidebars, 229
small caps, 116
spacing, 310-312
special characters, 117-118
styles, 147-149
subscript, 99, 116, 304
superscript, 99, 116, 304
wrapping around graphic, 312-313
text blocks, 102, 301
    aligning, 144
    deleting, 131
    linked, 102
    moving, 126-127
    reflowing, 288
    resizing, 128-131, 302
Text tool, 43-44, 83, 91
Text Wrap command, 86, 107, 178, 243, 312
Text Wrap dialog box, 178-182, 184, 312
text-flow modes, 109
text-placement icon, 103, 108-109
ThePage journal, 289
thumbnails, 201-202
    printing, 320
TIFF files, 17-19, 160, 163-165, 172, 185-187, 195-196, 212, 214, 261, 265, 287
    modifying, 187-190
    placing, 287
tiling, 204-205, 320
tips
    adding color with Kroy, 288
    adding handwritten signatures to documents, 287-288
    binding publications, 288-289
    converting pages to EPS files, 286
    drawing white lines, 287
    improving laser-printed output, 287
    on-line support, 289-290
    placing TIFF files, 287
    recovering from crash, 285-286
    reflowing blocks, 288
    ThePage journal, 289
    updating stories with word processor, 286
toolbox, 42-46
    hiding, 45, 292
Toolbox command, 45, 292
tools
    circle, 44
    cropping, 44-45
    diagonal-line, 43
    drawing, 166-170, 293
    perpendicular-line, 43
    pointer, 42-43

    rounded-rectangle, 44
    square-corner, 44
    square-corner rectangle, 82
    Text, 43-44, 83, 91
type
    all caps, 304
    attributes, 113
    changing specifications, 303-304
    kerning, 97, 119-120
    reversing, 304
    selection for newsletters, 257-258
    small caps, 304
    styles, 112-117, 236-237
Type menu, 83, 90, 99, 101, 113-114, 119, 134-136, 138, 141, 143-145, 148, 151, 303-307, 310-311, 313-315
Type Size menu, 90, 115, 206, 243
Type Specifications dialog box, 90, 99, 113-115, 134, 147, 243, 303-304, 313-314
Type Specs command, 90, 114, 134, 303-304, 313
Type Style command, 83, 303-304
typefaces, 20-21, 112-113

U-Z

Undo command, 73, 125-126, 151
Undo Page Setup command, 71
Unibind Thermal Binding Machine, 288-289
utilities
    Filter Installer, 98
    Font/DA Mover, 206

window
    scroll bars, 292
    Get Info, 284
word processing software, 17
    updating stories, 286
words
    spacing, 144-146, 311
wrap all sides text-flow icon, 179
wrapping text around graphic, 312-313
WriteNow, 17, 98, 122

Zero Lock command, 47, 75, 300
zero point on rulers, 47, 75, 300

More Computer Knowledge from Que

LOTUS SOFTWARE TITLES

1-2-3 QueCards	21.95
1-2-3 QuickStart	21.95
1-2-3 Quick Reference	6.95
1-2-3 for Business, 2nd Edition	22.95
1-2-3 Command Language	21.95
1-2-3 Macro Library, 2nd Edition	21.95
1-2-3 Tips, Tricks, and Traps, 2nd Edition	21.95
Using 1-2-3, Special Edition	24.95
Using 1-2-3 Workbook and Disk, 2nd Edition	29.95
Using Symphony, 2nd Edition	26.95

DATABASE TITLES

dBASE III Plus Handbook, 2nd Edition	22.95
dBASE IV Handbook, 3rd Edition	23.95
dBASE IV Tips, Tricks, and Traps, 2nd Edition	21.95
dBASE IV QueCards	21.95
dBASE IV Quick Reference	6.95
dBASE IV QuickStart	21.95
dBXL and Quicksilver Programming: Beyond dBASE	24.95
R:BASE Solutions: Applications and Resources	19.95
R:BASE User's Guide, 3rd Edition	19.95
Using Clipper	24.95
Using Reflex	19.95
Using Paradox, 2nd Edition	22.95
Using Q & A, 2nd Edition	21.95

MACINTOSH AND APPLE II TITLES

HyperCard QuickStart: A Graphics Approach	21.95
Using AppleWorks, 2nd Edition	21.95
Using dBASE Mac	19.95
Using Dollars and Sense	19.95
Using Excel	21.95
Using HyperCard: From Home to HyperTalk	24.95
Using Microsoft Word: Macintosh Version	21.95
Using Microsoft Works	19.95
Using WordPerfect: Macintosh Version	19.95

APPLICATIONS SOFTWARE TITLES

CAD and Desktop Publishing Guide	24.95
Smart Tips, Tricks, and Traps	23.95
Using AutoCAD	29.95
Using DacEasy	21.95
Using Dollars and Sense: IBM Version, 2nd Edition	19.95
Using Enable/OA	23.95
Using Excel: IBM Version	24.95
Using Managing Your Money	19.95
Using Quattro	21.95
Using Smart	22.95
Using SuperCalc4	21.95

HARDWARE AND SYSTEMS TITLES

DOS Programmer's Reference	24.95
DOS QueCards	21.95
DOS Tips, Tricks, and Traps	22.95
DOS Workbook and Disk	29.95
IBM PS/2 Handbook	21.95
Managing Your Hard Disk, 2nd Edition	22.95
MS-DOS Quick Reference	6.95
MS-DOS QuickStart	21.95
MS-DOS User's Guide, 3rd Edition	22.95
Networking IBM PCs, 2nd Edition	19.95
Programming with Windows	22.95
Understanding UNIX: A Conceptual Guide, 2nd Edition	21.95
Upgrading and Repairing PCs	24.95
Using Microsoft Windows	19.95
Using OS/2	22.95
Using PC DOS, 2nd Edition	22.95

WORD-PROCESSING AND DESKTOP PUBLISHING TITLES

Microsoft Word Techniques and Applications	19.95
Microsoft Word Tips, Tricks, and Traps	19.95
Using DisplayWrite 4	19.95
Using Microsoft Word, 2nd Edition	21.95
Using MultiMate Advantage, 2nd Edition	19.95
Using PageMaker IBM Version, 2nd Edition	24.95
Using PFS: First Publisher	22.95
Using Sprint	21.95
Using Ventura Publisher, 2nd Edition	24.95
Using WordPerfect, 3rd Edition	21.95
Using WordPerfect 5	24.95
Using WordPerfect 5 Workbook and Disk	29.95
Using WordStar, 2nd Edition	21.95
WordPerfect Macro Library	21.95
WordPerfect QueCards	21.95
WordPerfect Quick Reference	6.95
WordPerfect QuickStart	21.95
WordPerfect Tips, Tricks, and Traps, 2nd Edition	21.95
WordPerfect 5 Workbook and Disk	29.95
Ventura Publisher Tips, Tricks, and Traps	24.95
Ventura Publisher Techniques and Applications	22.95

PROGRAMMING AND TECHNICAL TITLES

Assembly Language Quick Reference	6.95
C Programming Guide, 3rd Edition	24.95
C Quick Reference	6.95
DOS and BIOS Functions Quick Reference	6.95
QuickBASIC Quick Reference	6.95
Turbo Pascal Quick Reference	6.95
Turbo Pascal Tips, Tricks, and Traps	19.95
Using Assembly Language	24.95
Using QuickBASIC 4	19.95
Using Turbo Pascal	21.95
AutoCAD Quick Reference	6.95

Que Order Line: **1-800-428-5331**

All prices subject to change without notice. Prices and charges are for domestic orders only.
Non-U.S. prices might be higher.

SELECT QUE BOOKS TO INCREASE YOUR PERSONAL COMPUTER PRODUCTIVITY

Using Excel

by Mary Campbell

Functioning as both a step-by-step tutorial and a comprehensive reference, *Using Excel* offers a thorough examination of Microsoft's powerful spreadsheet for the Macintosh. This book presents the features of Excel in a logical manner with clear, easy-to-understand examples. You will learn how to navigate through the Excel worksheet, use windows, set up a database, create graphs, and develop timesaving macros. Use Que's *Using Excel* to progress from simple program installation to advanced application design—and become a Macintosh spreadsheet master!

Using Microsoft Word: Macintosh Version

by Steve Lambert and Marsha L. Miliman

A complete guide to Microsoft Word on the Macintosh, *Using Microsoft Word: Macintosh Version* leads you step-by-step from Word basics to the advanced capabilities of Word 3.0. You will learn how to format documents, add headers and footers, merge text, develop customized menus, outline documents, and create a table of contents. Complete with a handy Quick Reference Guide and information on Word's desktop publishing features, this book is an excellent tutorial and lasting reference. Develop your word-processing skills with Que's *Using Microsoft Word*!

Using HyperCard: From Home to HyperTalk

by W. Tay Vaughan III

Move beyond the Home card to advanced HyperTalk programming with Que's new *Using HyperCard: From Home to HyperTalk*. This comprehensive guide serves as a complete tutorial and lasting reference to all aspects of HyperCard. Using HyperCard introduces you to HyperCard basics, shows you how to create new stacks, teaches you the fundamentals of the HyperTalk programming language, and presents techniques for improving the performance of HyperCard applications. Learn all there is to know about HyperCard with Que's *Using HyperCard*!

Using Microsoft Works

by Ronald Mansfield

Microsoft Works is the program for the Macintosh that combines word processing, database, spreadsheet, and communications into one easy-to-use package. *Using Microsoft Works* is the book that makes Works easy to learn and easier to use. Combining Quick Start tutorials with more advanced tips and techniques, this book shows you both basic and advanced features of each of Works' four applications, and teaches you how to copy and merge data between applications. Whether you are a Works novice or an experienced Works user, *Using Microsoft Works* is the book for you!

R949—*Using PageMaker: Macintosh Version*

REGISTRATION CARD

Register your copy of *Using PageMaker: Macintosh Version* and receive information about Que's newest products. Complete this registration card and return it to Que Corporation, P.O. Box 90, Carmel, IN 46032.

Name _____ Phone _____

Company _____ Title _____

Address _____

City _____ State _____ ZIP _____

Please check the appropriate answers:

Where did you buy *Using PageMaker: Macintosh Version*?
- ☐ Bookstore (name: _____)
- ☐ Computer store (name: _____)
- ☐ Catalog (name: _____)
- ☐ Direct from Que _____
- ☐ Other: _____

How many computer books do you buy a year?
- ☐ 1 or less
- ☐ 2-5
- ☐ 6-10
- ☐ More than 10

How many Que books do you own?
- ☐ 1
- ☐ 2-5
- ☐ 6-10
- ☐ More than 10

How long have you been using PageMaker?
- ☐ Less than 6 months
- ☐ 6 months to 1 year
- ☐ 1-3 years
- ☐ More than 3 years

What influenced your purchase of *Using PageMaker: Macintosh Version*?
- ☐ Personal recommendation
- ☐ Advertisement
- ☐ In-store display
- ☐ Price
- ☐ Que catalog
- ☐ Que mailing
- ☐ Que's reputation
- ☐ Other: _____

How would you rate the overall content of *Using PageMaker: Macintosh Version*?
- ☐ Very good
- ☐ Good
- ☐ Satisfactory
- ☐ Poor

How would you rate *Chapter 4: Quick Start: Creating a Newsletter*?
- ☐ Very good
- ☐ Good
- ☐ Satisfactory
- ☐ Poor

How would you rate *Chapter 8: Formatting and Enhancing Graphics*?
- ☐ Very good
- ☐ Good
- ☐ Satisfactory
- ☐ Poor

How would you rate *Special Section: Additional Tips and Techniques*?
- ☐ Very good
- ☐ Good
- ☐ Satisfactory
- ☐ Poor

What do you like *best* about *Using PageMaker: Macintosh Version*?

What do you like *least* about *Using PageMaker: Macintosh Version*?

How do you use *Using PageMaker: Macintosh Version*?

What other Que products do you own?

For what other programs would a Que book be helpful?

Please feel free to list any other comments you may have about *Using PageMaker: Macintosh Version*.

_____
_____
_____
_____

FOLD HERE

Place Stamp Here

Que Corporation
P.O. Box 90
Carmel, IN 46032